T5-BQA-031

Library of
Davidson College

THE
FUTURE
OF
FREE SPEECH LAW

THE
FUTURE
OF
FREE SPEECH LAW

R. George Wright

QUORUM BOOKS
New York • Westport, Connecticut • London

342.73
W952F

Library of Congress Cataloging-in-Publication Data

Wright, R. George.
   The future of free speech law / R. George Wright.
     p. cm.
   Includes bibliographical references.
   ISBN 0-89930-539-3 (lib. bdg. : alk. paper)
   1. Freedom of speech—United States. I. Title.
KF4772.W75 1990
342.73'0853—dc20   89-49430
[347.302853]

British Library Cataloguing in Publication Data is available.

Copyright © 1990 by R. George Wright

All rights reserved. No portion of this book may be
reproduced, by any process or technique, without the
express written consent of the publisher.

Library of Congress Catalog Card Number: 89-49430
ISBN: 0-89930-539-3

First published in 1990

Quorum Books, 88 Post Road West, Westport, CT 06881
An imprint of Greenwood Publishing Group, Inc.

Printed in the United States of America

The paper used in this book complies with the
Permanent Paper Standard issued by the National
Information Standards Organization (Z39.48-1984).

10 9 8 7 6 5 4 3 2 1

92-5853
ACF-7172

Copyright Acknowledgments

The author and publisher gratefully acknowledge permission to use the following materials written by R. George Wright:

"*Hustler Magazine v. Falwell* and the Role of the First Amendment," 19 *Cumberland Law Review* (1988).

"*Fowler v. Board of Education: The Scope of Teachers' Free Speech Rights,*" 15 *Northern Kentucky Law Review* (1988).

"The Unnecessary Complexity of Free Speech Law and the Central Importance of Alternative Speech Channels," 9 *Pace Law Review* (1989).

"Speech on Matters of Public Interest and Concern," 37 *DePaul Law Review* (1987).

"Judicial Responses to Long-Term Societal Decline," 30 *Arizona Law Review* (1988). Copyright © 1988 by the Arizona Board of Regents. Reprinted by permission.

"Defining the Obscene: The Criterion of Value," and "Free Speech Values, Public Schools, and the Role of Judicial Deference," 22 *New England Law Review* (1987). Copyright © New England School of Law 1987. All rights reserved. Reprinted by permission.

"Racist Speech and the First Amendment," 9 *Mississippi College Law Review* (1988).

"A Rationale from J.S. Mill for the Free Speech Clause," *1985 Supreme Court Review* (1986). Copyright © 1986 by the University of Chicago. All rights reserved.

Contents

viii Contents

Acknowledgments

There are a number of people to whom I owe thanks for reading and commenting on portions of the material in this book. I owe them as well an equal obligation to avoid imputing any agreement on their part with anything that follows. I therefore thank, and simultaneously exculpate, Becky Anthony, Howard Bromberg, Sharon Donaldson, Ed Fletcher, Marjorie Heins, Ellen Howard, Philip Kurland, David Langum, Judge Hans Linde, Mari Matsuda, Mary Mitchell, Sheldon Nahmod, Jack Nelson, David Smolin, Dean Geoffrey Stone, Cass Sunstein, Howard Walthall, Dean Parham Williams, and Ann Woolhandler. For assistance of various sorts, I gratefully thank Judy McAlister. For, among other things, her patience and forbearance, this book is dedicated to my wife Mary.

Introduction

This is a book about free speech law that is meant to be a bit more disturbing than most. It calls into question some important assumptions underlying much of contemporary free speech case law. The basic thesis is that courts have increasingly tended to lose track of why we value freedom of speech in the first place. The courts have instead gradually expanded the scope of protection afforded by the free speech clause to encompass all sorts of phenomena that do not significantly implicate any of the several goals of the free speech clause. This expansionist tendency is one of the reasons why free speech case law has become pathologically complex.

Some kinds of expansion of the coverage of the free speech clause are perfectly legitimate. In a sense, there is within free speech law an inherent dynamism that legitimately carries it beyond what one might imagine to be its otherwise appropriate bounds. Free speech law, for example, should obviously keep up with new technologically generated ways of speaking. And while "speech" might literally suggest a restriction of the concept solely to verbal forms of idea communication, this limitation would of course be unjustifiable. Some of our most vital political speech has taken the form of pictures, sculptures, or non-verbal symbolism of various kinds. These principles, whether we call them extensions of more basic principles or not, are amply justifiable by recurring to the basic purposes, goals, or values normally thought to underlie our desire to protect freedom of speech.

Perhaps, however, one might suggest that there is a more radical sense in which the logic of free speech protection overflows its own banks. Consider, as posed by Professor Larry Alexander, the case of a natural rock formation that provokes some viewers to political reflection, or of the site of a nuclear power plant accident.[1] Suppose that the government bars all access to both sites, solely on the grounds that some persons will draw a politically undesirable message from their viewing either site. Are these not quintessential free speech cases? And yet do they not lack a speaker, or a speech, or an intent to speak, or any kind of "sending," or an act of speaking? Does a free speech case really require none of these components?

If we are uncomfortable with Professor Alexander's examples as free speech cases, we can probably dispose of them on, say, right to travel grounds, or even on free press grounds. After all, the freedom of the press must include a right of access to natural objects and to events and places for purposes of investigation, and not merely to listen to speech. If we must dispose of Professor Alexander's examples on free speech grounds, however, we should do so without dispensing with speech, speakers, or the act of speaking. Presumably, the free speech clause protects written reflections and tentative jottings intended solely for the writer's own use in later developing a more public presentation. But the audience for those mere notes is only the writer of the notes. The only speech is, to the present point, "internal." Perhaps, then, the least misleading way of analyzing Professor Alexander's examples under a free speech rubric would be to condemn the government's interference with the reflections and thought processes of potential viewers, where we think of those viewers as potentially thinking or speaking particular thoughts disfavored by the government, or where we think of such a viewer as a potential communicator of thoughts to other people. This analysis would preserve the presence of a potential speaker and of an act of speech. The government regulations would be scrutinized under the free speech clause because of their impact on real or potential speech to an audience that may or may not be identical to the speaker. On this analysis, we do not have a free speech case without speech, or without an intent of some sort by a speaker to at some point communicate or convey some sort of idea. Relatedly, we might note that if someone speaks, but without the slightest intent to convey any sort of idea, then unless that lack of intent itself reflects some illicit engineering by the government, any free speech rights violated by the government in regulating that speech must be those of the audience, or of some third party, and not those of the speaker.

Admittedly, there will be cases that unsteady some familiar analyses of what freedom of speech involves. Consider a government that is able, through drugging the water supply, to create an utterly docile populace, one without the slightest desire, on any conceivable occasion, to think or say anything critical of the government, or even of the drugging program itself. This is presumably a grotesque violation of free speech rights, yet we are missing the ordinary elements of legal restraints, actual speech, threats, punishments, a desire to speak, conflicting desires, disagreements, and such. Yet the basic framework of speakers and speech and audience, actual or potential, still seems to suffice to express what is intolerable about such a situation. In this case, potential speakers are prevented from developing an intent to speak. In this sense, then, there is no dynamic inherent within the concept of free speech that necessarily leads to the continuous expansion and extension of the logic of the idea of freedom of speech.

Ultimately, relentless judicial expansion of the free speech clause may, by diluting the essential seriousness of the free speech clause, and by ignoring the values or goals underlying freedom of speech, eventually tend to erode public support for freedom of speech as a fundamental principle. Increasingly, the case law of freedom of speech is grounded only in one sort or another of relativist or subjectivist thought. The long-term risk is that our adoption of freedom of speech may come to be seen as an ultimately arbitrary societal preference without morally binding character in any traditional sense.

Each of the chapters below develops some aspect of this argument. Some of the chapters are broadly theoretical in character. Others focus illustratively on a concrete fact situation. Throughout, the argument appeals to common sense rather than to some sort of esoteric ideology. The book seeks to be of value not merely to academics of various sorts interested in freedom of speech, but to practicing lawyers who must present arguments about free speech issues to trial courts. In striving to stay close to common sense, the book may help the lawyer who must present an argument to any judge inclined to resist calls for the sacrifice of the elemental logic of freedom of speech.

NOTE

1.   _See_ Alexander, _Low Value Speech_, 83 _Nw_. _U.L_. _Rev_.
547, 553 (1989).

1

Speech in the Constitutional Sense

INTRODUCTION

My primary purpose in this chapter is to defend a
simple if unpopular thesis. I assume that the free
speech clause of the first amendment has an
appropriate range of applicability. The thesis is
simply that the scope of coverage of the free speech
clause should be determined by the broadest range of
purposes or values that can coherently be thought to
underlie the free speech clause. Where free speech
values are not significantly implicated by any given
expression or conduct, the expression or conduct is
not entitled to protection under the free speech
clause. The distinction between expression that is
not within the scope of the clause and expression to
be accorded at least some limited free speech
protection is often not difficult to recognize. When
properly drawn, this distinction should expedite the
sound resolution of many free speech cases.

The unpopularity of this argument flows from its
incompatibility with two schools of thought. The
first school effectively substitutes "expression" for
"speech," and rightly considers tolerance and
pluralism as goods to be aggressively furthered
whenever possible. It therefore detects speech, and
free speech issues, in the most curious of contexts.
This school tends toward one form or another of
relativism or subjectivism and flirts with
constitutionalizing libertarianism in general social
conduct in order, it is alleged, to protect more
securely genuine speech in a narrow sense. The
second, opposing school, of less current practical

influence but with strong intellectual credentials, would limit the protection of the free speech clause to a few selected free speech values. Both schools impose unnecessary long-term social costs.

"Speech" for free speech purposes is of course not an unproblematic concept in all contexts. It is simultaneously broader and narrower than speech in its literal sense of the spoken or written word. Free speech values may conflict in a given case, tugging a given instance of expression simultaneously toward or away from recognition as "speech." The approach offered here, however, aims at increased analytical simplicity while preserving the possibility of vigorous application of the free speech clause within its proper and legitimate sphere.

FREE SPEECH VALUES

Were we able to ask the drafters or ratifiers of the first amendment, "Now, when you refer to freedom of speech, do you mean to include, say, commercial nude dancing as a form of speech?" the answer, one suspects, would square poorly with current judicial decisions. But the possibility remains that the drafters chose the open-textured term "speech" just so that we, of a later generation, could include such activities within its purview.

It seems evident that "[w]e know very little of the precise intentions of the framers and ratifiers of the speech and press clauses of the first amendment."[1] Under these circumstances, one approach that might set constitutional theory on a sound jurisprudential basis would be to turn to the classic texts in defense of first amendment activities for guidance in delimiting the concept of speech; Socrates, John Milton, Locke, Hume, and John Stuart Mill would be obvious sources. We should be disturbed if the classic philosophical exponents of freedom of thought and discussion cannot be fairly enlisted in general support of our contemporary free speech case law.

This course, however, is rarely taken directly or explicitly, both because there is ample free speech case law precedent, and because it can hardly be claimed that someone like Mill, however titanic his stature, influenced the drafters of the first amendment. Moreover, the classic texts are themselves not without difficulties of interpretation. The reader may therefore wish to interpret the term "Millian" values used below as referring simply to all coherently defensible values particularly underlying the free speech clause.

There is at least a fair consensus as to the

major contemporary and historical candidates for free speech values or underlying purposes. One broad formulation refers to: "1. The development of the faculties of the individual; 2. The happiness to be derived from engaging in the activity; 3. The provision of a safety valve for society; and, 4. The discovery and spread of political truth."[2] Another frequently cited broad formulation holds:

> Maintenance of a system of free expression is necessary (1) as a method of assuring individual self-fulfillment, (2) as a means of attaining the truth, (3) as a method of securing participation by the members of the society in social, including political, decision-making, and (4) as a means of maintaining the balance between stability and change in the society.[3]

Other relatively inclusive formulations of first amendment or, more specifically, free speech values include those of Dean Stone, who cites the "search for truth," meaningful participation in self-government, and individual "self-fulfillment,"[4] and perhaps Chaffee, who refers to both an "individual interest" in "the need of many men to express their opinions on matters vital to them if life is to be worth living, and a social interest in the attainment of truth, so that the country may not only adopt the wisest course of action but carry it out in the wisest way."[5]

Before such broader formulations can be adopted, they must survive the critique of those who have taken any of a variety of narrower views of free speech, and they must have their own internal ambiguities resolved. What will be left in the end is a set of considerations with some surprising implications that I shall refer to as Millian values. To fail to implicate Millian values in some respect is, in that respect, not to be speech at all for free speech purposes.

Among the most eminent contemporary American scholars who have sought to limit the scope of coverage of the free speech clause have been Alexander Meiklejohn,[6] Alexander Bickel,[7] and Robert Bork.[8] Professor Meiklejohn's distinction between speech implicating the public welfare and speech implicating merely private goods[9] is perhaps elastic enough to encompass most of what would be considered protected speech under the broader free speech value conceptions.[10] But to the extent that for Meiklejohn the touchstone of free speech coverage is speech

bearing on "issues with which voters have to deal,"
Meiklejohn's theory is either unduly narrow or
misleadingly phrased.[11]

An exclusive concern with issues that we must or
may address as voters, expansive as such a category
may be, does not seem a felicitous way of capturing
what we recognize intuitively as at least one among
other free speech values: "[o]ur personal growth. . .
intellectual, emotional, aesthetic, professional,
vocational, civic, and moral."[12] While it is far from
true that everything implicating our emotional growth,
for example, or every expression of emotionality
implicates free speech values, certainly the category
of personal development is useful in accounting for
why a given expression counts as speech or as
protected speech.

Alexander Bickel may also be taken to have
restricted the broad free speech value formulations
when, in modifying Chaffee's formulation, he confines
the scope of the "social" interest to "the interest in
the successful operation of the political process."[13]
The political can obviously be defined in narrower or
broader terms, and conceptions of what is required to
successfully operate a constitutional government vary
in breadth.[14] Paradoxically, what is required to
operate the political process successfully probably
itself depends on the scope of constitutional
protection accorded to speech, so Bickel's formulation
may be of limited value. If the political process is
thought of narrowly, Bickel's formulation is
arbitrarily underinclusive, in that civic-minded
persons would, as civic-minded persons, tend to care
about and wish to express publicly their opinions on
nonpolitical matters as much as on political
concerns.[15]

In focusing attention on "explicitly and
predominantly political speech,"[16] Bork notes:

> The First Amendment indicates that there is
> something special about speech. We would
> know that much even without a first
> amendment, for the entire structure of the
> Constitution creates a representative
> democracy, a form of government that would
> be meaningless without freedom to discuss
> government and its policies. Freedom for
> political speech could and should be
> inferred even if there were no first
> amendment.[17]

The problem with proceeding thus to confine the scope
of the free speech clause is that this interpretation

assumes the clause's redundancy. While it is certainly possible to argue that the drafters inserted this express protection of political speech merely for reasons of expediency, and not genuinely to amend the Constitution, it is at least equally plausible to suggest that the free speech clause was intended to add something meaningful and that the drafters could well have inserted the qualifier "political" had they meant to so confine the clause.

Narrow formulations of the scope of and values underlying the free speech clause tend, therefore, to be unduly arbitrary. But this does not mean that the broader formulations of free speech values are unproblematic. Writers such as Martin Redish[18] have explicitly recognized that what is variously referred to as the value of self-realization, or development, or "self-fulfillment," or autonomy, conceals an ambiguity.[19] For convenience, this ambiguity will be referred to in terms of autonomy$_1$ and autonomy$_2$. Autonomy$_1$, which can safely be regarded as a Millian value and is at least arguably defensible as a coherent element of the set of distinctive free speech values, is connected with self-realization in the sense utilized by Mill and draws on the developmental dynamic that is described by writers as diverse as Aristotle and Hegel. This sense of autonomy or self-realization is associated with what Isaiah Berlin has referred to as "positive liberty."[20]

In contrast, autonomy$_2$, or autonomy in the broader sense, has no essential reference to progress, growth, development, or cultivation of one's higher powers and is associated more with simply doing as one likes, generally, or with an absence of socially imposed restraint on one's actions and choices. Autonomy$_2$, or Berlin's "negative liberty," however valuable it may be, is simply too broadly conceived to support a free speech principle above and beyond a general libertarianism. Then, too, it will be a rare case indeed in which suppression of the freedom of speech of one group does not simultaneously advance the broad "negative liberty" or autonomy$_2$ of another, perhaps larger, group. Autonomy$_2$ may therefore be at most of limited usefulness in deciding free speech cases or in deciding what is to count as speech.

Even the theorists subscribing to a broader conception of free speech values have occasionally been subject to criticism for excessively restrictive categorization. Professor Tribe has warned that

> [h]owever tempting it may be to resist governmental claims for restricting speech by retreating to an artificially narrowed

zone and then defending it without limit,
any such course is likely in the end to
sacrifice too much to strategic maneuver:
the claims for suppression will persist, and
the defense will be no stronger for having
withdrawn to arbitrarily constricted
territory.[21]

The trick, of course, is to tell artificial from
principled constriction, and it will be argued here
that the "Millian values" help us to do so.

In the meantime, artificially expanding the zone
of protected speech beyond that justified by the
principles and purposes underlying freedom of speech
may disserve those values and impose costs in other
ways.   Strategically, it is not true that the free
speech "army" cannot overextend its position.[22]   It is
certainly plausible to argue, as against Tribe, that a
refusal to trivialize or debase the free speech clause
by extending its application beyond the bounds of its
coherent, identifiable purposes helps to enhance and
dignify the invocation of the Clause within the full
extent of its legitimate scope.   If we wish to honor
its intrinsic importance, we do so by supporting free
speech principles intensively, on every appropriate
occasion.   We do not do so by converting all sorts of
mundane social activities into "speech" in the
constitutional sense.

MILLIAN VALUES AND THE REQUIREMENT OF A SOCIAL IDEA

The recognizable, distinctive values or purposes
underlying a free speech principle, tied together as
Millian values, impose certain requirements on what is
to count as speech.   In terms of Millian values, for
something to be speech it must embody or convey a more
or less discernible idea, doctrine, conception, or
argument of a social nature, where "social" is
understood to include broadly political, religious,
ethical, and cultural concerns.   For language or
gesture or conduct to be speech, it must carry
implications beyond the speaker's individual and
immediate circumstances.   Speech must communicate; it
must be, at least potentially, socially "fertile," and
not socially sterile or exclusively ego-referential.

Speech, certainly, can be almost purely factual
and empirical or normative and evaluative, or
informal, or false, or internally inconsistent, or
pernicious, or irresponsible; it can go unheard or
even be intended for an audience of only the speaker.
It may take the form of preliminary, personal notes or
journal entries.   What it cannot be is patently

socially sterile, without any intended implication for our collective arrangements and institutions, broadly understood.   Self-servingness is not definitive, however; self-serving speech in a commercial marketplace may well not be protected speech, but self-serving speech about the commercial marketplace generally is.[23]

Generalizations about putative speech in particular contexts, such as commercial speech or, as discussed below, in the context of nude dancing or other entertainment, or disorderly conduct arrests, should only be drawn inductively by examining a run of individual cases, judicially decided on a case-by-case basis.   The stakes involved, the risks of either trivializing the guarantee or of suppressing legitimate speech, are so high that conclusively presuming putative speech in any particular social context to be or not to be first amendment speech seems ill advised.

While speech can be vague, or equivocal, or metaphorical, or guarded, or aesopic, this does not mean that the presence of speech depends on the efforts, or successful efforts, of an intended audience, bystanders, or third parties.   A verbalization may causally provoke or incite action or inspire thought, speech, or action in others without being speech in the constitutional sense.   A glimpse of a starving child may inspire an ethical debate or change a foreign policy without the child's presence being speech, just as a flower placed in a crannied wall may inspire the poet without speaking or amounting to speech.   If one has no significant social message to impart, however confused or apparently foolish or inarticulate or ill formed, the creativity of the listener cannot constitute one's words as speech in this sense.   If one has sent a social message, however, even if none was received, or if an entirely different message was received, one has engaged in speech, even if imperfectly.

If talk or conduct does not rise to the level of speech, symbolic or otherwise, this does not mean that such talk or conduct is without any sort of practical, statutory, or even constitutional protection.   If talk is genuinely or even widely perceived as sterile, there may be little incentive for a government to expend resources in suppressing it.   Even where such incentives exist, other constitutional safeguards apart from the free speech clause may come into play. These may include, beyond due process, the free exercise of religion clause, the equal protection clause, the right to vote, the right to travel, free assembly and the right to petition, as well as freedoms of association and privacy, or even freedom of the press, if this is thought to rest on a basis different from that of freedom of speech.[24] Whatever the constitutional concept, there may be some comfort to be secured from the strong historical tendency of dictatorial regimes to suppress precisely on the grounds of the alleged harmfulness, or falsity, or unorthodoxy, or reactionary character of the idea, none of which denies the presence of a social idea of some sort. Selective enforcement problems are minimized because potential oppressors cannot resist the temptation to label opposing ideas as bad social ideas, thereby admitting that they are some sort of social ideas, and thereby giving the game away.

The reasons for placing these restrictions on the concept of speech reflect the nature of Millian values. Mill's defense of the regime of free speech or, more particularly, of liberty of thought and discussion, was informed not by an undifferentiated libertarianism but by a vision of the progressive enlightened development of a society. Victorian progressives such as Mill were perhaps not so sanguine as to believe that humanity's "prospects of creating a rational and enlightened civilization [were] virtually unlimited,"[25] but it is clear that Mill's thinking is not adequately reflected by focusing on a condition of "negative liberty" or on a mere absence of restraint. The end sought by Mill is not perpetually increasing diversity for its own sake, or social fragmentation, but social progress through individual character development. Without suggesting, of course, that good character should generally be legally enforced, Mill believed that character could be better or worse, higher or lower, and his approach to free speech is inseparable from this assumption.

Mill indeed presupposes a "prior ideal of excellence for human beings further realized by allowing liberty of action and thought."[26] This is reflected in Mill's estimation not of mere idiosyncrasy of speech and behavior[27] but of "individual growth"[28] and the "due study and preparation"[29] typically required therefor.

Mill recognizes that not all forms and instances of speech in the literal sense significantly implicate the values and aims underlying freedom of speech. For example, "[t]he scope of Mill's defense of freedom of expression does not cover the dissemination of information, whether true or false, about a person's private life which has no bearing on the scientific, moral, political, religious, and social issues with which he is concerned."[30]

Outside the context of his narrow discussion of

free speech, but with implications for current free
speech issues, Mill observed unhesitatingly that

> there are many acts which, being directly
> injurious only to the agents themselves,
> ought not to be legally interdicted, but
> which, if done publicly, are a violation of
> good manners, and coming thus within the
> category of offenses against others, may
> rightly be prohibited. Of this kind are
> offenses against decency on which it is
> unnecessary to dwell.[31]

This is plainly some distance from the late twentieth
century free speech jurisprudence that fashionably, if
ultimately incoherently, seeks to reject ethical
skepticism while settling for an historically unstable
ethical relativism or subjectivism in which one
person's indecency is commonly another person's lyric.
It also reinforces the necessity of some sort of
social idea for protected speech to be present. For
Mill, the indecent is, at least sometimes,
recognizable and to be shunned not only as a matter of
unconstrained moral preference, but also by
authoritative legal prohibition.

Even where the issue is not one of legal
prohibition, Mill is not reluctant to distinguish
greater and lesser value on grounds other than mere
subjective preference. He unselfconsciously asserts
that "[i]t may be better to be a John Knox than an
Alicibiades, but it is better to be a Pericles than
either; nor would a Pericles, if we had one in these
days, be without anything good which belonged to John
Knox."[32]

This, again, is to suggest not that Mill
advocated the legal proscription of all that he
considered decadent or depraved but merely that there
can be no Millian reasons for barring any legal action
against that which does not implicate Millian values.
Within the sphere of liberty of thought and
discussion, Mill is concerned essentially with that
which rises to the level of "doctrine," as when he
asserts at his most radical that "there ought to exist
the fullest liberty of professing and discussion, as a
matter of ethical conviction, any doctrine, however
immoral it may be considered."[33]

For speech in a literal sense to be speech in a
protectable, first amendment sense, however, it must
rise to the level of recognizable doctrine or of
factual assertion or evaluative opinion that may in at
least some sense be either true or false. This much
is clear even from Mill's famous recapitulation of his

arguments for liberty of thought and discussion, where he iterates his arguments on infallibility, on the likelihood of partial truth, and on the necessity of vigorous contest to promote vital, as opposed to thoughtless, merely prejudiced belief.[34]   If the putative speech cannot be envisioned as some sort of direct, if minor, contribution to a social or intellectual debate continuing over time, in which there is perhaps a consensus or an array of contesting schools of thought that now approach, now recede from the truth, Millian values are not significantly implicated.

We resist this clear understanding of Mill largely on the assumption that Mill, like many of us, must have subscribed to a sort of nonjudgmental, nonhierarchical general libertarianism.   But this is inconsistent not only with Mill's arguments and their underlying premises but also with the unmistakable tone or flavor of Mill's language throughout On Liberty.   Mill insists on the capacity for "being improved"[35] as a prerequisite to the regime of free speech.[35]   He appeals "to the permanent interests of man as a progressive being."[36]   His emphasis is on not merely thinking for oneself but also thinking for oneself "with due study and preparation."[37]   He approves Humboldt's exaltation of "the highest and most harmonious development of [humanity's] powers to a complete and consistent whole" as the dictate of reason.[38]   Choosing one's "plan of life" calls for "observation to see, reasoning and judgment to foresee, activity to gather materials for decision, discrimination to decide, and...firmness and self-control to hold to [one's] deliberate decision."[39]

Mill refers without embarrassment to "human excellence"[40] and goes on to specify that "individuality is the same thing with development."[41] He is careful to link eccentricity with "strength of character"[42] and to observe that "the amount of eccentricity in a society has generally been proportional to the amount of genius, mental vigor, and moral courage it contained."[43]   The ultimate aim remains "cultivation of higher nature."[44]

This is not to suggest that only that which is universally recognized as decent and uplifting can be entitled to special protection.[45]   The point is merely to elaborate on Millian values, in the absence of which there is no point in according special constitutional protection to a given instance of expression.

It is occasionally suggested that a linkage between the free speech clause and Millian or other values is illegitimate and not textually warranted. William Van Alstyne has said:

> The first amendment does not link the protection it provides with any particular objective and may, accordingly, be deemed to operate without regard to anyone's view of how well the speech it protects may or may not serve such an objective. The second amendment expressly links the protection it provides with a stated objective...and might, therefore, be deemed to operate only insofar as the right it protects...can be shown to be connected with that objective.[46]

The problem is that if we try to remain agnostic about the aims, purposes, or values underlying the free speech clause, there is no reliable, nonarbitrary guide for inclusion or exclusion as "speech." Literalism fails us, since a Morse Code message or sign language may plainly implicate first amendment values without being speech in a literal sense.[47] Can something be "symbolic" speech?[48] Recourse to the purposes of the free speech clause, as recognized by one or more drafters or ratifiers or by other persons, is necessary in order to decide. At least some sort of ultimate reference to ascertainable purposes is necessary to limit the potential for arbitrariness in following or distinguishing established case law. Nor should we expect a society to perpetually accept the sacrifices often required by free speech jurisprudence if no authoritative reference to the aims or purposes underlying the free speech clause is permitted.

Bearing the Millian values in mind not only permits the principled resolution of free speech cases but also permits, in many instances, their more expeditious and less logically tortuous resolution as well. The complexity of the Supreme Court's treatment, in various contexts, of "low value" speech, meriting some, but only limited, free speech protection, has been described by Dean Stone.[49] At least some "low value" speech is, in the absence of any significant implication of Millian values, actually "zero value" or, more simply, nonspeech, meriting no free speech clause protection at all.

Something of the logic underlying this approach was applied, whether correctly on the facts or not, by Chief Justice Rehnquist's dissent in the recent widely discussed flag-burning case of <u>Texas v. Johnson</u>.[50] Chief Justice Rehnquist observed that "[f]ar from being a case of 'one picture being worth a thousand words,' flag burning is the equivalent of an inarticulate grunt or roar that, it seems fair to say, is most likely to be indulged in not to express any particular idea, but to antagonize others."[51]   It may be that the speaker in <u>Johnson</u> had available to him alternative means of expressing whatever his communicative point may have been that were just as good from the standpoint of his own free speech values.[52]

Courts should pursue the suggestion that speech in the form of, say, published articles may implicate Millian values more deeply than mass oratory or placards, as a general rule.   The general hierarchy seems clear: books, articles, and leaflets may tend to be more precise, richer, more articulate, or self-incriminating intellectually, than placards, slogans, banners, and bumper stickers.   The world may, in free speech terms, be better off to the extent that there is a reasonably social class-neutral minimal legal incentive to write or argue, rather than merely to sloganeer.   Articulateness is not the sole Millian value, or even the dominant or controlling Millian value, but it is a Millian value.

Frederick Schauer has denied the wisdom of drawing this general qualitative distinction in constitutional terms.   His argument is that we are bombarded with so much speech nowadays that in order to be heard, we must each perhaps speak more offensively, or literally or figuratively raise our voice above the din of other speech to acquire or maintain an audience.[53]   The general futility of this advice seems clear; one might as well counsel all spectators at a football game to stand up in order to see better.

ENTERTAINMENT AND MILLIAN VALUES

Entertainment is not necessarily beyond the compass of the free speech clause.   Some instances of entertainment, such as protest songs or satiric comedy, clearly tend to implicate Millian values.   But many forms of entertainment do not.   It is unmistakably the law that even, or especially, in a commercial context, "nude dancing is not without its First Amendment protections from official regulation."[54]   While this result has not been universally acclaimed, it seems solidly entrenched.[55] The problem is that not all nonobscene commercial nude dancing, for example, purports to convey a social idea in the relevant sense, nor need Millian values otherwise be significantly implicated.   As a result, the courts feel "bound to treat topless dancing as a form of expression which is protected at least to some

extent by the first amendment," while recognizing that
"'few of us would march our sons and daughters off to
war' to protect that form of expression."[56]

It has been suggested in a broader context,
however, that sexually related "speech" "will almost
invariably carry an implicit, if not explicit, message
in favor of more relaxed sexual mores.... In our
society, the very presence of sexual explicitness in
speech seems ideologically significant, without regard
to whatever other messages might be intended."[57] It
would seem, however, that advocacy of relaxed sexual
mores is something imputed to commercial nude dancing
or something invested by third parties in the concept,
rather than a message in any sense sent and received.
One clue is that "sexual mores" is obviously broader
than the activities encompassed by commercial nude
dancing. One might even cynically suspect that the
hidden agenda of commercial nude dancing may be not
the relaxation of sexual mores, but keeping them the
way they are so that the customers will be motivated
to return and pay to watch again. Then again, it is
likely that there may be no intent, explicit or
implicit, in operation other than merely to
commercially profit or merely to entertain; diversion
for its own sake, rather than to make a point.[58] If
the social idea is not expressed by or integrated into
the nude dance routine but is merely "worn about the
neck" to ward off constitutional attack, then only the
readily severable social idea communication itself
should be protected by the free speech clause. There
is generally no need to inquire whether the invokers
of the free speech clause really believe in, or even
vaguely understand, their own protected and protective
social idea.

If the message of commercial nude dancing is so
shadowy and equivocal, however, it is too attenuated
and insubstantial to significantly implicate Millian
values.[59] Further, and perhaps more controversially,
there is no reason necessarily to assume that the
Millian pointlessness of commercial nude dancing must
depend on a finding of bad taste, lewdness, indecency,
obscenity, or widespread offensiveness. A claim of
free speech protection for a given activity may
"trivialize"[60] the free speech clause because of the
Millian pointlessness of the activity, and not because
the activity is judged immoral, or harmful, or lewd,
or misleading.[61]

In a slightly different context, the Eleventh
Circuit has detected no advocacy or expression of
ideas in connection with nude sunbathing, despite
plaintiffs' claim that nude sunbathing "is the
practice by which they advocate and communicate their

philosophy that the human body is wholesome and that nudity is not indecent."[62]   The plaintiffs sought to analogize their situation to that involved in the protected commercial nude dancing cases, but the Eleventh Circuit rejected the argument on the grounds that the nude dancing cases, unlike nude sunbathing, involved "nudity in combination with a protection form of expression."[63]   A problem lies in the fact that non-sexually oriented social or recreational dancing is generally not accorded any free speech protection at all, despite the ability of articulate persons to generate plausible messages, such as antipuritanicalism, that might be imputed to recreational or social dancing.[64]

Sorting these cases out, it appears that the courts attach crucial first amendment significance to a strict separation of performer and audience. Persons in a group of social dancers are not viewed as performing for themselves or for each other as an audience.   Performance dancing, nude or presumably otherwise, with an audience, is protected, unlike social dancing, and it does not lose its expressive, protected quality when associated with nudity. Sunbathing clad, however, is not an otherwise free speech protected activity, and nudity adds or subtracts nothing in the way of free speech protection to the sunbathing.   The cases can probably thus be reconciled.   What should not be overlooked, however, is that there is no Millian value-based rationale available to defend the results obtained if it is recognized that the courts often protect putative speech that does not even purport to convey any social idea.

If one turns to the video game free speech cases, one finds that the possible analogy of video game screens to movies is generally downplayed and that video games, at least at the present state of technology, are typically said to fall afoul of the requirement that, to enjoy free speech protection, the entertainment be intended to convey some idea or information.[65]   This is an eminently sensible result from a Millian standpoint and, despite contentions that some video games vaguely inculcate recognizably martial values, should stand until the video screen conveys, in a manner inextricable with what is sought to be prohibited, some sort of recognizable social idea.

The idea or information requirement tends to go out the window, however, in other entertainment contexts, such as musical performances.   The first amendment, it has been held, protects the right to produce jazz concerts.[66]   Similarly, the bands marching in Philadelphia's Mummers Parade, complete with "thematic arrangement," are engaged in a "form of expressive entertainment" protected by the first amendment.[67]   The problem in focusing on the expressiveness or performance aspect of the entertainment is, of course, the determination to ignore the absence of any social idea.   Expressive entertainment in the form of juggling, plate balancing, and the swallowing of swords or goldfish cannot be distinguished in principle from the above sorts of performances.   If anything is clear about the first amendment, it is that such activities, however captivating, are simply not speech.

The First Circuit has, in a somewhat different context, stated quite soundly that "[a]n act not intended to be communicative does not acquire the stature of first amendment-protected expression merely because someone, upon learning of the act, might derive some message from it.   Nor is such an act entitled to special protection merely because others speak about it."[68]

Again, however, the generalizations drawn above are subject to some exceptions.   One could theoretically employ plate balancing as a medium of social criticism.   Since there are substantial risks, potentially, in erroneously deciding free speech cases for or against the speaker, which may be summed as the risks of decadence or loss of purpose versus the risk of suppression, a case-by-case determination process without the aid of specific presumptions seems called for here, even if most cases of plate balancing do or do not turn out to involve speech in the constitutional sense.

The logic of the entertainment cases is ultimately derived from the now rather quaint "crime magazine" case of Winters v. New York.[69]   The Court indicated, in a free press clause context, that

[w]e do not accede to appellee's suggestion that the constitutional protection for a free press applies only to the exposition of ideas.   The line between the informing and the entertaining is too elusive for the protection of that basic right.   Everyone is familiar with instances of propaganda through fiction.   What is one man's amusement, teaches another's doctrine.[70]

The Court in Winters was otherwise confident, of course, of its ability to reliably detect the lewd, the indecent, and the absence of social value in a publication.[71]   Its otherwise consistent judicial modesty, however, is appropriate only with respect to recognizable borderline cases. Obviously, propaganda in the guise of fiction is ordinarily protectable speech on any theory. But it is unreasonable to suggest that since there are undeniably borderline cases, it is either impossible or pointless to recognize the substantial numbers of instances in which the absence of any intent to convey a social idea can be fairly and reliably detected.

PROFANITY AND THE ABUSE OF COPS, METER MAIDS, AND CIVILIANS: THE CONJUNCTION OF CHAPLINSKY AND COHEN

It may be that the very triviality of much pure entertainment perversely inspires first amendment protection: If it is socially inconsequential, why permit its suppression? This brings into issue the judicial refusal to defer to the legislative balancing of the benefits and costs associated with the literally pointless prohibited activity. There are a wide variety of cases of allegedly socially pointless "speech" in which the alleged associated harms range from public "pollutant" effects, such as a general coarsening in the tenor of public discourse, to the taking of justified personal offense, to the threat of physical violence.[72]

It must be conceded at the outset that, while the well-known _Cohen_ case should not be defended in unduly romantic terms, _Cohen_ was probably correctly decided at least on the issue of the presence of speech.[73] In _Cohen_, a jacket bearing an increasingly common nominally sexual reference[74] inspired a divided court to observe that it is "often true that one man's vulgarity is another lyric,"[75] and to decline to "indulge the facile assumption that one can forbid particular words without also running a substantial risk of suppressing ideas in the process."[76] Whether or not an attempt to generally forbid any particular words was ever at issue, the Court in effect constitutionalized protection of the emotive, as opposed to cognitive, force of language.[77]

But the _Cohen_ result is on this issue defensible as a recognition of a particular phrase, in historical context, that barely made it into the category of "speech" by expressing a remarkably vague social idea about a reasonably clearly specified social phenomenon, the draft. More enthusiastic defenses of _Cohen_'s logic on this issue seem questionable.

It is suggested, for example, that "Resist the Draft" would not have conveyed the same meaning,[78] or that Cohen's expression says it twice as well,[79] or that the manner of expression in _Cohen_ is "more powerful,"[80] or that, more generally, "[t]he use of profanity...is often an effective means for individuals to convey dramatically otherwise inexpressible emotions."[81] It is pointed out that "[n]ot everyone can be a Daniel Webster."[82]

None of these arguments is without point.   Yet each can easily be oversold.   Despite its non-McCluhanesque tenor, there is some sense in the observation that "[a] requirement that indecent language be avoided will have its primary effect on the form, rather than the content, of serious communication.   There are few, if any thoughts that cannot be expressed by the use of less offensive language."[83]   If a surgically neat form-content distinction is admittedly impossible, it remains true that the slope connecting the proscribing of Cohen's language in that particular context and banning or regulating Thoreau is not terribly slippery.

The more central problem is that without projecting our own sentiments into Cohen, we simply cannot tell what Cohen's expression means well enough to pass informed judgments as to its power, aptness, or effectiveness. We can, admittedly, dispute at the margins what Thoreau meant in a literal sense. But Cohen's language, while it conveys enough meaning of a social character to cross the line into speech, is not far from a blank sheet of paper. Does it mean, roughly, as C. L. Stevenson might suggest, "I strongly disapprove of the draft, do so as well"? Perhaps it means, in alienated fashion, "I strongly disapprove of the draft, but/and I don't care what you think": an entirely different message and one to which we know Thoreau would not have subscribed.

The grounds of Cohen's objection to the draft are not hinted at.   The draft may be disfavored or abhorrent for a variety of moral reasons, or out of practical self-interest. Obviously, a slogan can say only so much, and it is unreasonable to expect a speaker to pack an expository essay into a slogan, but this only bespeaks the limited communicative value of slogans and the riskiness at best of assuming that a slogan, profane or otherwise, is likely to be particularly apt in expressing deep frustrations. If we can't tell what Cohen meant at some level of detail, how can we know how well his slogan expressed his feelings?

It is interesting to note that Cohen's expression scans well only with moderate-level alleged evil as a target. Analogous vulgarities conjoined with, say, "Nazism," "Genocide," "Slavery," or "Terrorism" are uninspiring partly because of the abstractness of the institution denounced, but also because they are

immediately recognizable as adolescent-minded
trivializations of the evils involved. We would not
view them as effective or powerful statements.

A dubious assumption at work in the defense of
Cohen is that a person's willingness to consciously
violate basic norms of social propriety, etiquette, or
concern for the sensibilities of others, including
those of some of one's allies, implies that the person
must feel more strongly, deeply, or intensely than the
rest of us, or than Thoreau did, or than the person
himself does on many other subjects.

This is a fallacy, though. Some of us simply
have a low threshold of resort to predictably socially
offensive behavior, quite apart from the intensity of
our feelings. Consider the facial expression of the
next person who violates the rules and breaches
decorum by playing his radio aloud on the local bus.
Does he seem to have an unusually intense devotion to
music that has resulted in the dictates of social
propriety being outweighed? The feelings of others
may simply not be thought to matter much. So even if
we are to accord free speech protection to emotions,
as opposed to ideas, we must not assume the emotion
from the willingness to offend.

Occasionally, the more enthusiastic defenders of
Cohen discuss social trends and touch on the
incentives set up by Cohen.[84] One court has observed
that "[w]hat is vulgar to one may be lyric to
another....Some people spew four-letter words as their
common speech such as to devalue its currency;
Billingsgate thus becomes commonplace."[85] This sort
of argumentation, along with the observation that many
words are less shocking now than they used to be, is
curiously reversible in its import.[86] It would seem,
all else equal, that the degeneration of language or
of the quality of discussion is to be avoided. Any
process of having to outbid one's competitors for
linguistic shock effect, or other merely
perlocutionary effect, worked out as a kind of
Gresham's Law among the tokens of language, would
similarly seem a bad thing.

Lost amid the relativism of Cohen is the obvious
point that even if we cannot reliably tell vulgarity
from lyric, we can reasonably well predict that what
we view as lyric will or will not be found
gratuitously offensive by substantial numbers of
reasonably tolerant people. Protected speech may be
rude or offensive, particularly where the rudeness or
offensiveness is inseparable from the message. But
elevating or at least maintaining the level or quality
of the debate is a Millian value. It remains so even
though it is virtually ignored by contemporary free

speech jurisprudence. While not all of us can rise to the level of a Daniel Webster or a Thoreau, this is not what the detractors of <u>Cohen</u> would require. The question is whether it would be constitutionally permissible, under the free speech clause, to require an even slightly closer approach to the level of a Daniel Webster than <u>Cohen</u> manifests if we are to address the public. The aim is not to ban any usage per se or to disenfranchise the inarticulate but to require of all speakers a certain minimum, universally easily attained level of civility or respect for the feelings of many among the audience.

It has been suggested that

> [O]ffensiveness is often an important part of a speaker's message. Use of offensive language reveals the existence of something offensive and ugly, whether in the situation described by the speaker or in the speaker's mind itself. In either event, the language reveals an important though unpleasant truth about the world. Suppressing this language violates a cardinal principle of a free society, that truths are better confronted than repressed.... We cannot expect to have, nor should we require, true civility in discourse until we achieve civility in society.[87]

Of course, an assassination attempt on a popular political figure may also reveal an important truth, but the issue is whether the price is worth paying. By the time of Cohen's speech, the "truth" about the draft, that it was profoundly immoral, let us say, had already been "said" and was already generally "known." From contrary speech, we also already generally "knew" the "truth" that the draft was a fine thing. What we actually learned from Cohen's speech was mostly about Cohen, and, as we have seen, Cohen's speech told us very little about him or the state of his mind at all. What we learned probably qualifies as neither particularly unpleasant nor important.

At the time of Cohen's speech, no one doubted the controversiality of the draft or the willingness of increasing numbers of persons to speak indecorously. Nor is there, ultimately, any clear reason to hold a minimal civility in public discourse hostage until such a time as we have achieved civility in society. The former has not been shown to be an impediment to achieving the latter, and it may perhaps be its prerequisite. If the two forms of civility are causally independent, why not enjoy the former while

we await the arrival of the latter? At a minimum, it
is unclear why we are bound by the free speech clause
never to accord the effect of a given speech on the
level of discussion any weight at all, even where the
effect on the level of debate is undisputed.

Perhaps on the theory, however, that grievances
are better aired than compulsorily bowdlerized, a more
recent Louisiana Court of Appeals case has, on the
strength of Cohen, given free speech protection to the
display on a pickup truck bumper of a sticker with a
vulgar sexual reference to Charles Foti, Jr.[88] Mr.
Foti was a local sheriff.   The court displayed no
great interest in the possibility of distinguishing
Cohen, perhaps on the grounds that, while a jacket may
be discreetly taken off and folded up, there may be a
felt necessity to park a truck in a given space
regardless of the presence of, say, a school yard or
playground in the vicinity.

Actually, it may be that the only way of
distinguishing the case is to take the direct route.
Except under rare circumstances not discussed in the
Foti opinion itself, vulgar sexual references to most
individuals not the center of controversy do not
convey even a rudimentary social idea.   Whether such
an expression is printed on a bumper sticker,
inscribed on a jacket, or chiseled in marble on the
author's front lawn, it is, in most circumstances,
simply too diffuse and open to significantly implicate
Millian values, even granting that it rises in
significance above mere random lettering.   Unlike
Cohen's expression, it does not necessarily even
psychologically tie in with or trigger thoughts on any
particular social issue.   Attempts at selective
enforcement should be obvious where the political
context suggests that a particular idea, far from
being so diffuse and open as to be unrecognizable, is
actually being suppressed as unpopular or disfavored
by the judge.

A much more common instance of Millian nonspeech
involving the police, though often adjudicated as
protected "low-value" speech, is that of directing
streams of epithets, sometimes for remarkably
prolonged periods of time, at an arresting or
investigating police officer. Typically, the speaker
is indignant, for reasons that are only rarely
ascertainable from the judicial opinion, at the prior
arrest of himself or a friend or relative.[89] One
suspects that, in some of the cases, the motivation is
simply the inconvenience associated with being
arrested.   Often, the purported speech is associated
with a physical disturbance or resistance to arrest.
Sometimes a crowd gathers. In a noteworthy proportion

of the cases, the speaker appears to have been
drinking immoderately. Despite perhaps even an intent
to offend, and the absence of any social idea being
communicated,[90] the purported speech is often
judicially protected as free speech,[91] the disorderly
conduct or breach of peace charge dismissed, and any
"reasonably necessary" force used physically to resist
the "illegal" arrest immunized. When such results are
reached, the most typical rationale is that the police
are or should be inured to abusive language, that they
did not in fact react to the verbal provocation, and
that they are paid to not be provoked and are under a
legal duty in that regard. The case is therefore held
not to fall within the scope of the "fighting words"
exception laid down in Chaplinsky. Sometimes the
strand of the Chaplinsky test focusing on the tendency
of the language to inflict injury drops out of the
analysis entirely.

An example, selected for the moderation, and not
the extremity, of its facts, would be the case of
State v. Montgomery.[92] The appellant in Montgomery
initiated the incident by loudly shouting a series of
profanities at 10:50 p.m. on a cold February night in
downtown Seattle as the two targeted police officers
were passing by on patrol in their car. When the
police stopped to investigate, the appellant, who was
eventually charged with possession of marijuana,
continued in a similar linguistic vein. Eventually,
it was determined that a recent drinking citation had
left the fifteen-year-old appellant irate.

Despite repeated attempts to settle the appellant
down, he continued to express himself loudly.
Eventually a crowd gathered, which, though sizable
enough to block the sidewalk, was not itself
threatening or hostile. The appellant did not
physically threaten the officers and was not carrying
a weapon. Largely because of the sidewalk blocking,
the appellant was, after a total of about five to ten
minutes, arrested and charged with disorderly conduct
and possession of a controlled substance.

On appeal, the convictions for disorderly conduct
and for possession of marijuana were reversed on free
speech grounds,[93] with the court citing Chaplinsky and
Cohen and determining that the appellant's conduct
deserved moral, but not legal, "censure and rebuke."[94]
The majority, unmoved by a dissenter's observation
that "I fail to see that the 'freedom of speech'
contemplated by the First Amendment has anything
whatsoever to do with this case,"[95] instead noted the
"commonplace" nature of the language employed.[96]

The logical centerpiece of the majority's own
independent analysis of the issues noted that "were

the use of the invectives and vulgarisms used by the defendant to be held to be grounds for arrest, a number of professional tennis players and other public figures in sports and entertainment would be subject to arrest for their language, oft repeated."[97] Shrinking from this disturbing prospect, the Court in effect constitutionalized its own weighing of the competing interests involved. Because there are some sound, practical reasons for not arresting tennis players, free speech must be involved. Perhaps part of the problem is that affirming a disorderly conduct or breach of peace conviction involves at least some modest cost to the particular, identifiable individual defendant, whereas on the other side of the ledger, a presumably desensitized police officer aside, there are only abstract, longer-term principles and broader policy considerations, the validity of many of which cannot be rigorously demonstrated.

But it is not a mere verbal quibble to distinguish, for Millian value or free speech purposes, between the proposition that fifteen-year-olds, including the speaker, should be permitted publicly to drink or to smoke marijuana, and the almost purely emotive expressions of a negative attitude, of some sort, toward one's own arrest, or the essentially perlocutionary intent merely to inflict pain through words rather than fists. If no particular grounds for concluding that the original arrest was unfair or discriminatory or arbitrary or illegitimate are given, we are left merely with a negative attitude toward one's own arrest, in particular, principle aside. Merely verbalizing this attitude does not rise to the level of a recognizable attempt to convey or express a social idea in the relevant sense. If a social idea is not present, the fact that the target of verbal abuse did not or, if reasonable, would not be expected to breach the peace in response is not relevant to the adjudication of the free speech constitutional claim.[98]

CONCLUSION

Understandably, we should be leery about not crediting a free speech claim. But it should be clear that not every principled attempt to limit the expansion of the scope of coverage of the free speech clause reflects a desire to impose orthodoxy or to root out ideological error. While the scope of the free speech clause should not be artificially circumscribed, as by narrowing its coverage to plainly political issues, neither should it be assumed that the free speech clause has a scope unrelated to its recognizable purposes. It may be that confining the application of the free speech clause to its defensible and proper scope might well vaguely and minimally advantage some persons and disadvantage others in certain contexts, but these effects cannot in principle extend to conflicts between recognizable interest groups, parties, classes, or political forces and causes. Social cause speech remains within the scope of speech, and cannot be legitimately exiled as nonspeech.

NOTES

1. Ollman v. Evans, 750 F.2d 970, 996 (D.C. Cir. 1984) (en banc) (Bork, J., concurring), cert. denied, 471 U.S. 1127 (1985).

2. Bork, Neutral Principles and Some First Amendment Problems, 47 Ind. L.J. 1, 24-25 (1971).

3. T. Emerson, The System of Freedom of Expression 3 (1970). See also Baker, Scope of the First Amendment Freedom of Speech, 25 UCLA L. Rev. 964, 990-91 (1978); Bloustein, The Origin, Validity, and Interrelationships of the Political Values Served by Freedom of Expression, 33 Rutgers L. Rev. 372, 373 (1981); Greenawalt, Free Speech Justifications, 89 Colum. L. Rev. 119 (1989); Solum, Freedom of Communicative Action: A Theory of the First Amendment Freedom of Speech, 83 Nw. U.L. Rev. 54 (1989).

4. Stone, Content Regulation and the First Amendment, 25 Wm. & Mary L. Rev. 189, 193 (1983).

5. Z. Chaffee, Free Speech in the United States 33 (1967).

6. See, e.g., A. Meiklejohn, Political Freedom 26-27, 79-80 (1965).

7. See A. Bickel, The Morality of Consent 61-75 (1975).

8. See Bork, supra note 2, at 23-25.

9. See A. Meiklejohn, Free Speech and Its Relation to Self-Government 94 (1948).

10. See Meiklejohn, The First Amendment Is an Absolute, in 1961 Sup. Ct. Rev. 245, 262-63 (P. Kurland ed. 1962).

11. A. Meiklejohn, supra note 9, at 93-94.

12.   Bloustein, _supra_ note 3, at 373.

13.   A. Bickel, _supra_ note 7, at 62.

14.   _See_ Perry, _Freedom of Expression: An Essay on Theory and Doctrine_, 78 _Nw. U.L. Rev._ 1137 (1983); Wellington, _On Freedom of Expression_, 88 _Yale L.J._ 1105, 1112 (1979).

15.   _See_ Members of City Council v. Taxpayers for Vincent, 466 U.S. 789, 816 (1984).

16.   Bork, _supra_ note 2, at 26.

17.   _Id._ at 23.

18.   _See_ Redish, _The Value of Free Speech_, 130 _U. Pa. L. Rev._ 591, 593 (1982).

19.   _Cf._ F. Schauer, _Free Speech: A Philosophical Enquiry_ 56-58 (1982) (not acknowledging a broader and narrower sense of autonomy but rejecting autonomy as a value underlying a distinctive free speech principle). The ambiguity at issue is illustrated by Emerson's use of the phrase "the affirmation of self." T. Emerson, _supra_ note 3, at 5, and by Scanlon's use of "autonomy" in Scanlon, _A Theory of Freedom of Expression_, 1 _Phil. & Pub. Affairs_ 204 (1972).

20.   _See_ Berlin, _Two Concepts of Liberty_, in _Four Essays on Liberty_ 118, 122-31 (1969).   But _cf._ MacCallum, _Negative and Positive Freedom_, 76 _Phil. Rev._ 321 (1967) (critically placing Berlin's negative versus positive freedom distinction in proper perspective).   _See also_ C. Bay, _The Structure of Freedom_ (1958); R. Flathman, _The Philosophy and Politics of Freedom_ (1987); F. Oppenheim, _Dimensions of Freedom_ (1961).

21.   _See_ L. Tribe, _American Constitutional Law_ 789 (2d ed. 1988).

22.   _Cf._ F. Schauer, _supra_ note 19, at 134-35 ("[t]he broader the scope of the right, the more likely it is to be weaker, largely because widening the scope increases the likelihood of conflict with other interests, some of which may be equally or more important").

23.   _But see_ the apparently fairly broad free speech protection extended to commercial marketplace speech that goes beyond merely _proposing_ a commercial

transaction by the Court in Board of Trustees of State Univ. v. Fox, 109 S. Ct. 3028, 3036 (1989).

24. See A. Meiklejohn, supra note 6, at 79.

25. T. Emerson, supra note 3, at 14.

26. R. Ladenson, A Philosophy of Free Expression and Its Constitutional Implications 152 (1983).

27. Id. at 150 ("it is . . . a non-sequitur to hold that someone who opposes conforming to custom merely as custom must also believe that people should be encouraged to be idiosyncratic simply for the sake of being idiosyncratic").

28. See Scanlon, Freedom of Expression and Categories of Expression, 40 U. Pitt. L. Rev. 473, 483 (1974) (Mill's focus on "true belief and individual growth;" concern for "fostering the development of better (more independent and inquiring) individuals").

29. J.S. Mill, On Liberty 33 (D. Spitz ed. 1975).

30. C.L. Ten, Mill on Liberty 136 (1980).

31. J.S. Mill, supra note 29, at 91. See also C.L. Ten, supra note 30 at 106-7; Honderich, 'On Liberty' and Morality-Dependent Harms, 30 Pol. Studies 504 (1983). A computer research session suggests that this interesting passage has been quoted only once in recent reported American jurisprudence, and that, appropriately, in dissent. See In re Excelsior Pictures Corp. v. Regents of the University of State, 3 N.Y.2d 237, 256, 144 N.E.2d 31, 43, 165 N.Y.S.2d 42, 58 (1957) (Burke, J., dissenting). But cf. A. Solzhenitsyn, A World Split Apart, in East and West 50-51 (1980) (reference to "destructive and irresponsible freedom" being granted "boundless scope").

32. J.S. Mill, supra note 29, at 59. See also J.S. Mill, Utilitarianism 12-13 (G. Sher ed. 1977) ("no intelligent human being would consent to be a fool . . . even though they should be persuaded that the fool is better satisfied with his lot than they are with theirs").

33. J.S. Mill, supra note 29, at 17 n.2.

34. Id. at 50.

35. J.S. Mill, supra note 29, at 11.

36. *Id.* at 12.

37. *Id.* at 33.

38. *Id.* at 54.

39. *Id.* at 56.   None of this is to suggest, of course, that Mill would seek to suppress the speech of those who disagree with the worthiness of Millian values or with any particular conception of their realization.

40. *Id.* at 59.

41. *Id.* at 60.

42. *Id.* at 63.

43. *Id.*

44. *Id.* at 64.

45. *See, e.g.,* Pring v. Penthouse Int'l, Ltd., 695 F.2d 438, 443 (8th Cir. 1982), *cert. denied,* 462 U.S. 1132 (1983).

46. Van Alstyne, *A Graphic Review of the Free Speech Clause,* 70 *Calif. L. Rev.* 107, 112 n.13 (1982).

47. *See H. Hart, The Concept of Law* 124, 126 (1961) on the logic and practical necessity of recourse to underlying purposes.

48. *See, e.g.,* Clark v. Community for Creative Non-Violence, 468 U.S. 288 (1984) (prohibition of demonstrators from sleeping in Lafayette Park); Tinker v. Des Moines School Dist., 393 U.S. 503 (1969) (wearing black armband in school); United States v. O'Brien, 391 U.S. 367 (1968) (draft card-burning case).

49. *See* Stone, *supra* note 4, at 194-96.   *See also* Stone, *Restrictions of Speech Because of Its Content: The Peculiar Case of Subject-Matter Restrictions,* 46 *U. Chi. L. Rev.* 81 (1978).

50. 109 S. Ct. 2533 (1989).

51. *Id.* at 2553 (Rehnquist, C.J., dissenting).

52. For the implications of this possibility, *see infra* Chapter 8.   For a standard defense of a less speech-restrictive approach, *see* Ely, *Flag Desecration: A Case Study in the Roles of*

Categorization and Balancing in First Amendment
Analysis, 88 Harv. L. Rev. 1482 (1975).

53. See F. Schauer, supra note 19, at 201-2.

54. Schad v. Borough of Mount Ephraim, 452 U.S. 61,
66 (1981).

55. See, e.g., Judge Richard Posner's reiterated
misgivings in Douglas v. Hustler Magazine, Inc., 769
F.2d 1128, 1141 (7th Cir. 1985), cert. denied, 475
U.S. 1094 (1986) ("Art...even of the artless sort
represented by `topless' dancing--today enjoys
extensive protection in the name of the First
Amendment") (contrasting an alternative of protecting
only "political" speech); Piarowski v. Illinois
Community College Dist. 515, 759 F.2d 625, 628 (7th
Cir.), cert. denied, 474 U.S. 1007 (1985).

56. Krueger v. City of Pensacola, 759 F.2d 851, 854
(11th Cir. 1985) (quoting Young v. American Mini
Theaters, 427 U.S. 50, 70 (1976)).

57. Stone, supra note 49, at 111-12. But cf. the
sexually explicit, but ideologically pointless,
language of the "cop abuse" cases discussed infra.

58. See, e.g., State v. House, 676 P.2d 892, 896
(1984) (en banc) (Rossman, J., dissenting), aff'd, 299
Or. 78, 698 P.2d 951 (1985).

59. The assumption that commercial nude dancing is
ordinarily sought to be suppressed because of its
"content," in the same sense in which a regime might
seek to suppress Das Kapital or Mein Kampf because of
dislike of or unpopularity of its content, seems
doubtful. See Krueger, 759 F.2d at 854.

60. Highway Tavern Corp. v. McLaughlin, 105 A.D.2d
122, 139, 483 N.Y.S.2d 323, 338 (1984).

61. Of course, the state is understandably required
to show more than mere triviality before obtaining a
criminal conviction. See, e.g., State v. Jacobson,
459 So. 2d 1285, 1290 (La. Ct. App. 1984) (obscenity conviction).

62. South Florida Free Beaches, Inc. v. City of
Miami, 734 F.2d 608, 609-10 (11th Cir. 1984). In
contrast, a Florida court has recognized a free speech
right to beg alms for oneself, despite the presumably
limited message content involved. See C.C.B. v.
State, 458 So. 2d 47, 48 (Fla. Ct. App. 1984).

63.   734 F.2d at 610.

64.   See, e.g., Jarman v. Williams, 753 F.2d 76, 78 (8th Cir. 1985) (assuming that the "message" intended is merely that dancing is not wrong); Kent's Lounge, Inc. v. City of New York, 104 A.D.2d 397, 398, 478 N.Y.S.2d 928, 929 (1984) ("recreational dancing is not a form of speech protected by the First Amendment") (further noting the absence of free speech protection for roller-skating).

65.   See, e.g., Marshfield Family Skateland, Inc. v. Town of Marshfield, 389 Mass. 436, 450 N.E.2d 605, 609, cert. dismissed, 464 U.S. 987 (1983).

66.   See Fact Concerts, Inc. v. City of Newport, 626 F.2d 1060, 1063 (1st Cir. 1980), rev'd on other grounds, 453 U.S. 247 (1981).

67.   See Tacynec v. City of Philadelphia, 687 F.2d 793, 796 (3d Cir. 1982), cert. denied, 459 U.S. 1172 (1983).

68.   Redgrave v. Boston Symphony Orchestra, Inc., 855 F.2d 888, 895 (1st Cir. 1988), cert. denied, 109 S. Ct. 869 (1989).

69.   333 U.S. 507 (1948).

70.   Id. at 510.

71.   Id.

72.   See, e.g., Archibald Cox's argument that the expression at issue in Cohen imposed social costs in the form of a lowering of the standard of public debate, in A. Cox, The Role of the Supreme Court in American Government 47-48 (1976).

73.   Cohen v. California, 403 U.S. 15 (1971).

74. Evidently, Cohen was not the author of the inscription at issue, and the jacket in question was covered with writing, among which the language at issue did not particularly stand out. See Farber, Civilizing Public Discourse: An Essay on Professor Bickel, Justice Harlan, and the Enduring Significance of Cohen v. California, 1980 Duke L.J. 283, 286 & 286 n.21. These details accord rather poorly with the image of a protester so overwrought with intensity of indignation that he, unlike, say, Henry David Thoreau in Civil Disobedience, could not reasonably be expected to convey this depth of feeling through mere

nonprofane speech.

75.   403 U.S. at 25.   Despite its judicial modesty in this respect, the Court remains fully inclined to review judgments that distinguish protected material that "provokes only normal, healthy sexual desires" from material that arouses "morbid" and presumably unhealthy responses. See Brockett v. Spokane Arcades, 472 U.S. 491, 498 (1985).

76.   403 U.S. at 26.

77.   Id.

78.   See, e.g., Rutzick, Offensive Language and the Evolution of First Amendment Protection, 9 Harv. C.R.-C.L. L. Rev. 1, 19 n.98 (1974) (quoting Haiman, Speech v. Privacy: Is There a Right Not to Be Spoken To? 67 Nw. U.L. Rev. 153, 189 (1972)).

79.   See Van Alstyne, supra note 46, at 142.

80.   See Redish, The Content Distinction in First Amendment Analysis, 34 Stan. L. Rev. 113, 141 (1981).

81.   Stone, supra note 4, at 244.

82.   People v. Callahan, 168 Cal. App. 3d 631, 214 Cal. Rptr. 294, 296 (1985), cert. denied, 474 U.S. 1081 (1986).

83.   FCC v. Pacifica Found., 438 U.S. 726, 743 n.18 (1978) (opinion of Stevens, J., joined by Burger, C.J., and Rehnquist, J.).

84.   403 U.S. at 25. See also Bollinger, Free Speech and Intellectual Values, 92 Yale L.J. 438, 470 (1983).

85.   Callahan, 168 Cal. App. 3d at 634, 214 Cal. Rptr. at 295.

86.   Id.

87.   Farber, supra note 74, at 302.

88.   See State v. Meyers, 462 So. 2d 227, 227 (La. Ct. App. 1984).

89.   It is difficult to envision the typical defendant as exercising autonomy in the literal form of Kantian legislation. See I. Kant, The Fundamental Principles of the Metaphysics of Ethics 38, 47, 52 (Manthey-Zorn

ed. 1966).

90. Occasionally, a brief, unelaborated reference to the race of one or more of the officers is made. See, e.g., State in re W. B., 461 So. 2d 366, 368 (La. Ct. App. 1984). A coherent focus on the unjustness of "the system" would also help the defendant in Millian terms.

91. See, e.g., Harbin v. State, 358 So. 2d 856 (Fla. Ct. App. 1978); Rutzick, supra note 78, at 22-27. Police restraint or indifference, however, does not add social content to the prior "speech." Occasionally, the invective is defended on a theory of the beneficial effects of catharsis. See, e.g., Redish, supra note 18, at 626. Experimental support for such theories is limited at best. See J. Goldstein, Aggression and Crimes of Violence 36, 48, 50, 53, 55, 164 (1975). It is certainly equally plausible to suppose that tolerating, if not actually rewarding, prolonged screaming at police officers legitimizes or encourages such behavior. In any event, this kind of theorizing would not seem to fall within the special competence of the judiciary.

92. 31 Wash. App. 745, 644 P.2d 747 (1982).

93. Id. at 760, 644 P.2d at 756.

94. Id. Courts often seek to have it both ways. In one case, the conviction was reversed, but the defendant was solemnly informed that the special restraint required of the police "does not give the public a right to abuse a police officer." People v. Justus, 57 Ill. App. 3d 164, 167, 372 N.E.2d 1115, 1118 (1978). Presumably, a constitutional right is indeed some sort of a right.

95. 31 Wash. App. at 761, 644 P.2d at 757.

96. Id. at 756 n.2, 644 P.2d at 754 n.2. Courts rarely pause to inquire whether there may be any connection between the increasing frequency of "reprehensible and disgraceful" language and their own increasing inclination to protect it on free speech grounds. See id. at 760, 644 P.2d at 756.

97. Id.

98. The sociological richness of the large number of "fighting words" cases is only hinted at by the examples cited above. See also Wilson v. Attaway, 757

F.2d 1227 (11th Cir. 1985); Bovey v. City of Lafayette, 586 F. Supp. 1460 (N.D. Ind. 1984), _aff'd mem_., 774 F.2d 1166 (7th Cir. 1985).

2

Hustler Magazine v. Falwell and the Hypertrophy of Free Speech Protection

INTRODUCTION

The decline of an institution such as freedom of speech is generally not measured out in detectable stages, or by discrete events. There may be occasional exceptions to this general rule, however. In <u>Hustler Magazine v. Falwell</u>,[1] the Supreme Court, through an opinion by Chief Justice Rehnquist, held with virtual unanimity[2] that

> public figures and public officials may not recover for the tort of intentional infliction of emotional distress by reason of publications such as the one...at issue without showing in addition that the publication contains a false statement of fact which was made with "actual malice," <u>i.e.</u>, with knowledge that the statement was false or with reckless disregard as to whether or not it was true.[3]

The publication at issue was a parody of a Campari Liqueur advertisement, the gist of which portrayed Reverend Falwell as having engaged in "a drunken incestuous rendezvous with his mother in an outhouse,"[4] and as being a habitual drunk. The ad parody was accompanied by a disclaimer indicating that it was "'not to be taken seriously,'"[5] and the magazine's table of contents listed the parody as "'[f]iction.'"[6] The plaintiff Reverend Jerry Falwell's attention was drawn to the ad parody by a reporter, and Falwell shortly thereafter filed suit alleging libel, invasion of privacy, and intentional infliction of emotional distress. The defendants, Hustler Magazine and publisher Larry Flynt, were granted a directed verdict on the invasion of privacy claim and were found not liable on the libel claim, but the jury found both defendants liable for $100,000 compensatory damages and $50,000 punitive damages on the claim of intentional infliction of emotional distress.[7] The judgment was affirmed by the Fourth Circuit, but was reversed by the Supreme Court.

The opinion for the court drew, at least implicitly, a number of controversial conclusions. First, it is questionable whether Flynt's ad parody should be treated as speech within the meaning, intent, or purposes and values of the First Amendment. That is, it is unclear whether Flynt's parody is actually speech in the constitutional sense. Second, assuming that Flynt's parody is speech in the constitutional sense, it is unclear why the court gave this speech the high level or degree of protection that it did. The Court has frequently sought to distinguish between "high-value" speech, or speech close to the core of the free speech clause, and "low-value" speech, or speech on the periphery of, if not entirely outside the purposes of, the free speech clause. This distinction is not unproblematic, but the court has often suggested that low-value speech may be constitutionally subject to state regulation on any one of a variety of relatively undemanding, nonrigorous constitutional tests. It is unclear why the Court did not view Flynt's parody as being within one of the "low-value" speech categories or at least as being analogous to speech ordinarily within those categories.

The Hustler Court's controversial conclusions may be examined primarily by reference to the broad range of purposes or values that might be thought to underlie the free speech clause. This focus raises a number of other controversial aspects of the Hustler opinion, including the relevance and application of a free speech-based concern for the value of individual self-realization; the relevance, for free speech purposes, of the falsity and unbelievability of Flynt's speech; and the possible analogy between Flynt's speech and invidious racial epithets. This chapter then considers whether any legitimate free speech concerns raised by the tort of intentional infliction of emotional distress could be addressed by nonconstitutional restrictions on the tort or, at least, by constitutional restrictions less dramatic than those imposed in Hustler. If the tort of intentional infliction of emotional distress is to be

"constitutionalized," then the most defensible
approach is to immunize only those otherwise tortious
speech-acts addressing a matter of public interest and
concern, regardless of whether the plaintiff-victim is
thought to be a public figure or not.

SPEECH AND NONSPEECH FOR CONSTITUTIONAL PURPOSES IN THE HUSTLER CONTEXT

By implication, the court in Hustler determined that
Flynt's parody was, at least as alleged, more like a
written defamation or libel than a psychological
battery and thus deserving of similar constitutional
treatment.[8]   Intentional   infliction   of   emotional
distress, even to the extent that it is inflicted in
some communicative manner, does not require that the
defendants have made some false assertion of fact.[9]
The Court nonetheless saw fit to subsume the tort of
intentional infliction of emotional distress within
the constitutional restrictions on the tort of libel.
Specifically, as quoted above, the Court required that
public official or public figure plaintiffs claiming
intentional infliction of emotional distress show not
only the elements of that tort, but also that the
defendant made a false statement of fact, and that the
defendant did so with actual malice.[10]
     The Court thus constitutionalized the tort of
intentional infliction of emotional distress in a
peculiarly inapposite way.   The Court grafted the
extraneous modern defamation element of falsity
incongruously onto the tort of intentional infliction
of emotional distress, and anticlimactically required
that the false statement be shown to have been made
with reckless disregard for its falsity.   However,
there is no organic, necessary, or even recurring
relationship between any communicative inflition of
emotional distress and the truth or falsity of any
statement of fact the defendant may happen to make.
In other words, there is no particular reason, if one
is inclined to verbally inflict emotional distress, to
do so in a way that requires or is attended by a false
statement.
     The emotional distress of someone in Falwell's
position is not assuaged by the understanding that
most or all readers do not believe the literal truth
of the factual assertions; the plaintiff's reputation,
or his distress over a decrease in his reputation, is
not the issue.   Further, we may be sure that no one
contemplating inflicting emotional distress on a
public official or public figure who is aware of the
Court's rule in Hustler will be so foolish as to
expose himself to the only possibility of plaintiff's

recovery by gratuitously including an arguably false
assertion of fact.   There will always be ways of
inflicting severe emotional distress on public
officials or public figures other than through false
factual claims.   For all practical purposes, the
Court's holding in Hustler grants reasonably
sophisticated perpetrators essentially complete and
absolute constitutional protection.

The relevance in this context of false statements
of fact by the defendant will be discussed further
below, but it is worth speculating why the Court might
have been led to essentially graft a portion of the
tort of defamation onto the tort of intentional
infliction of emotional distress.   Perhaps the Court
assumed that there was no harm in doing so since the
torts of defamation and intentional infliction of
emotional distress are often thought of as somehow
mutually equivalent[11] or at least as on a par with
each other constitutionally.[12]

The problem is that the two kinds of tortious
conduct might be entitled to the same degree of
constitutional protection without the elements of the
torts, such as a false statement, being transferable
between the torts in any nonarbitrary way.   The torts
of defamation and of intentional infliction of
emotional distress plainly serve different purposes;
the falsity of an assertion of fact is generally
relevant, in principle, only to defamation.   As one
commentator has rightly observed, "[t]he emotional
distress tort...is designed to protect the victim's
emotional well-being, as distinct from the
reputational interests historically protected in
defamation law."[13]   Intentional infliction of
emotional distress is more in the nature of a kick or
a punch and need not involve any true or false
assertion of fact.

This analogy between intentional infliction of
emotional distress and the tort of battery impeaches
the constitutional logic of Hustler at its deepest
level.   Most of us would be reluctant to ever
categorize any punch or kick as "speech" within the
meaning of the First Amendment, or to afford such
action even a limited degree of constitutional
protection.   We are reluctant to classify a punch as
"speech" even though some punches are provoked by the
literal speech of one's political opponent.   A punch
may, in at least some cases, convey a general attitude
or state of mind, and the person throwing the punch
may intend this, nor need any of this be lost on the
victim of the punch.   Arguably, the punch may be a
reaction or a response to a political speech with
which one heatedly disagrees.

But if a punch or, for that matter, a merely negligent elbowing, does not amount to speech in the constitutional sense, why must "written speech" be treated as speech within the meaning of the Constitution if the "written speech" is nothing more than a surrogate for the punch? If, in a particular instance, "written speech" is demonstrably intended to merely have the same functions and effect as a punch, shouldn't the law recur to substance rather than to form?[14]

As we have seen, the free speech clause has been widely interpreted by commentators to serve either a narrower or a broader range of purposes. Interpreted broadly, the free speech clause is, again, thought to operate to protect the workings of a representative process of government, to promote the detection and dissemination of truth at least in the political realm, and to accommodate and promote the important value of individual self-realization. As a first approximation, a court should be reluctant to classify "written speech" as speech in the constitutional sense where the utterance, apart from its popularity or unpopularity, cannot plausibly be construed as implicating any of the recognized purposes or functions of the first amendment.

The Court in Hustler did not consider the relation between the ad parody and the purposes or functions of the first amendment presumably because it assumed that Flynt's parody, however distasteful and controversial, qualified as speech in the constitutional sense. Such an assumption seems warranted only if one focuses only vaguely on the speaker and the addressee, both well-known, politically controversial public figures who are natural political adversaries, in a broad sense of the term "political." But if the focus is instead placed on the actual speech and its context, the Court's assumption seems more doubtful.

Regardless of whether one accepts the view that "Hustler is not a bona fide competitor in the 'marketplace of ideas,'"[15] it seems clear that the contents of the magazine, exclusive of any obscene material, cannot all be considered constitutional speech. In light of the recognized purposes of the free speech clause, we should again impose a minimum requirement that for something to count as speech in the constitutional sense, it must itself embody or seek to convey some discernible social idea, where both "social" and "idea" are interpreted with reasonable breadth. The Court has in fact come close to endorsing this requirement in several cases, such as the obscenity case of Paris Adult Theatre I v.

Slaton,[16] in which the Court concluded that "[w]here communication of ideas, protected by the First Amendment, is not involved,...the mere fact that, as a consequence, some human 'utterances' or 'thoughts' may be incidentally affected does not bar the State from acting to protect legitimate state interests."[17]

Chaplinsky v. New Hampshire[18] established the classic "fighting words"[19] category and at least arguably held such speech to be completely outside the meaning of the First Amendment. The Court in Chaplinsky referred to fighting words as "no essential part of any exposition of ideas . . . ,"[20] thereby at least suggesting a linkage between constitutional protection and the presence of an idea of some unspecified sort. Requiring that constitutionally protected speech seek to convey some rudimentary social idea is consistent with most of the familiar rhetoric of the free speech case law. Protecting written speech that embodies the requisite social idea is perfectly consistent with protecting allegedly outrageous, unpopular, or offensive ideas, or foolish and immoderate speech, or the conveyance of ideas dependent upon satire, imagination, exaggeration, or caricature, or speech that does not in fact persuade or even attempt to persuade some or all of one's immediate audience.

It is not at all obvious that Flynt's immediately retracted depiction of Jerry Falwell as engaging in drunken incest with his mother meets the "social idea" requirement. Consider an argument made on behalf of Hustler magazine in another context, on the issue of defamatoriness. The material is said to be nondefamatory because it is so patently absurd and nonsensical on its face that no reasonable reader could believe it to be true.[21] While the intended and appreciated inanity of a statement of a nominally factual sort may save it from being defamatory, it hardly suggests that the statement should be treated as a contribution to public discussion or debate.

To argue that Flynt's speech would be widely thought of as offensive, and particularly offensive to Reverend Falwell, by itself hardly suffices to supply the requisite social idea. While the Court majority may have seen fit to extend free speech protection to the arguably offensive terse anti-draft imprecation in Cohen v. California,[22] and while Cohen sought to extend protection to the emotive as well as the cognitive aspects of the speech, Cohen seems easily distinguishable.[23] The defendant in Cohen at least expressed, if without much pretension to articulateness, an opinion, or reaction, to some obviously significant political issue or debate, along with, if not by means of, his emotive meaning. Cohen is thus perhaps best read as protecting emotive meaning expression as long as there is some minimally sufficient grounding in cognitive meaning. But Flynt's speech in Hustler lacks the requisite cognitive meaning about some topic of potential public interest, even if, as seems questionable, it was intended to convey some recognizable emotive meaning, as opposed to merely inflicting a perlocutionary injury.

Courts have occasionally been led to overlook this simple logic on the dubious assumption that "all statements that are not factual must be categorized as opinion."[24] Perhaps the most straightforward analysis of Flynt's speech would recognize that it did contain one assertion of fact, however ludicrously false. But even if we assume, as the Court did in Hustler, that no recklessly false assertion of fact is contained within Flynt's speech,[25] it is a fallacy to assume, as the Court does, that Flynt's speech therefore falls into the category of "robust political debate,"[26] or "debate about public affairs,"[27] or speech on "public issues."[28] Why must speech that is neither true nor false necessarily qualify as some sort of opinion on a particular public issue? Presumably, an ordinary joke or riddle would fall into neither the fact nor opinion category.

Of course, Flynt's speech names or is about an incontestably public figure. This, however, does not mean necessarily that Flynt's speech sought to convey some social idea. Even speech by one public figure about another, antithetical public figure need not qualify as conveying a social idea. The Supreme Court has observed elsewhere that the mere background presence of political controversy or ideological debate, "lurking" in the broader cultural context of an instance of speech, does not itself necessarily change the speech's category.[29]

If Flynt's speech were interpreted generously, it could be seen to indicate not merely distilled irresponsibility, or inarticulate animosity, but a more particular message, perhaps along the lines of a hyperbolically formulated accusation of broad, unprincipled hypocrisy on the part of Reverend Falwell. If Flynt's language were reasonably susceptible to such a meaning, it would certainly meet the minimum requirements for speech in the constitutional sense. But Flynt's speech cannot genuinely sustain any such meaning. Initially, Flynt's speech appears to be speech in the constitutional sense, in that it expressly, or by reasonable inference, accuses or associates Falwell

Library of
Davidson College

with drunken incest contrary to Falwell's pretensions.
Flynt, however, wants to assert, for free speech
purposes, that this sort of implication was not meant
seriously and could not be taken seriously by a
reasonable audience, which seems plausible if
"reasonable" is defined restrictively.[30]   There is
certainly   no obvious reason why Flynt should be
allowed inconsistent positions on this issue.
However, if the "unprincipled hypocrisy" claim is not
fairly attributable to Flynt's speech, no other
cognizable social idea remains, except that which
unusually creative persons, or Flynt's attorneys, may
gratuitously bestow upon the speech after the fact.
    Finally, one can of course easily envision
Flynt's deriving a great deal of personal
gratification, if not individual self-fulfillment,
from the speech in question, and individual
self-fulfillment is, as we have seen, often considered
among the primary values underlying the free speech
clause. The problem with this view, even if we assume
that Flynt's speech promoted his self-fulfillment as
much as it might have predictably impaired that of
Falwell, is that not everything that promotes a value
underlying the free speech clause is necessarily
speech in the constitutional sense. Even if Flynt's
ad parody promoted Flynt's self-fulfillment in some
relevant sense recognizable to Aristotle, or Rousseau,
or John Stuart Mill, which seems doubtful in the
extreme, one might presumably derive comparable
self-fulfillment from a vigorous session of chopping
firewood or from leading a scout troop on a hike.
These latter activities are hardly speech in the
constitutional sense, and Flynt's ad parody is only a
marginally closer case.
    To put the point in perspective, one might note
that Flynt's putative speech simply does not lend
itself to classic free speech policy analysis. What
would be the point, for example, of suggesting that
Falwell's situation, or the welfare of the public
generally, would be promoted by "counterspeech" or a
rebuttal by Falwell of whatever assertions or opinions
are thought to be conveyed by Flynt's speech?[31]
Certainly, the public interest might be served by
Falwell's reacting to Flynt's speech in a way that
delegitimizes Flynt's approach, but this is hardly the
same as answering Flynt's speech on its own terms.
Similarly, it would be impertinent to suggest that to
avoid or minimize the injury, Falwell should have
avoided "further bombardment" by averting his gaze
from the ad parody.[32]   Furthermore, it would be
genuinely odd to ask, for example, such questions as
whether Flynt had available, at reasonable cost,

sufficient alternative channels or means of conveying his message in undistorted fashion beyond the means he actually chose. If Flynt had some cognizable social message to impart, he would, of course, have the resources and notoriety to convey his message in ways not involving the intentional infliction of emotional distress. If, on the other hand, Flynt intended neither to convey a social idea, nor to arbitrarily joke about a controversial public figure he disliked, but to inflict emotional distress on a designated victim, obviously no alternative means less subject to governmental regulation were available to him.

LOW-VALUE SPEECH VERSUS HIGH-VALUE SPEECH FOR CONSTITUTIONAL PURPOSES

A cold-eyed analysis suggests that Flynt's ad parody probably does not bear classification as speech within the meaning of the First Amendment. But even if Flynt's parody comes within the scope of the First Amendment, if it can be classified, apart from its controversiality or unpopularity, as "low-value" and not "high-value" speech, it should be subject to state regulation on grounds less stringent than those adopted by the Court in Hustler.

The low-versus high-value speech distinction, perhaps traceable to Chaplinsky,[33] assumes that in light of first amendment values, different types or categories of speech deserve different degrees of protection.[34] Speech central to, or at the core of,[35] the First Amendment merits stringent protection, while speech less central, or at the periphery of the first amendment, merits less protection.[36] The low-versus high-value determination does not reflect some essentially controversial judicial assessment of the merits or cogency of the idea being expressed, but rather the degree of relationship of the speech to the purposes underlying the free speech clause. Dean Stone indicates that among the low-value free speech categories are "express incitement, false statements of fact, obscenity, commercial speech, fighting words, and child pornography."[37] In this context, "obscenity" presumably refers generally to sexually explicit or pornographic materials; "obscenity" is often used to refer to the legal characterization of materials as failing to meet the relevant constitutional test, and therefore not at all protected. Characterizing express incitement as low-value speech also does not seem inevitable. At least some speech expressly inciting illegal acts would seem most logically classified as core political speech, crisply articulating an important approach to important public affairs, and therefore high-value speech. It is just that at least some such speech may fail the appropriate constitutional test, one that is very demanding on the government, as befits high-value speech.[38]

Whether one chooses to call the language of express incitement high-or low-value speech depends upon whether one focuses on its crucial political content and viewpoint, or upon its counseling of seriously harmful illegal acts. This choice itself is presumably not crucial, as long as the burden on the government to justify suppressing the speech is a heavy one, as with incontestably core speech. Obviously, other sorts of activities accorded constitutional protection by some provision other than the free speech clause are not typically divided judicially into high-value manifestations and low-value manifestations of that activity. One reason, however, for not classifying both obscene materials and express incitement to rebellion as low-value speech is that it makes the low-value speech classification nearly useless as an independent predictor of the degree of protection against government suppression that the speech is entitled to. On such an analysis, we know from the low-value speech classification only that the speech is entitled to either no, or virtually no, free speech protection (obscene materials), or the most stringent sort of protection, no less protective than any kind of high-value speech (express incitement), or else requires protection of an intermediate degree (e.g., commercial speech). The low-versus high-value distinction thus loses much of its meaning. The same point might be made, incidentally, with respect to the distinction between content-based and content-neutral restrictions on speech, in which knowing that a government restriction on speech is content-based tells us very little, if anything, about the stringency or laxity of the government's constitutional burden in suppressing the speech.

Perhaps the most useful analysis of what makes particular kinds of speech low-value speech for constitutional purposes is that of Professor Sunstein, who suggests the relevance of four factors. These four factors are as follows: first, that the speech be remote from the central first amendment focus on popular control of public affairs or the governmental process; second, that the speech be largely noncognitive rather than cognitive, or knowledge-imparting, in nature; third, that the speaker not be intending to convey a message; and finally, that the speech fall into a class where it is relatively unlikely that the government's motive in seeking to regulate the speech is constitutionally impermissible.[39]

While these four factors are not susceptible to invariably uncontroversial application, they do collectively suggest as unequivocally as can reasonably be hoped for that Flynt's speech in the Hustler case qualifies at best as low-value speech. First, although Falwell and Flynt are both public figures who frequently publish ideas about public affairs and public policy, Flynt's speech in the Hustler case does not reasonably seek to convey any of these governmental process-related ideas. Second, Flynt's speech is either wildly false by admission or utterly devoid of cognitive or knowledge-imparting content. Third, any coherent message is brought to Flynt's speech by the creative reader, rather than reasonably drawn from it. Finally, the theory that an illegitimate government motive played any significant role in regulating the defendant's speech is implausible. The regulation was, after all, initiated by a private party plaintiff in a civil suit whose claims must often filter their way through the jury process. The government's own role in regulating the kind of speech at issue in Hustler simply reflects the widespread view that there should be at least some minimal form of civil tort redress for the intentional infliction of severe emotional distress.

Professor Sunstein's four factors thus suggest that Flynt's speech should at best be classified as low-value speech and should not be given the practically absolute constitutional protection conferred on it by the Court. Flynt's parody is certainly entitled to no greater protection than arguably offensive speech that constitutes an independent common law tort. In the past, the Court has permitted state regulation of nonobscene but arguably offensive sexually oriented speech, based on its content, without imposing a demanding constitutional test. State regulation is allowed on the assumption that such speech is low-value speech[40] on the periphery of first amendment concerns.[41] In sexually oriented speech cases, the Court has recognized that it would be idle pedantry to suggest that regulating profanity in appropriate contexts imposes some appreciable burden or disadvantage on speakers who wish to convey a particular viewpoint, or even on those who wish to convey a particular speech "content."[42] As Justice Stevens has observed, "[a] requirement that indecent language be avoided will have its primary effect on the form, rather than the content, of serious communication. There are few, if any, thoughts that cannot be expressed by the use of less offensive language."[43]

Some conceptions of what constitutes "core" or high-value speech are more expansive. One commentator has suggested, for example, that "[e]xpressions of dislike or disrespect for another are precisely the type of ideological communications that are within the very core of the protection accorded by the first amendment."[44] Doubtless some expressions of dislike or disrespect may qualify as high-value speech, depending, among other considerations, on the content of the speech. But some instances of speech conveying disrespect, as we may assume Flynt's does of Falwell, are so "open" and undifferentiated, essentially all that Flynt "says" of Falwell is immediately "retracted" by Flynt's disclaimer,[45] that the values underlying the free speech clause are at best not strongly implicated.

This conclusion is independent of one's sympathy, or lack thereof, for Flynt or Falwell or the ideas ordinarily associated with either. Regardless of the identity or popularity of the speaker or the target, "few of us would march our sons and daughters off to war to preserve the citizen's right"[46] to commit the common law tort of intentional infliction of emotional distress by means of words or drawings that are, by admission, as devoid of any seriously intended meaning or public issue content as Flynt's were.[47] From the standpoint of the public interest, it seems appropriate to require, in exchange for granting immunity from liability for the tort of intentional infliction of emotional distress on a public figure or public official, that the speaker at least take the trouble to attempt to reasonably convey some particular public interest-related idea.

The Court thus had ample reason to classify Flynt's speech as low-value speech, at best, and accord it less than the practically absolute protection that it did. In addition, despite the important difference between the two torts, many of the individual and social costs of false and defamatory speech about public figures and public officials that have been identified in the libel context[48] are also relevant in the context of the Hustler case. If the risk of defamation, or unprovable defamation, constitutes a disincentive to public service, so does the risk of speech like Flynt's that is now essentially immunized by the Supreme Court.[49]

It should be noted that the arguments presented above do not rely in the slightest on any social interest in maintaining or elevating the level of

public discourse or in promoting public civility.
While such an interest has been given central
importance by such champions of liberty as John Stuart
Mill, there unfortunately seems to be little current
enthusiasm for such an apparently anachronistic
approach.[50]   This state of affairs may eventually
change if the judiciary begins to conclude that the
quality of public debate, particularly at the lower
ranges, is tending to systematically deteriorate over
time. If and when this occurs, the Court's logic in
Hustler may become more controversial.

It has been said that "[o]nly small men are
afraid of small writings."[51]   Writers of the stature
of Warren and Brandeis, however, have expressed
reasonable fear of material less inanely virulent than
Flynt's.[52]   Referring to personal gossip in general,
Warren and Brandeis classically warned that

> Even gossip apparently harmless, when widely
> and persistently circulated, is potent for
> evil. It both belittles and perverts. It
> belittles by inverting the relative
> importance of things, thus dwarfing the
> thoughts and aspirations of a people....
> Easy of comprehension, appealing to that
> weak side of human nature which is never
> wholly cast down by the misfortunes and
> frailties of our neighbors, no one can be
> surprised that it usurps the place of
> interest in brains capable of other
> things.[53]

Obviously this kind of assertion is not verifiable
with the degree of empirical rigor normally associated
with the ability to predict the occurrence of lunar
eclipses. But the rigorously verifiable is not
synonymous with the real. If there is a public
interest in diminishing the scope and pervasiveness of
mere idle gossip, there is an even more substantial
public interest in providing only limited
constitutional protection for intentional infliction
of severe emotional distress.

Finally, it is possible to argue for relatively
great constitutional protection for otherwise tortious
intentional infliction of emotional distress on the
grounds that such conduct amounts merely to "blowing
off steam," thereby avoiding the risk of more serious
harm by the defendant.[54] Even if we assume, however,
that this essentially Aristotelian theory of catharsis
is psychologically sound and that the harms of such
speech are slight, this argument should give us pause.
If the courts provide more than quite modest

constitutional protection in accordance with this theory, the courts are essentially paying off to an implicit threat by defendants, many of whom, including Flynt, are acting with deliberation rather than impulse, to wreak even more serious havoc on their targets, or on others, if their otherwise tortious conduct is not strongly immunized. Adopting the "blowing off steam" rationale is, therefore, even more objectionable than according a "heckler's veto" to those who point to their own responses to disfavored speech.[55]   Ultimately, the only sensible judicial response to those who feel some irresistible impulse to blow off steam is to insist that they do so by means of relatively high-value speech, of which defendants such as Flynt are presumably readily capable, or else that they accept a more modest level of free speech protection.

One controversial area of the law in which the claim of intentional infliction of emotional distress is sought to be countered in part by a "blowing off steam" rationale is that of abusive, racially charged epithets or invective. Any attempt to sort out instances of personally directed racial invective deserving greater and lesser degrees of protection is apt to be difficult. At least as to public official or public figure plaintiffs, the logic of the Court in Hustler will be clear: the defendant's speech will be immunized as long as the defendant is not so unwary as to gratuitously include a false, but plausible, statement of fact about the plaintiff.

This rule, however, is less than fully satisfactory, especially when it is recognized that the category of "public officials" is often defined expansively, so to include, for example, ordinary police officers.[56]   One can certainly imagine that continually repeated vicious racial invective directed at a black police officer by a superior officer in the police hierarchy could be sufficient to establish the common law elements of intentional infliction of emotional distress.[57]   Rather than simply regretting the large social cost of such speech, borne disproportionately by ethnic minorities, one might consider whether a reduced level of constitutional protection could ever be appropriate in such cases.

In accordance with the basic distinction drawn in this chapter, courts should assume the quite manageable task of considering whether the speech at issue involves "pure" racial invective or racial invective severable from any social idea reasonably conveyable without resort to racial epithets. Not all racial invective is constitutionally alike. Our free speech traditions will often require protection, for example, for the misguided eugenics policy advocate. They do not require substantial protection for the speaker whose point or message involves no more than simply announcing that the particular listener-victim is indeed quite uncontroversially a member of some racial or ethnic group to which the speaker attaches, for utterly unspecified reasons, a pejorative appellation. That a person $\underline{A}$, who is a member of group $\underline{B}$, is referred to by the speaker as a (member of group) $\underline{B_1}$, without more, where $\underline{B_1}$ is merely a rude name for $\underline{B}$, is not itself a sufficient social idea, however much it may resonate or fit in with a broader cultural element of an actually articulated racial ideology.

This distinction would often protect speech not involving a severable racist epithet that, for example, attempts to give a reason for the view that members of group $\underline{B}$ are somehow objectionable or even speech that asserts that some or all $\underline{B}$s possess some objectionable quality. Under this distinction, such speech would be protected even if the speech is addressed only to one of the members of $\underline{B}$ whom the speaker has no realistic hope of persuading. Otherwise protected speech directed only to implacably opposed listeners, or that is not even intended to convince that particular audience, should not for that reason alone lose its protected character. The value of free speech is not solely dependent upon the prospect of changing minds; one might seek instead to preserve one's integrity by taking a definitive stand on some controversial public issue, even to an unalterably hostile audience, perhaps partly out of a desire to avoid hypocrisy or patronizing one's audience. One might also object that this approach protects the articulate or the reason-giving racist. The objection is largely correct, but it is a result that seems consistent with free speech values and purposes. And at least for the moment, the alternative accepted by the majority of the Supreme Court, in the case of public officials and public figures, is more solicitous of even the most painful, inane racial invective as long as the speaker does not inadvertently make a false, but plausible, factual claim. The obviously vexed question of restrictions on racist speech will be taken up again in more detail in the following chapter.

LIMITING THE SCOPE OF THE TORT BY NONCONSTITUTIONAL MEANS

It would be perfectly sensible to have misgivings about reducing, if not eliminating, constitutional protection for Flynt's speech if the courts would, as a result, be left with insufficient means of controlling potential jury excesses in cases not involving the expression of any social idea. But this is not the case. The courts have at their disposal a number of nonconstitutional means of reducing the potential for abuse of the tort of intentional infliction of emotional distress.

The essential legitimacy of the tort of intentional infliction of emotional distress is well established,[58] and Professor Prosser suggested in his seminal article in 1939 that up until that time, the tort had been well policed and generally not used as an instrument of abuse.[59] Recently, however, the fear has arisen that plaintiffs might use the tort of intentional infliction of emotional distress to avoid short statutes of limitation, circumvent restrictions on punitive damage awards, unduly expand privacy concepts, or generally appeal to juror prejudice, among other potential abuses.[60]

Each of these potential problems, however, can readily be controlled by insistence on appropriate common law restrictions. One commentator has observed, for example, that "the strict requirements of the outrageousness standard"[61] may account for the paucity of successful emotional distress suits against media defendants. The common law requirement that the plaintiff show severe emotional harm[62] and that the defendant's conduct be extreme and outrageous, over and above showing the defendant's intent, functions as an effective nonconstitutional limitation on the range of the tort.[63]

Accordingly, a showing of defendant's intent does not substitute for a showing of outrageousness, and a showing of outrageousness does not substitute for showing the requisite intent.[64] Similarly, neither intent nor outrageousness substitutes for a showing, perhaps even on a standard of "convincing" evidence,[65] of the seriousness or gravity of the emotional harm inflicted.[66] If, despite the possibility of judicial supervision of the elements, further restrictions on the tort are necessary, the courts could simply limit or bar the availability of punitive damages. This limitation could perhaps be based on the theory that the legal distinction between merely being liable for this tort, and appropriately being subject to punitive damages, is essentially arbitrary.[67] As has been suggested in the libel area, the states might simply impose a reasonable statutory maximum on the amount of total damages recoverable for intentional infliction of emotional distress.[68] Finally, the tort can have a short statute of limitations no longer than the period applicable to the most closely related torts.[69]

CONCLUSION

The threat to free speech values posed by potential tort liability for speech akin to Flynt's is minimal, especially if the courts and legislators adopt the available nonconstitutional means of restricting potential excesses. The Court in Hustler chose instead to protect almost absolutely, in a practical sense, language intended merely to inflict severe emotional distress on public figures and public officials.

One reason for this approach, beyond the continuing tessellation of public moral standards, the coarsening of public discourse, and our cultural enthusiasm for any extension at all of the First Amendment, may be the Court's prediction that such a course would help avoid subjecting the Court to superintending yet another stream of free speech cases. The problem is that it is probably not much easier to judicially identify public officials and public figures for such purposes than it is to tell whether particular language seeks to convey a cognizable social idea. For example, suppose a television reporter emotionally abused Jessica McClure, the toddler famous for falling into a well. Would the case really hinge on the presence or absence of a plausible false statement of fact, or would the court instead find a way to deny her public figure status? This example suggests that public figure versus private figure status is only loosely associated with the essential concerns underlying the free speech clause, which are captured more accurately by a concern for the presence of the requisite social idea.

It is initially surprising, though, in view of Chief Justice Rehnquist's heavy reliance on libel precedents,[70] that no member of the Court chose to pursue the possibility of imposing different constitutional standards based upon whether the speech at issue was on a matter of public interest and concern or on a matter of private or personal interest and concern. This approach is suggested by recent cases in the area of libel.[71] On reflection, however, the Court's disinclination to pursue this avenue may be explained on the basis of the poor fit between these categories and the actual speech in Hustler. It is probably safe to say that Flynt's speech itself was not on some matter of public interest or concern. But it also fits uneasily within the category of merely private or personal interest speech. It is not as though Flynt had stopped to inform Falwell that he had dropped his car keys or was, say, merely expressing annoyance over Falwell's reassigning him to a less prestigious job. Finding it difficult to categorize Flynt's speech as either public or private, the Court might have seen no point in applying the distinction.

The problem with this logic, however, is that the Court has implicitly adopted the wrong "default" setting. Even if the Court could not classify Flynt's speech as either public or nonpublic interest speech, it should not have effectively classified it as public interest speech by strongly constitutionalizing it. The Court should constitutionalize only such speech which it has affirmative reason, in light of basic free speech values, to protect. Speech that is not public interest speech, all else equal, should not be strongly constitutionalized because the "default" position, for unclassifiable speech, should be for the federal courts to respect the interest balancing inherent in state common law adjudication of tort claims, especially where a contrary approach may ultimately serve to degrade, rather than strengthen, the cultural institution of freedom of speech.

NOTES

1.   108 S. Ct. 876 (1988).

2. Justice White filed an opinion concurring in the judgment in which he appeared to broadly reject Chief Justice Rehnquist's approach to the case, while leaving to a more propitious moment the task of suggesting why the First Amendment required Chief Justice Rehnquist's result.   _Id_. at 883 (White, J., concurring). Justice Kennedy had not joined the Court in time for argument and took no part in deciding the case.

3.   _Id_. at 882.

4.   _Id_. at 878.

5.   _Id_.

6.   _Id_.

7.   _Id_.

8. For an analogy of intentional infliction of emotional distress to battery, _see_ Collin v. Smith, 578 F.2d 1197 (7th Cir.), _cert. denied_, 439 U.S. 916

(1978). For a discussion of the illegitimacy, from a free speech value standpoint, of relying on perlocutionary meaning, or the essentially broadly coercive or manipulative effects of certain kinds of speech, see Solum, Freedom of Communicative Action: A Theory of the First Amendment Freedom of Speech, 83 Nw.U.L. Rev. 54, 88-97 (1989).

9. See, e.g., Restatement (Second) of Torts § 46 (1977); W. Keeton, D. Dobbs, R. Keeton & R. Owen, Prosser and Keeton on the Law of Torts § 12 (5th ed. 1984) [hereinafter Prosser and Keeton].

10. Hustler, 108 S. Ct. at 882. Presumably, the defendant's actual malice must be shown by clear and convincing evidence, as required by the constitutional libel case of New York Times Co. v. Sullivan, 376 U.S. 254, 285-86 (1964).

11. See Dworkin v. Hustler Magazine, Inc., 668 F. Supp. 1408, 1420 (C.D. Cal. 1987).

12. Pring v. Penthouse Int'l, Ltd., 695 F.2d 438, 442 (10th Cir. 1982).

13. Mead, Suing Media For Emotional Distress: A Multi-Method Analysis of Tort Law Evolution, 23 Washburn L.J. 24, 27 (1983).

14. See, e.g., Bowen v. Gilliard, 107 S. Ct. 3008, 3019 (1987).

15. Herceg v. Hustler Magazine, Inc., 814 F.2d 1017, 1026 (5th Cir. 1987) (Jones, J., concurring in part and dissenting in part), cert. denied, 108 S. Ct. 1219 (1988). But cf. S. Brownmiller, Against Our Will: Men, Women and Rape 394-95 (1975) (pornography characterized as antifemale propaganda).

16. 413 U.S. 49 (1973).

17. Id. at 67.

18. 314 U.S. 568 (1942).

19. See, e.g., L. Tribe, American Constitutional Law § 12-8, at 837 (2d ed. 1988). See also Harry Kalven, Jr.'s reference to Chaplinsky as "a case which bespeaks the gentility of a bygone era." H. Kalven, A Worthy Tradition: Freedom of Speech in America 78 (J. Kalven ed. 1988).

20. Chaplinsky, 315 U.S. at 572. Professor Kalven pointed out that the unanimous Court opinion in Chaplinsky, whatever its current authority, was joined by Justices Black and Douglas, whose sensitivity to free speech values seems undeniable. See H. Kalven, supra note 19, at 79.

21. Hustler, 108 S. Ct. at 879.

22. 403 U.S. 15 (1971).

23. Id. at 26.

24. Dworkin, 668 F. Supp. at 1415 (citing Koch v. Goldway, 817 F.d 507, 509 (9th Cir. 1987)).

25. Hustler, 108 S. Ct. at 882.

26. Id. at 879.

27. Id. at 880.

28. Id.

29. See Pittsburgh Press Co. v. Pittsburgh Comm'n on Human Relations, 413 U.S. 376, 385 (1973) (gender-labeled help wanted ads as merely commercial speech, rather than political speech, even though the notion of the propriety of gender-stereotyped job categories is plainly implicated).

30. Hustler, 108 S. Ct. at 878. The true inanity of Flynt's language is recognized in Smolla, Emotional Distress and the First Amendment: An Analysis of Hustler v. Falwell, 20 Ariz. St. L.J. 423, 424 (1988 (Flynt's speech as "a bad, dirty joke"), but Professor Smolla thenreinvests Flynt's speech with coherent cognitive meaning in id. at 425 (message of Flawell's alleged hypocrisy and Flynt's associated distaste for Falwell). But see Fein, Hustler Magazine v. Falwell: A Mislitigated and Misreasoned Case, 30 Wm. & Mary L. Rev. 905 (1989). Fein's own theory that Flynt's speech was unprotected "fighting words," see id. at 911, 917, must fail in view of the general restriction of the "breach of the peace" element to circumstances involving immediate, fact-to-face confrontations between plaintiff and defendant at the time of the speech. See supra notes 18-19. For a different perspective, see LeBel, Emotional Distress, The First Amendment, and "This Kind of Speech": A Heretical Perspective on Hustler v. Falwell, 60 Colo. L. Rev. 315 (1989).

31. For the importance in other contexts of counterspeech, see Whitney v. California, 274 U.S. 357, 375 (1927) (Brandeis, J., concurring), overruled on other grounds, Brandenburg v. Ohio, 395 U.S. 444 (1969) (per curiam); see also Dworkin v. Hustler Magazine, Inc. 668 F. Supp. 1408, 1421 (C.D. Cal. 1987).

32. Cf. Note, First Amendment Limits on Tort Liability for Words Intended to Inflict Severe Emotional Distress, 85 Colum. L. Rev. 1749, 1749-50 (1985) (noting the possibility of a defendant's making it impossible for a public figure to avert her attention). But cf. Cohen v. California, 403 U.S. 15, 21 (1971) ("[t]hose in the Los Angeles courthouse could effectively avoid further bombardment of their sensibilities simply by averting their eyes") (establishing, in parallel with a few cases involving dangerous canines, a "one bite" rule).

33. 315 U.S. at 572 (referring to certain categories of speech as being of only "slight social value as a step to truth").

34. For a recent academic exposition, see Stone, Content-Neutral Restrictions, 54 U. Chi. L. Rev. 46, 47 & nn.2 & 4 (1987).

35. For a recent reference to the concept of the "core" of the First Amendment, see Boos v. Barry, 108 S. Ct. 1157, 1162 (1988) (the category of classic "political speech" as at the core).

36. For a recent example, see Curtis v. Thompson, 840 F.2d 1291, 1297-98 (7th Cir. 1988) (regulation of the category of "commercial speech" based on its content as "less problematic" than regulation of political speech based on its content).

37. Stone, Content Regulation and the First Amendment, 25 Wm. & Mary L. Rev. 189, 194 (1983).

38. See Brandenburg v. Ohio, 395 U.S. 444 (1969) (per curiam); see also American Booksellers Ass'n v. Hudnut, 771 F.2d 323, 331 (7th Cir. 1985) (pornography cannot be considered low-value speech if it is sought to be suppressed because of its alleged influence on political and social attitudes), aff'd per curiam, 475 U.S. 1001 (1986). But see Dennis v. United States, 341 U.S. 494, 544-45 (1951) (Frankfurter, J., concurring) (express incitement of overthrow of the government as low-value speech).

39. _See_ Sunstein, _Pornography and the First Amendment_, 1986 _Duke L.J_. 589, 602-06.

40. _See_ Young v. American Mini Theatres, Inc., 427 U.S. 50, 70 (1976) (plurality opinion).

41. _See_ FCC v. Pacifica Found., 438 U.S. 726, 743 (1978) (opinion of Stevens, J.). The Court more recently took a similar approach in analyzing a school district's regulation of offensive or vulgar speech by a public high school student in Bethel School Dist. No. 403 v. Fraser, 478 U.S. 675, 683 (1986).

42. _See Pacifica Found._, 438 U.S. at 743 & n.18.

43. _Id_. at 743 n.18. _But cf_. Cohen v. California, 403 U.S. 15, 26 (1971) ("words are often chosen as much for their emotive as their cognitive force").

44. Gard, _Fighting Words as Free Speech_, 58 _Wash. U.L.Q_. 531, 569 (1980).

45. _Hustler_, 108 S. Ct. at 879.

46. _Cf_. Young v. American Mini Theaters, Inc., 427 U.S. 50, 70 (1976) (plurality opinion) (referring to the right to see sexually explicit nonobscene materials at a convenient local theater).

47. _Hustler_, 108 S. Ct. at 878.

48. _See, e.g._, Epstein, _Was_ New York Times v. Sullivan _Wrong?_, 53 _U. Chi. L. Rev_. 782, 797-801 (1986).

49. _See id_.

50. One commentator has stated flatly that "[t]he societal interest in purifying or raising the level of discourse is not a sufficient justification for regulating speech. The abstract interest in civility is too weak to justify such explicit content regulation." Note, _supra_ note 32, at 1762 n.71 (citing Cohen v. California, 403 U.S. 15, 25 (1971)).

51. Faloona v. Hustler Magazine, Inc., 607 F. Supp. 1341, 1360 n.58 (N.D. Tex. 1985) (quoting Pierre de Beaumarchais), _aff'd_, 799 F.2d 1000 (5th Cir. 1986), _cert. denied_, 107 S. Ct. 1295 (1987).

52. _See_ Warren & Brandeis, _The Right to Privacy_, 4 _Harv. L. Rev_. 193 (1890).

53. Id. at 196; see also A. Bickel, The Morality of Consent 61-75 (1975).

54. See Prosser, Intentional Infliction of Emotional Suffering: A New Tort, 37 Mich. L. Rev. 847, 887 (1939) ("[S]ome safety valve must be left through which irascible tempers may blow off relatively harmless steam.").

55. See, e.g., Terminiello v. Chicago, 337 U.S. 1 (1948).

56. See Fleming v. Benzaquin, 390 Mass. 175, 454 N.E.2d 95, 104-5 (1983) (concluding in dicta that the weight of authority so holds) (citing Note, Police Defamation Suits Against Citizens Complaining of Police Misconduct, 22 St. Louis U.L.J. 676, 684-85 (1978)).

57. See the private employee case of Bailey v. Binyon, 583 F. Supp. 923, 932-34 (N.D. Ill. 1984) (distinction between actionable emotional distress and the unpleasantness of mere insults, annoyances, or indignities) (discussing no free speech issues).

58. See Yeager v. Local Union 20, Int'l Bhd. of Teamsters, 6 Ohio St. 3d 369, 453 N.E.2d 666, 670 (1983) (unanimity of adoption among the states).

59. Prosser, supra note 54, at 888-89.

60. See Mead, supra note 13, at 25.

61. Id. at 53.

62. See Fudge v. Penthouse Int'l, Ltd., 840 F.2d 1012, 1021 (1st Cir. 1988).

63. See, e.g., Ross v. Burns, 612 F.2d 217, 273 (6th Cir. 1980) (absence of "extreme and outrageous" conduct found as a matter of law); Cape Publications v. Bridges, 423 So. 2d 426, 428 (Fla. Ct. App. 1982) (same), cert. denied, 464 U.S. 893 (1983). But see Boos v. Barry, 108 S. Ct. 1157, 1164 (1988), in which the Court reiterated its view, adopted in Hustler, that an outrageousness standard would be too "inherently subjective."

64. See, e.g., Chuy v. Philadelphia Eagles Football Club, 595 F.2d 1265, 1275 (3d Cir. 1979) (en banc); Godbout v. Cousens, 396 Mass. 254, 485 N.E.2d 940, 946 (1985) (not requiring a showing that the defendant's intention was to cause particularly severe emotional distress).

65.   _See_ Prosser, _supra_ note 54, at 888.

66.   _See_ _id._; _see_ _also_ Mead, _supra_ note 13, at 48.

67.   _See_ the discussion in _Chuy_, 595 F.2d at 1277.

68.   _See_, _e.g._, Epstein, _supra_ note 48, at 815.

69.   _Cf_. Yeager v. Local Union 20, Int'l Bhd. of Teamsters, 6 Ohio St. 3d 369, 453 N.E.2d 666, 672 (1983).

70.   _Hustler_, 108 S. Ct. at 878-82.

71.   _See_, _e.g._, Dun & Bradstreet, Inc. v. Greenmoss Builders, 472 U.S. 749 (1985) (plurality opinion).

3

The Problem of Racist Speech

INTRODUCTION

The course of history following the Civil Rights Act of 1964 reminds us of the evolving, rather than static, nature of societal racism.[1] One group of problems of increasing public concern focuses on the proper legal response to what may be thought of as racist speech. Putatively racist speech has become the subject of potential litigation in a variety of contexts, including the workplace,[2] ordinary commercial transactions,[3] public policy debate,[4] the public schools,[5] and the college campus.[6] However it is defined, racist speech takes a number of forms. It imposes or threatens a number of harms. As a result, a variety of legal strategies have been devised to address the problems of racist speech. The consistency of such solutions with the Constitution's free speech clause is controversial, however, and this issue is central to the discussion that follows.[7]

Initially, several legal strategies appear to have promise in deterring, punishing, or obtaining compensation for racist speech. Depending partly upon context, one might look to the torts of group defamation[8] or intentional infliction of emotional distress,[9] or to civil[10] or criminal[11] anti-discrimination statutes, while making appropriate use of the "fighting words" doctrine developed by the Supreme Court in <u>Chaplinsky v. New Hampshire</u>.[12] This chapter surveys these legal strategies and discusses the constitutional free speech and other legal constraints on the use of these strategies, as well as the likely practical costs and disadvantages associated with their use. The chapter then proposes some elements of a theory of restrictions on racist speech consistent with the requirements of the first amendment. This theory seeks to take into account the particular features of the predominant strains of contemporary racism as it is currently practiced, and seeks also to give appropriate weight to the society's recognition of the sheer moral wrongness of racist speech, as distinguished from the possible harmful social and psychological consequences of such speech in particular cases.

In particular, this chapter suggests that the use of crudely insulting racist invective, in the form of invidious racial epithets, alone or in the context of other speech, remains a significant problem. Most or all of such speech may constitutionally be restricted, chiefly on the grounds that such speech, inherently or in its context, does not amount to an attempt to communicate any particular social idea and therefore fails to fall within the class of speech in the constitutional sense, or speech the legal protection of which promotes the range of values or purposes that might be thought to underlie the free speech clause. In most or all cases in which racial epithets occur in the context of a more extended speech, which by itself or in conjunction with the racial epithet communicates a sufficient social idea to otherwise qualify for free speech protection, it will ordinarily be possible to disaggregate the speech into a protected ideational component and an unprotected racist epithet component. Such speech may then be restricted not insofar as it conveys a particular social idea, but insofar as the racist epithet's use either imposes social or psychological harms on its target or victim, or, more importantly, is thought of by the society as an act of deontic moral wrong.

It is of course possible to argue that at least in some contexts, the social idea will be analytically inseverable from the invidious racial epithet, or that the racial epithet itself necessarily bespeaks or implies or conjures up and seeks to convey a sufficient social idea. Perhaps surprisingly, in a number of the litigated cases, these claims are simply implausible. More importantly, though, it will be seen that proscribing racial epithets is crucially unlike proscribing words such as "Solidarity," or "Jefferson." The latter may perhaps be examples of· linguistic tokens that are indispensable, in the sense that at least at a particular time and place, there are no substitutes for them that can as adequately communicate the speaker's intended message, insofar as protection of the utterance of that message promotes what we have referred to as free speech values. But there are adequate alternatives, or semantic substitutes, for racist epithets, insofar as what is sought to be conveyed through the epithet is a social idea, without distorting, subduing, or diluting either the social idea itself or the rhetorical power of conviction, or emotive force, with which it is conveyed. One might well wish to employ a racist epithet for reasons other than those purposes protected by the free speech clause, for example, simply to inflict emotional pain or to vent frustration, unrelated to any social idea one has. But such purposes do not implicate significantly the purposes or values underlying the free speech clause.

The practically available alternatives to sheer racist epithets will often in fact be superior, from a free speech values standpoint, from the speaker's own perspective. It must be admitted, however, that it cannot be conclusively demonstrated in advance that there will never be a case in which, from the speaker's own standpoint, there is no combination of available English words that does not significantly distort at least the emotive meaning of the message, by comparison with the alternative of precisely a racist epithet, insofar as the emotive meaning falls within the range of the free speech values. While the racist epithet itself may not be perfect, it might conceivably be marginally better.

In this rare case, in which even the most fiery, impassioned rhetoric cannot convey the protected meaning as well as rhetoric involving the use of a racial epithet, the constitutional case for tolerance is at its strongest. But the trade-off involved in such a case should be made clear. In protecting such speech we forfeit the societal interest in preventing or redressing the deontic wrong, as well as the psychological and social injury attributable to the distinctive features of the racist epithet, in order to protect not the expression of the speaker's message but the difference between the message conveyable using the racist epithet and the message conveyable using the best available substitute language, from the speaker's standpoint.

This chapter will thus argue that any unavoidable trade-offs between free speech values associated with the use of racial epithets and conflicting cognizable values will be both rare and, from the standpoint of free speech values, minimal in severity. If one seeks to impose broader restrictions, however, the costs in terms of free speech values, as well as other values, begin to mount up considerably, at least in the longer term. To seek to authoritatively suppress a range of allegedly racist social ideas, in the absence of recognizable racial epithets, is to invite a variety of unintended adverse consequences of varying degrees of severity. And while such a project of broad suppression of arguably racist speech, where such speech is not otherwise actionable as an act of, say, employment discrimination, is in some respects historically timely, in other respects it is of historically diminishing utility. Whether one thinks of racism as waxing or waning overall, it seems clear from the evidence that the problem of the expression of relatively crude racist social ideas, beyond racist epithets, of a type that it is plausible to imagine society's legally suppressing, is of historically diminishing importance, as a general tendency, whatever its absolute magnitude of importance.

Apart from the problem of racial epithets, then, as societal racism has become subtler, more refined, and more equivocal, it has become less responsive to a broad speech-suppressive legal strategy, beyond enforcing familiar civil rights and antidiscrimination statutes. Attempts at broad legal suppression of disfavored ideas in this context, whether successful or not, would likely engender a range of adverse consequences discussed below that would discourage even the proponents of such suppression, at least over the long term.

This chapter concludes that the legal suppression of racist epithets is generally consistent with the free speech clause and may in fact be well advised. This conclusion is tested by reference to Dean Lee Bollinger's sustained argument for the salutary effects of tolerating extremist speech.[13] However, to extend even successful legal suppression much beyond such a line is likely, we shall conclude, to become largely self-defeating.

THE LIMITATIONS OF CONVENTIONAL RESTRICTIONS ON RACIST SPEECH

Racial Group Defamation

In exploring the inadequacies of various approaches, including that of racial group defamation, it may be useful to envision a concrete example of unmistakable, crude, contemporary racist speech. Imagine a black undergraduate student walking alone on a predominantly white college campus. As a car passes, the driver sees fit to hurl an opprobrious racial epithet at the black student. We shall assume that only the targeted student hears the remark, and that the student has some sort of unspecified psychological reaction.

As ordinarily conceived, a racial group defamation approach to such an incident must falter on a number of grounds. This is so even if it is assumed that prosecution for racial vilification poses no greater free speech problems today than it did in 1952 when the Supreme Court decided <u>Beauharnais v. Illinois</u>,[14] although this premise is seriously questionable.[15] One scholar has recently concluded that the constitutional reasoning in <u>Beauharnais</u> "was crippled by <u>New York Times Co. v. Sullivan</u>, and its holding was unmistakably undone by <u>Philadelphia Newspapers, Inc. v. Hepps</u>."[16] But the problems faced by a racial group defamation approach to the incident described above extend far beyond issues of actual malice or the burden of proof on the issue of truth or falsity.

To begin with, the opprobrious racial epithet does not seem most plausibly characterized as conveying a true or false statement of fact, either explicitly or by fair inference. Typical racial epithets, however evocative, are preeminently harsh, crudely insulting expressions of the speaker's negative evaluation of the target, by virtue of the target's race. Whether the epithet seeks to communicate a reasonably coherent particular social idea or not, it will at most rise to the level of what is considered in the law to be a statement of opinion, and thus not to be any more actionable in racial group defamation[17] than in individual defamation.[18] The most vitriolic, psychologically damaging racial invective need not assert any statement of fact. If it does not, it will generally not be actionable on a group defamation theory.[19]

The example cited above would thus likely be immune from attack on a racial group defamation theory on at least this ground. But the example could be changed. Suppose that the speaker abjures racial epithets but delivers a scurrilous tirade consisting not of opinion exclusively, but in material part of true or false assertions of general fact about his target racial group. Even here, the choices are unattractive. Regardless of whether truth is made a defense, or falsity an element,[20] there are obvious prudential reasons counseling against making the truth or falsity of carefully phrased invidious racial assertions a central element in the case. It is difficult to imagine a forum better suited to the demagogue and the seeker of publicity. The factual assertions may raise complex, subtle, unresolved issues of natural or social science beyond the ken of most scientists, let alone most juries.[21] The risk of error, or of public misimpression from a jury finding that the factual claims are not provably false, with an ensuing propaganda harvest, seems large.[22]   The misconceived factual inquiry would predictably come to dominate the trial, until such time as the presiding judge risked accusations of censorship and suppression by limiting the scope and length of the defendant's presentation on the issue of falsity.   This is all quite aside from the fact that the judicial inquiry into the truth or falsity of the defendant's claims is likely to be inherently demeaning to the targeted group.

One possible response to this problem would be to revive the tradition of libel prosecutions in which truth or falsity is legally irrelevant.[23]   Just as a defendant might defame or otherwise injure through speech an individual member of a racial group, or the racial group itself, without making any assertion of fact, so an individual member of a group, or the group itself, may be injured by speech that is at least technically true, if grossly incomplete or misguided. While such an approach would minimize a number of the problems noted above, it obviously faces substantial free speech and due process hurdles, and it suggests that some tort theory other than group defamation is perhaps more appropriate.[24]   At the pragmatic level, the possibilities for martyrdom of a defendant who is found civilly or criminally liable for speaking what he will attempt to portray as an important alleged social truth seem substantial.

Of course, a racial group defamation approach to the racial epithet incident posed above faces other problems as well.   If the action is thought of as civil in nature, it is not clear whether the proper plaintiff would be the individual target addressed or all persons encompassed within the scope of the racial epithet employed.[25]   This choice raises issues not only of standing, but also of the theory and measure of damages, as well as even more basic issues.   If the group allegedly defamed cannot show that the language employed fits into a limited number of traditional categories, it may have to show actual damages to the group caused by the defendant's language in order to recover.[26]   Actual damages causally attributable to the particular defendant's remarks, in the absence of some concert of action theory that allows the plaintiff to rely on the harms attributable to racist speech generally, may be difficult to show.

In the racial epithet incident postulated above, there is, of course, no actionable defamation because the allegedly defamatory language was by hypothesis not published to a third party.[27]   If the theory is racial group defamation, there is arguably still no

publication if the racial epithets are addressed
exclusively to even a large audience of only the
verbally targeted race. As well, it is at least
arguable that invidious racial epithets heard only by
target group members are not defamatory, at least in
the traditional sense, in that such language, in those
circumstances, would not tend to impair the target
group's reputation in the community or to deter others
from dealing with the target group,[28] however morally
wrong, offensive, or psychologically damaging the
epithets were. Such language, under such
circumstances, impairs dignity, self-esteem, or a
number of other crucial values,[29] but not
reputation.[30]

The defamatory character of even the most
venomous racial epithets may in fact remain at least
contestable if the epithets are also heard by
nontarget group members. If the hearers who are not
target racial group members can be shown already to
have been racially prejudiced against the target
group, the target group's reputation may well have
been unaffected or reinforced, but not impaired or
diminished by the racist invective.[31] But if the
nontarget group members were not racially prejudiced,
their natural reactions may range from mild disdain to
shock and outrage toward the speaker, and at worst
from indifference, to active sympathy, for the
targeted group.[32] Defamation, or the damages flowing
from defamation, may even under these circumstances be
contestable.

Intentional Infliction of Severe Emotional Distress

The strategy of reliance on the tort of outrage,
or intentional infliction of severe emotional
distress, has had at best limited success to date in
the context of racist invective. The tort itself is
ordinarily defined in narrow, restrictive terms.[33] One
commentator has accurately observed that

> Courts generally impose strict culpability
> requirements, permitting such actions only
> where the defendant intentionally or
> recklessly caused the plaintiff mental
> suffering. Further, the cause of action is
> normally limited to those cases in which the
> plaintiff has suffered a severe degree of
> emotional distress as the result of the
> defendant's "extreme and dangerous" conduct
> exceeding all reasonable bounds of
> decency.[34]

In elaborating on the degree of severity of emotional distress required, one court has observed that the distress must be "so severe that no reasonable man could be expected to endure it. The intensity and the duration of the distress are factors to be considered in determining its severity."[35]

Some plaintiffs have successfully stated a cause of action on this theory in cases involving the defendant's use of racial epithets and racial invective against the plaintiff, but such cases generally involve other sorts of allegedly outrageous conduct in addition to the verbal epithets,[36] as well as special circumstances and a special relationship between the plaintiff and defendant not characteristic of our archetypal campus racial epithet case.[37] Whether even the repeated use of racial epithets would have sufficed to constitute intentional infliction of severe emotional distress must remain unclear as long as the plaintiff also alleges such grounds as arbitrary, groundless demotion or dismissal from the job.[38] Similarly, it is unclear whether verbal abuse of a stranger will suffice if those plaintiffs who have successfully stated a cause of action have also alleged employee status, as well as the defendant's knowledge of the plaintiff's particular susceptibility to emotional distress, and violation of union status.[39]

At least in the absence of a relevant special relationship or special "aggravating" circumstances, courts have been reluctant to allow "mere" use of racial epithets to reach a jury on a theory of intentional infliction of severe emotional distress.[40] The typical judicial analysis has involved a denunciation of the racial epithets as objectionable,[41] but a characterization of the use of racial epithets as merely offensive, insulting "namecalling,"[42] for which, in light of the typically modest physical or psychological symptoms resulting,[43] no recovery may be had.

As the tort of intentional infliction of severe emotional distress is traditionally understood, these results are generally predictable, and in that sense justified. Of course, the courts err in suggesting that the use of racial epithets by a member of a historically dominant racial group against a member of a traditionally explicitly subordinated racial group, in the American historical context, is essentially indistinguishable from mere rude forms of address or mere offensive namecalling.[44] But the problem is not so much insensitive or unduly constricted application of the tort, but its substantial misdirectedness even in theory. One may argue that the use of racial

epithets is not so "extreme,"[45] at least in the sense
of so statistically infrequent, as to fit within the
tort, and one may point out that even predictable
adverse psychological and social consequences flowing
from the tort will not suffice unless the plaintiff's
reaction can be characterized as "severe."[46]

All of this hardly establishes that the
defendant's conduct cannot reasonably be thought of as
tortious. Instead, it merely demonstrates that the
tort of intentional infliction of severe emotional
distress is an inapt vehicle, and is poorly designed
for the job. As this chapter suggests more generally
below, the essence of what is wrong with the use of
racial epithets is not that it is offensive,[47] or that
it is offensive and is becoming less common
historically,[48] or even that it is offensive and is
becoming, in the minds of its targets, increasingly
so.[49] The essence of the public policy underlying the
wrongness of the use of racial epithets is instead
precisely that it is morally wrong, largely
independent of its degree or popularity or
offensiveness. There would be good grounds in public
policy for holding such activity tortious even if it
were quite common, and even if its victims had been
socialized, or impelled by circumstances, to regard it
as only minimally offensive.

Similarly, the essence of what is condemnable
about racial epithets is not, as we shall see below,
that they can by themselves be proved to inflict
genuinely grievous, severe psychological injury on
their targets, in some subjectively perceived sense.
All this may be difficult to show in any particular
case, despite the undoubtedly devastating, profound,
and subtle short-and long-term consequences of
American racist patterns and practices generally.[50]
Whether it is scientifically demonstrable fact or not,
it is certainly at least conceivable that persons who,
as a group, are continually subjected to racist
treatment, including racist epithets, tend to adapt in
various ways so as to reduce their sensitivity in
terms of the largely psychological shock effects
measured by the tort of outrage. Even if no exotic
psychological defense mechanisms are called into play
to reduce one's direct psychological vulnerability to
such shocks, the shocks might at least conceivably be
reduced by the ordinary process of inurement through
repeated exposure.[51]

But it is hardly a decisive argument against a
legal restriction of racist epithets that the victims
of such epithets tend to adapt, perhaps in
self-defeating, self-destructive ways, such as by
identifying with their tormentors,[52] or with reduced

levels of self-esteem,[53] to racist depredations, merely because such adaptations reduce the severity of the victim's emotional distress in the ways for which the tort of outrage provides redress. Of course, these adaptations are in response to racism generally, and not distinctively in response to racist speech, let alone the type of racial epithet speech that is the focus of this section. This is irrelevant to our point, which is that even if we assume that victims adapt to racial epithet speech in ways that minimize the sorts of injuries traditionally central to severe emotional distress, such speech could still sensibly be viewed as tortious on some revised, alternative theory. At least in this context, the legal system should not single out, among all possible victim reactions, near hysteria as the sole compensable reaction, while ignoring the possibility of more severe, but less spectacular, less overtly manifested, or less outwardly directed, victim reactions. More fundamentally, the law should not ignore what a hard-won societal consensus has established as the elemental wrongness of the use of racial epithets, independent of any emotional distress or other psychological reactions they may cause. At the very least, as we shall see, the free speech clause does not preclude the recognition of a tort that focuses not so much on the tort's "unendurability" in virtue of the victim's reaction,[54] but on the tort's unendurability in terms of the clarity with which basic social norms have been flouted.

Criminalizing racist speech has the advantage of shifting the focus from the relations between a particular victim and perpetrator to the question of the wilful violation of basic norms from which the community derives not only stability, but its legitimacy, as a community respectful of the elemental dignity of its constituent members. The use of racist epithets, in particular, is ordinarily a knowing, wilful breach of minimal community solidarity, and it is appropriate that the judicial response take the form of an authoritative expression of repudiation in the name of the community itself.

However, drafting a practically workable criminal statute that can be effectively used to vindicate the community's rejection of racist speech, however defined, while respecting the recognized free speech rights and interests of speakers, the audience, and the public generally has proven unexpectedly difficult. Adverse consequences and intractable dilemmas, both anticipated and unanticipated, loom large. While other countries continue to experiment with limited success,[55] statutory criminalization of racist speech has had limited appeal for American states.[56]

Some of the recurring problems associated with criminalizing racist speech can be briefly illustrated as choices confronted by the statutory drafters. First, one must overcome the daunting challenge of defining the target kind of speech, the necessary state of mind or intent on the part of the defendant, the undesirable result of the speech that is sought to be suppressed, the nature and kind of causation between speech and result, and the degree to which those results must have been predictable.[57]   Apart from any concerns for freedom of speech, one must draft a reasonably broad-ranging, efficacious statute, lest the statute become merely an empty symbol, while providing fair notice of its scope, and not criminalizing speech which under the circumstances may seem justifiable or excusable, at least in the eyes of a jury.

A number of these problems do not seem resolvable by experimental tinkering with the wording of the criminal statute.   For example, one might reduce the difficulty of proving the defendant's intent by statutorily emphasizing the actual or probable consequences of the defendant's speech.   But the more extreme and outrageous the racist speech, hence the greater the speech's vulnerability to suppression, the greater the likelihood that the prosecution will not be able to prove beyond a reasonable doubt that the probable or actual consequences of the defendant's speech were predominantly something other than indifference, revulsion toward the speaker, or sympathy for the targets of the speech.[58]

There is as well the irresolvable conundrum of the defense of truth.[59]   Perhaps in recognition of the truth that racism is in part a matter of how one looks at, explains, or interprets selected undenied facts, a statute criminalizing racist speech might deny the relevance of a defendant's claim of the truth of his statements.[60]   This would limit the potential for a criminal prosecution's turning essentially into an awkward, degrading, pseudo-scientific judicial trial on the merits of the group targeted by the speech, with the facts being found by amateurs, and the initiative being held largely by the defendants. Declining to recognize truth as a defense might also convey the public sentiment that some values simply outrank unrestricted freedom of speech, even in the absence of a public emergency.[61]

On the other hand, the inclination to view the truth status of propositions addressing issues of pubic policy as irrelevant, or of secondary importance, is uncomfortably alien to the best traditions of Plato, John Milton, Thomas Jefferson, and John Stuart Mill. Certainly, any government assertions of the essential falsity of the racist speech will inevitably ring hollow with substantial segments of the public if the government even creates the arguable appearance of not itself being sufficiently convinced of the speech's falsity to allow such falsity to be judicially exposed through the adversary process, even if the government's motivation is actually quite otherwise. There is thus some force to the argument that just as the question of clear and present danger must be determined judicially, in each particular case, so the balance between the pursuit of political truth and various arguably incompatible values must be made judicially in each particular case, rather than once and for all by the legislature for the broad category of racist speech.[62] Weighing the value of truth against that of solidarity, or of legally enforced solidarity, seems less manageable in the abstract than in particular cases.

Similarly difficult issues are posed by the question of whether the criminal statute should require that all prosecutions be brought only with the consent of some designated relatively high-placed public official.[63] While the higher authorities may be more sensitive to the importance of free speech concerns than local prosecutors charged with preventing disruptive incidents,[64] and while requiring higher approval might well result in more politically astute selection of cases for prosecution, as well as affirming the value of equal dignity from the highest levels of government, there are obvious costs in imposing such a requirement. If local authorities are inclined to prosecute, the failure of higher authorities to acquiesce, even for justified reasons,[65] may be perceived as legitimizing, if not endorsing, the content of the speech. Declining to prosecute because of realistic fears of the weakness of the government's case on perhaps only a single element may well be read by some of those most deeply concerned as indicating bias, insensitivity, or cowardice on the part of the highest governmental authorities. The government's choice will often be difficult, because the most influential or most popular racist speakers, successful prosecution of whom might create the greatest benefit, will tend to be those whose unsuccessful prosecution may be both relatively likely and politically most disastrous.[66]

Finally, there is the controversial issue of whether the criminal statute should by its terms apply to racist speech directed by members of historically oppressed groups against groups not historically oppressed, or what would otherwise be racist speech if such historical power relationships did not obtain. While this general problem is not unique to a criminal law response to racist speech, a criminal statute opposing racist speech poses the problem in particularly stark fashion.   There is a certain superficial evenhandedness in criminalizing both anti-black and anti-while speech, but the costs of successful prosecution of black speakers where some arguably comparable white speakers are acquitted or left unprosecuted may be substantial.[67]   More fundamentally, it is deeply questionable whether black victims of racist speech are genuinely similarly situated with at least those whites who are targeted as members of an undifferentiated white community.   In many particulars, this debate must recapitulate the currently not fully resolved controversy between formal or color-blind neutrality and more compensatory or historically-oriented strategies of affirmative action.[68]   It is, at least, hardly self-evident that anti-black and anti-white speech must rationally be regarded as symmetrical harms in nature and degree.

In sum, if the inescapable constitutional problems, including free speech problems associated with criminalizing racist speech, are set aside, the primary disincentive to adopting a criminal law restricting racist speech is not any single insuperable theoretical obstacle, but the discouragement induced by having to confront a series of difficult subordinate choices.   Whether the cumulative cost of these choices becomes excessive may well depend upon one's appraisal of the constitutional permissibility of such statutes, the free speech dimensions of which are explored below.

DEONTIC TORTS AND THE PROBLEM OF SPEECH THAT DOES LESS OR MORE THAN CONVEY A SOCIAL IDEA

One reason why racist insults, or insults of persons as members of historically subordinated groups, are distinguishable from mere insults and other such offenses is that "'they conjure up the entire history of racial discrimination in this country.'"[69]   But an incident, or an image, or an object can conjure up a broad history, or a social idea, without itself being speech in the constitutional sense.   Despite the accumulated cultural baggage toted by racial epithets, in many concrete instances, the plainest interpretation of the racist epithets involved is that they amount to "general [verbal] abuse" rather than

constitutional speech.[70]   Speech that does not seek to
communicate at least some sort of social idea does not
ordinarily implicate the purposes or values underlying
the free speech clause and therefore falls outside the
compass of the free speech clause.   Professor Paul
Chevigny has suggested that "[t]he essence of the
notion of 'speech' for purposes of political
protection is that it puts forth an argument that must
be understood, that is susceptible to explanation or
response through other arguments before any other sort
of action is taken."[71]   One need not even adopt this
rigorous formulation to recognize that the point, from
the standpoint of the purposes of the free speech
clause, of protecting at least some instances of the
use of racial epithets is obscure.

Racial epithets may be resorted to, for example,
in the context of an ordinary dispute over a parking
space,[72] or in an ordinary dispute over a department
store lay-away ticket.[73]   Publicly embarrassing racial
references not involving racial epithets can also
occur in contexts not fairly suggestive of any intent
to convey any associated social idea.[74]   While it is
easy to assume that all earnest use of racial epithets
must be charged with a "view"[75] of some feature of
society or its proper ordering, this assumption is
universally sound only if we attribute to some speech
an implausibly sweeping intent.   The actual,
substantive social ideational content that is
necessarily implied, regardless of circumstances, by
any particular racial epithet is minimal at best.[76]

To illustrate the importance of this recognition,
we may take the example of the controversy over the
use of the restaurant trade name "Sambo's."   If the
government on some theory seeks to restrict the use of
that particular trade name as racially offensive, the
conventional legal response may be to assume not only
that all offense is alike for constitutional purposes,
but that offense and distaste are simply the
inevitable price of a robustly exercised freedom of
speech.[77]   But on our approach, a prior question must
be asked if free speech concerns are to be implicated:
were the owners of Sambo's Restaurants attempting to
communicate some recognizable social idea through the
use of that trade name?   If, as judicially appears to
be the case, they were not, their use of the trade
name "Sambo's" should not be thought to cognizably
implicate free speech concerns.   The record
establishes that the name "Sambo" was chosen because
of associations with pancakes, as well as the
coincidence of combining portions of the names of two
of the principals.[78]

It may seem curious to decline to classify some

literal speech, especially insofar as it may offend or
inflict suffering upon identifiable groups, as speech
in the constitutional sense. It is therefore useful
to remember what this claim does not amount to. It is
not a claim that literal speech falls outside the
scope of the free speech clause if it is primitive or
fallacious,[79] or if it offers social ideas of no
discernible "substance or merit,"[80] or if it touches
upon social ideas that threaten basic values[81] or that
must be regarded as settled.[82] Declining to extend
free speech protection to literal speech that does not
seek to convey any social idea is thus far removed
from assuming that some "fighting faith,"[83] the truth
of which we are at least for the moment convinced,
justifies us in suppressing some disfavored speech.

It must certainly be admitted, however, that not
all literal speech involving recourse to racial
epithets will be entirely outside the scope of the
free speech clause on this analysis. Racial epithets
themselves are predictably offensive and derogatory,
if only in an undifferentiated sort of way.[84] Beyond
this, at least some uses of racial epithets involve an
intent to communicate the social idea "that
distinctions of race are distinctions of merit,
dignity, status and personhood."[85] On some occasions,
racial epithets are employed in the immediate context
of at least tersely explicit statements of evaluative
or descriptive social propositional statements. Just
as "an intent to injure another can accompany the
expression of ideas,"[86] so the expression of ideas can
accompany an intent to injure.

In such cases, the government should not be
barred by the free speech clause from severing or
disaggregating the distinctive offense or distinctive
moral wrong of the racial epithet from the cognitive
or, to the extent constitutionally protected, the
emotive meaning of the speech. Such speech would not
be subject to restriction insofar as it sought to
convey a social idea, or in respect of its attempt to
convey a social idea, even if that idea, however
expressed, is inherently offensive to some degree.
But such speech would be subject to restriction
insofar as it involves the injury infliction or
deontic wrong of racial epithet speech.

This approach does not assume governmental
infallibility, or simply cast aside concerns for the
pursuit of truth, self-realization, political
participation, or other values thought to underlie the
free speech clause. These values would be jeopardized
only if governmental restriction of the use of racial
epithets suppressed or distorted, to a significant
degree, the cognitive or, to the extent otherwise

protected, the emotive meaning intended by the
speaker. The potential for suppression or distortion
of the social ideas sought to be conveyed by the
speech is essentially a function of the degree of
adequacy, from the standpoint crucially of the
speaker's own view of the best combination of free
speech values he or she wishes to exercise and
promote, of the alternative means or channels left
open and available for the speaker's use. As a matter
of logic, the courts should be reluctant to find a
free speech violation where the complaining party is
left with alternative means for conveying his or her
message that are essentially as good as the means
restricted, from the speaker's own perspective on the
relevant free speech values.

In a somewhat broader context, Justice Stevens
has observed that a "requirement that indecent
language be avoided will have its primary effect on
the form, rather than the content, of serious
communication. There are few, if any, thoughts that
cannot be expressed by the use of less offensive
language."[87] This is equally true in the context of
racial epithet speech, and it is true not merely for
the cognitive content of racist epithets, but for the
emotive content as well. Doubtless there is some
sense in which a change in form necessarily involves
some degree of change in content, and in which no
formulation of words is ever perfectly interchangeable
with another, in all respects and for all purposes.
But a government regulation that prohibited, for
example, the use of the phrase "looking glass," while
leaving open and unimpaired the availability of the
alternative admittedly not utterly indistinguishable
word "mirror," would leave most speakers with what
might be called a free speech value rough equivalent
means of communicating, regardless of the presence or
absence of any repressive government intent.

It is at least possible that a speaker may
plausibly claim that requiring the speaker to convey
the protected emotive force of the speaker's message
through means other than racial epithets not only
impairs the speaker's general autonomy, as would
virtually any police power regulation of any sort of
activity, but distorts the speaker's message to some
significant degree. Ordinarily, of course, it will be
far from clear why the profundity, fervor, and
certitude of one's convictions about any social issue
cannot be conveyed without recourse to racial
epithets. That one feels quite strongly, or is
willing to violate certain taboos because of the
fervency of one's belief, does not seem
incommunicable, to the extent it is relevant to free

speech values, by means other than racial epithets. At the very least, such emotive messages do not seem inherently susceptible to more accurate or more powerful conveyance through racial epithets, to the extent that the sentiments involved can be faithfully communicated by language at all. To the extent that one's sentiments or ideas or emotions cannot be successfully communicated by that person at all, government restrictions on his or her language in that context will generally not impair the speaker's freedom of speech, assuming the speaker's inarticulateness is not attributable to the government.

Some of the divergence in meaning between racial epithet speech and nonracial epithet speech will be sheer "noise," in the sense of meaning variance neither consciously nor unconsciously considered or intended by the speaker. Some of the remaining variance will implicate no social idea. Presumably a major reason why speakers of racist epithets would nonetheless object to restrictions on such speech would be their desire, at best irrelevant to if not generally destructive of free speech values, to inflict emotional pain on or otherwise somehow impair their targets. But to the extent that genuine free speech values are significantly implicated by such speech restrictions, any marginal loss in free speech values from the speaker's standpoint must be considered in light of any free speech value loss, including speech autonomy loss, on the part of the targets of racist epithets, as well as the importance attributed to the sheer moral disvalue of racist epithets. Just as a speaker's autonomy, as a speaker, may legitimately be restricted to the extent necessary to criminalize verbal fraud, bribery, and blackmail, so there is the possibility of justifying government restrictions on racist speech.[88] Ultimately, it must be remembered that the benefits of restricting racial epithet speech must reflect the continuing legally unrestricted availability of other offensive, immoral ways of discussing racial groups. The policy logic of not restricting such alternatives is discussed below. But it is equally necessary to remember that the free speech costs of restricting racial epithet speech must be discounted to reflect the availability of alternative means of speaking that may be superior, essentially as good, or nearly as good from a free speech values standpoint. Again, it is entirely possible that a government restriction on racist epithets may coerce a user of racial epithets into using a form of speech that is actually higher in free speech values from the speaker's own subjective standpoint than that of racial epithets, if the speaker's preference for racial epithets reflects values other than free speech values, such as the speaker's desire to lash out satisfyingly, to inflict pain, or to attract attention, of whatever sort, to the speaker.

Racial epithet speech may therefore in principle be subject to general restriction by government. The underlying rationale or justification for actually imposing such a restriction, given the constitutional legitimacy of doing so, is controversial, however. The approaches referred to earlier in this chapter tended generally to focus on concrete, individualized injuries to the particular plaintiff. While the interests served by such restrictions are occasionally referred to broadly, to the extent that such restrictions are aimed at promoting the "psychological well-being"[89] of the targets of racial epithets, the theory of restricting the speech may be misfocused. Restrictions of speech based on the content of the speech are generally disfavored.[90] Restricting racial epithet speech on the basis of contingent, speculative, unsystematic, causally obscure consequences for the broad psychological well-being of individual targets provides a relatively shaky foundation for such disfavored restrictions, and may be no truer to our underlying motivations for restricting racial epithet speech than the less contingent, more straightforward deontic approach emphasized in this chapter.

In some sense, it is doubtless true that "[t]he psychological or emotional harm alleged in [racial epithet] cases can be proved in the same manner as in other torts that protect psychological well-being."[91] However, most of the more serious potential psychological consequences of racist epithets, including social alienation, lower self-esteem, reduced aspirations, as well as effects on parenting practices, may be ascribable to racism generally in some form, but not identifiable in any particular case involving racist epithets.[92] Even if the plaintiff can show, by a preponderance of the evidence, a harm such as decreased self-esteem or less effective parenting, it will ordinarily be difficult at best for the plaintiff to show that the identified harmful psychological effects can be attributed not to his or her cumulative experience with disadvantage, poverty, racism, or to a long-term pattern of exposure to racist epithets from various persons not acting in any recognizable concert, but to the particular racial epithets of the particular defendant in the particular case.[93]

Even if the incremental harmful psychological effects of particular instances of the use of racial epithets could be shown, reliably and at a reasonable cost, such an approach to racial epithets would largely miss the point. The public sentiment that persons should not be legally required to endure racist epithets is not, or at least should not be, exclusively a reflection of the intensity, duration, or overall psychological severity of the injury or of a concern that the public esteem in which such victims are held will be diminished as a result of such epithets.[94] The public sentiment involved is not so dependent upon such contingent reactions of the victims or of other persons. Instead, such public sentiment more straightforwardly reflects the historically strengthening consensus that the use of racial epithets in typical cases involves a clear violation of an important public norm. It is not necessarily that racial epithets have become more abusive and insulting than formerly.[95] Rather, as a society we may be less willing than formerly to tolerate the same degree of abuse and insult of this kind, because of the society's changing moral conceptions.

Issues such as the peculiar emotional susceptibility of particular individual targets of racist epithets,[96] or of the potential for some violent or disruptive reaction by those subjected to racist epithets,[97] are on this approach of only tangential importance. If the targets of racist epithets had invariably become so desensitized by repeated exposure to racist epithets that they regarded such language with great equanimity, as a matter of course, or if such victims reacted invariably with passivity, or aggression turned inward only, so that the threat of a violent reaction to such epithets was nil, the use of such racist epithets would remain just as reprehensible, if not more so, and just as fittingly subject to some form of legal censure. As one commentator has observed with regard to the use of ethnic slurs, "[i]t is not merely a question of preventing fights or riots; it is a matter of dignity."[98]

The legal system's tendency to underplay what this chapter has referred to as deontic harms is illustrated, if not partially explained, by the fate of the two-pronged approach to "fighting words" in Chaplinsky v. New Hampshire.[99] Under Chaplinsky, it is reasonably clear that constitutionally unprotected fighting words may take the form either of words tending "to incite an immediate breach of the peace,"[100] or of words "which by their very utterance inflict injury."[101]   But the vitality of the latter, more deontic prong has been seriously questioned.[102] At least on occasion, the latter prong has been judicially ignored in favor of the former.[103]   And this is probably unfortunate, because, as Professor Hadley Arkes has suggested, judicial emphasis on the breach of the peace prong "teaches the worst lessons that a regime of law could possibly teach.   It suggests that, before citizens can expect the law to protect them or to vindicate their interests, they must be prepared themselves to use violence outside the law."[104]   As well, the absence of any violent reaction to racial epithets, along with interracial harmony generally,[105] may at least conceivably be due to morally objectionable socialization, if not outright repression, of the targeted victims.

Recognizing some sort of tort action, or some sort of criminal liability of some description, for deontic injuries of the sort discussed above, is a meaningful and appropriate response to racial epithet use.   A tort or criminal action in response authoritatively vindicates and reaffirms the hard-won community sentiment that the use of racial epithets involves a clear and fundamental moral wrong.   The individual victim is not left alone to fend for herself through some sort of "counterspeech" remedy, which itself lends legitimacy to the appropriateness of the use of racial epithets.   While there are less degrading means of reacting to some racially offensive speech, as when persons offended by the restaurant name "Sambo's" organize a boycott, such remedies will in some measure be insufficient.   Even in the case of racially offensive speech that lends itself to boycott, economic theory can offer no guarantees that the speaker can be persuaded by changed marketplace incentives to cease indulging in the taste for racially offensive speech.[106]   To the extent that the law can offer a remedy for the deontic harm of racial epithet speech that approaches more nearly a guarantee of redress, the nature of the deontic injury itself suggests that it should do so.

THE DISTINCTIVE COSTS OF LEGALLY SUPPRESSING RACIST POLITICAL SPEECH IN GENERAL

Thus far, the argument has sought to establish the logic, and the permissibility under the free speech clause, of legal restraints on the use of racial epithets, at least where the targets of such epithets are members of historically subordinated groups.   The interests at stake change, however, when it is suggested that the government should be empowered to restrict not only racist epithets, but at least some speech not involving the use of racist epithets that is nevertheless racially offensive, or racist, in communicating a recognizable social idea.   Such an extended claim, while not currently widely influential in the United States, at least has the virtue of recognizing that restricting racial epithet speech only leaves open the possibility of deliberate infliction of suffering and embarrassment on members of particular racial groups, if perhaps through speech conveying a social idea.   The approach argued for in this chapter, it might be said, puts a premium on avoiding only the crudest, most inane sort of racist speech.   One might argue that such an approach is therefore class-biased.

How telling such criticisms are is controversial. Before such a judgment can be made, however, we should consider at least briefly some of the potential costs and risks distinctively associated with governmental restriction of allegedly racist speech not involving racial epithets and conveying a recognizable social idea.   Most of the burden of any argument against censoring offensive, unpopular, or evidently false social ideas must be borne by the classic apologies for freedom of speech.   Perhaps the most pertinent theme that can be developed in our particular context is that the question of whether governmental restrictions should be imposed on allegedly racist speech generally is not a matter of the relative weights one attributes to freedom of speech and to racial equality.[107]   Freedom of speech, even for generally racist speech, may in fact tend to contribute to such racial equality as is practically attainable, and generalized legal censorship of racist speech may tend significantly to impair the cause of racial equality and community.

First, of course, the advocate of government restrictions on racist speech generally must choose among the possible ways of defining racist speech. Restricting all speech that tends to inflict even short-term discomfort on racial minorities, in their capacity as racial minorities, seems a well-focused approach, but such an approach would overlook the fact that receiving news, if only of one's neighbor's attitudes, that is unpleasant in the short term may be beneficial or even vital in the long run.[108]   On the other hand, presuming to know in concrete detail what speech is destructive of minority interests in the long run must prove generally unconvincing.   Avoiding these problems by defining racist speech to include only demonstrably fallacious claims may still occasionally involve pretensions to infallibility, as

well as leaving much racially offensive speech
untouched.   Ultimately, a reasonably workable
definition of racist speech that commands the
agreement of even the targets of such speech may be
practically unattainable, given that not only the
behavioral patterns associated with racism,[109] but the
nature or definition of racism itself may change
historically.[110] When one adds in the complications
that the racist quality of a speech may depend not
only upon context,[111] but upon the reputation or
intent of the particular speaker,[112] the problem of a
satisfactory practical definition of racist speech
seems daunting.

If a suitable definition of racist speech can be
settled upon, the problems of interpreting and
applying the legal standard to concrete situations
begin. One possible approach, of course, is that of a
continuing censorship bureaucracy.   In the end,
history teaches us that "the boundaries of the
forbidden cannot reliably be drawn."[113]   Professor
Chevigny points out that "[i]n the Old
South....freedom of thought withered, not only in
relation to slavery but generally as to all topics,
because no one could predict when a discussion might
suggest a new idea about slavery or race."[114]

Assuming that legal restraints on racist speech
deter racist speech, genuine social gains may result.
Enforced behavioral change, in the form of avoiding
racist speech, may tend to produce genuine attitudinal
change, as persons bring their attitudes into line
with their nonracist speech.[115] Even if no unpunished
racist speech occurs, however, there may be limits to
the society's ability to change attitudes through
enforced behavioral norms.[116]   Some residue of
alienated, resentful, seething, underground racist
speech and belief will likely remain, fortified by the
false conviction that opponents of racism are simply
afraid that their own alleged errors would be exposed
by an open debate that they therefore cannot permit.

Among the more subtle, but potentially serious,
problems that would remain is the loss of racist
speech as an indicator of social attitudes. Before a
society or an industry adopts a program of affirmative
action, for example, some sense of the program's
practical workability is desirable. But if no racist
speech, at least in a broadly defined sense, is
legally permitted, the government's sense of the
feasibility of such a program may be significantly
distorted, in either an unduly optimistic or
pessimistic way.[117] After all, an enforced absence of
public racist speech is compatible with either
widespread skepticism about the norm upheld, or with

its complete and universal voluntary acceptance. It may seem worth paying some price, even one borne disproportionately by innocent victims, in order to have an improved sense of the real attitudes of much of the society. It would be particularly unfortunate, for example, if the majority were genuinely receptive to more aggressive affirmative action programs, but little initiative were taken in that direction because, in its ignorance of genuine majority attitudes, the society overestimated the extent of underlying, unarticulated opposition.[118]

As well, it is predictable that at least in the long term, racial minorities and the cause of racial equality would suffer from the disease of any legally enforced secular orthodoxy, in which vitally and vividly held principles, tempered in the fire of intellectual combat, gradually approach the admitted extreme of lifeless platitudes and clichés which lose their power to inspire. The Pledge of Allegiance tends to descend, in public school classrooms, to rote, not merely because it is frequently repeated, but because it by necessity is perpetually unchallenged. Coherent speech propagating a social idea, at least in the absence of the gratuitous element of racial epithets, that is classified as racist, indispensably serves the function of preventing the decay of the thought and rhetoric of racial equality. Even if wholly false, racist speech is in the long term not without substantial value to the victims of racism itself, as John Stuart Mill has classically given us grounds to believe.

These arguments seem insignificant, of course, in the context of the societal harms wreaked by racist actions that were informed and justified by racist ideas. Racism in its most familiar senses is pernicious in the extreme. But the wisdom of suppressing racist speech does not easily follow from this, largely because it is possible to suppress much of the harm of racism by informal social sanctions, by education, and by the imposition of legal requirements and legal prohibitions in the various realms of social conduct, or action, as distinct from speech.[119] Doubtless it is frustrating to realize that the impact of false and misleading racist speech generally cannot invariably be immediately effaced from the minds of its audience.[120] But this is equally true of any false and misleading speech.

To these considerations should be added another. It is not surprising that as our tolerance as a society for racist speech decreases, the utility and practicality of confronting racism by restricting racist speech is diminishing. Whether racism is generally diminishing or not, it is apparently increasingly taking forms not susceptible to address by restrictions on speech.[121]   The kinds of racist speech most likely to inspire legal proscription will inevitably tend to be those crude, overt forms of blatantly racist speech that may be not only relatively unpersuasive, but of diminishing significance historically.

Whether or not racism is diminishing in any absolute sense, a consensus has developed that at least in the field of verbal public statements, the kind most amenable to legal control, there has over the past few decades been "a strong and steady movement of white attitudes from denial to affirmation of equality."[122]   The historical "decline in the expression of racist ideology and racist attitudes toward blacks"[123] has led to a "near universal affirmation of the inadmissibility of racial prejudice in public political discourse"[124] and the virtual public disappearance of an "explicitly segregationist, white supremacist view."[125]

Of course, the virtual absence from public discourse of the most crude, and therefore most legally sanctionable, expressions of racism does not mean that anonymous, clandestine, transient, underground expressions of crude racism no longer occur, even, or especially, on college campuses. Nor does it necessarily mean that racial prejudice has not simply been transformed into more subtle, "ostensibly nonracial"[126] sorts of expression of perhaps a "more insidious type of racial bigotry."[127] But "ostensibly nonracial" expressions of racism are obviously relatively difficult to prosecute, or to consistently hold tortious. Not surprisingly, it is only as the practical significance of relatively crude, objectively racist public speech has diminished that it has become possible to imagine legal restrictions on such speech becoming sufficiently popular to be practically workable. The evidence appears to establish that high and increasing percentages of white Americans regard minorities as able and competent[128] and prefer less invidious, and even collectively self-accusatory, explanations for the persistence of racial inequality.[129] Contemporary discrimination is likely to take the form of whites rating favorably perceived blacks more positively than favorably perceived whites.[130] However ultimately destructive such forms of bias may be, it is difficult to imagine a society's pressing its criminal or tort system beyond concern for discriminatory conduct, whether by omission or commission, to attack the social idea-communicating speech that underlies such forms of stereotyping.

CONCLUSION AND POSTSCRIPT: DOES THE VIRTUE OF TOLERANCE REQUIRE TOLERANCE OF RACIAL EPITHET SPEECH?

The argument sketched above has suggested that while arguably racist speech seeking to convey some recognizable social idea should generally be constitutionally protected, speech in the form of racist epithets need not be so protected, in light of the purposes or values underlying the free speech clause. The argument has also suggested a particular approach to the question of why restricting the latter sort of speech is not merely constitutionally permissible, but sound public policy as well. A number of objections have been anticipated and discussed above, but no extended reference was made to the well-regarded and already influential defense of the constitutional protection of extremist speech developed by Dean Lee Bollinger in his recent book, The Tolerant Society.[131] There is much more in Bollinger's book that is of value, and much more that is susceptible to plausible criticism, than a brief discussion can suggest. Here we will attempt no more than to briefly indicate the major theme of the book and suggest why its implications for the argument sketched above in this chapter are less significant than might be supposed.
    Bollinger's thesis is that many observers have rightly felt that particularly in certain cases involving extremist speech, such as in the litigation involving the proposed Nazi parade in Skokie, Illinois,[132] the principle of freedom of expression has been carried beyond the bounds suggested by the most familiar explanations for the protection of freedom of expression.[133] To satisfactorily account for why such deeply painful, necessarily unpersuasive speech is protected, Bollinger suggests that we must recognize that excessive intolerance, in the realm of speech and elsewhere, is a serious, looming threat,[134] and that the exercise of voluntary self-restraint involved in permitting extremist speech to go legally unimpeded is therefore healthful in strengthening the public capacity for the important virtue of tolerance.[135] The particular value of protecting speech as inanely virulent and profoundly offensive as that of the Illinois Nazis lies in recognizing the truth of the character-building maxim, "[t]o straighten a bent stick you bend it back the other way."[136]
    Recoiling from the impulse to excessive intolerance, in the particular context of extremist

speech, is thus meant to be educative, or public character-building, with benefits accruing far beyond the area of speech itself. Free speech is singled out for essentially practical reasons as "a discrete and limited context"[137] in which the costs of extraordinary self-restraint may be relatively low and the benefits relatively high.[138] This argument is, not surprisingly, set forth by Dean Bollinger with a good deal more subtlety and power than this brief account suggests, but this description may suffice for our limited purposes.

One might respond to Bollinger's thesis by suggesting that whatever civic virtues our society may be in acutely short supply of, the sort of tolerance and self-restraint in the realm of political ideas that Bollinger apotheosizes is not one of them. Certainly the students Professor Bloom describes in The Closing of The American Mind[139] tend more in the direction of an almost vacuous relativism than toward the tyranny of classic intolerance, at least in the realm of speech. But even if we assume that our contemporary inclination toward excessive intolerance is so pronounced that it is worth asking historically victimized groups in particular to pay the very real price that the cultivation of tolerance of extremist speech exacts, it does not follow that the realm of racial epithet speech is an appropriate venue in which to display such tolerance. Judicial toleration of racial epithet speech devoid of, or as distinct from, articulated social ideas is still too readily interpretable, at least to some, as bespeaking not the virtue of tolerance, but unconscious judicial insensitivity to the sensibilities and free speech potential of historically subordinated groups.

Of course, it is still possible to argue that many Americans have not fully internalized the principle of freedom of speech, and that they prefer that speech they find objectionable on the merits be legally restricted. In this sense, many Americans are indeed excessively intolerant, if nondisruptively so. It seems an odd strategy, though, to try to reduce such intolerance by demanding tolerance above and beyond the point at which tolerance can be justified independently. To press the demand for legal tolerance of speech beyond the point where tolerance can be justified by reference to the values and purposes traditionally thought to underlie the free speech clause risks merely confirming the intolerant in their view that freedom of speech has been pressed too far.

Ultimately, however, any excessive social intolerance we detect may simply not be attributable to excessive judicial intolerance of racial epithet speech, or of extremist speech generally. It may well be that whatever pedagogical benefits that can be drawn from the technique Bollinger recommends are in fact already being otherwise extracted. There is certainly no logical necessity that civic tolerance be enhanced particularly through the vehicle of restraint in even the broad area of speech. There is arguably already a remarkable excess of voluntary, quasi-principled self-restraint by the courts, as the agent of the broader society, in other areas of the law such as criminal sentencing. It can reasonably be argued that the sentences ordinarily actually served for violent crimes are not rationally explainable on any established theory of criminal sentencing, apart from a curiously indulgent sort of self-restraint or lack of moral seriousness on the part of society.[140] Plato was among the first to note roughly this phenomenon as characteristic of the democratic society in the course of its decline.[141] For a variety of reasons, then, Bollinger's argument does not establish the inadvisability of legal restraints on racial epithet speech.

NOTES

1. Pub. L. No. 88-352, 78 Stat. 243 (codified as amended at 42 U.S.C. §§ 2000(c)-2000(h) (6) (1982)).

2. See, e.g., Gaiters v. Lynn, 831 F.2d 51 (4th Cir. 1987).

3. See, e.g., Sambo's Restaurants, Inc. v. City of Ann Arbor, 663 F.2d 686 (6th Cir. 1981).

4. See, e.g., Dominguez v. Stone, 97 N.M. 211, 638 P.2d 423 (Ct. App. 1981).

5. See, e.g., Resetar v. State Bd. of Educ., 284 Md. 537, 399 A.2d 225, cert. denied, 444 U.S. 838 (1979).

6. See, e.g., Delgado, Words That Wound: A Tort Action For Racial Insults, Epithets, and Name-Calling, 17 Harv. C.R.-C.L. L. Rev. 133, 135 n.12 (1982); Report of the Committee on Freedom of Expression at Yale, 4 Hum. Rts. 357 (1975).

7. Compare, e.g., Delgado, supra note 6 (detecting only minimal free speech constraints) with Heins, Banning Words: A Comment on "Words That Wound," 18 Harv. C.R.0C.L. L. Rev. 585 (1983). For a sensitive treatment, see Matsuda, Public Response to Racist

Speech: Considering the Victim's Story, 87 Mich. L. Rev. 2320 (1989).

8.   See, e.g., Beauharnais v. Illinois, 343 U.S. 250 (1952).

9.   See, e.g., Contreras v. Crown Zellerbach Corp., 88 Wash. 2d 735, 565 P.2d 1173 (1977) (en banc).

10.   See, e.g., Bailey v. Binyon, 583 F. Supp. 923 (N.D. Ill. 1984).

11.   See, e.g., Cotterrell, Prosecuting Incitement to Racial Hatred, 1982 Pub. L. 378.

12.   315 U.S. 568 (1942).

13.   See generally L. Bollinger, The Tolerant Society: Freedom of Speech and Extremist Speech in America (1986).

14.   343 U.S. 250 (1952).

15.   See, e.g., Collin v. Smith, 578 F.2d 1197, 1205 (7th Cir.), cert. denied, 439 U.S. 916 (1978) and the cases collected in Sambo's Restaurants, Inc. v. City of Ann Arbor, 663 F.2d 686, 694 n.7 (7th Cir. 1981). But see Note, Group Vilification Reconsidered, 89 Yale L.J. 308 (1979).

16.   Post, Cultural Heterogeneity and Law: Pornography, Blasphemy, and the First Amendment, 76 Calif. L. Rev. 297, 330 (1988) (citations omitted). The Times case is reported at 376 U.S. 254 (1964), and Hepps at 475 U.S. 767 (1986).

17.   See Post, supra note 16, at 330.

18.   See Gertz v. Robert Welch, Inc., 418 U.S. 323, 340 (1974). For criticism of this result in the context of racial defamation, see Lasson, Racial Defamation as Free Speech: Abusing the First Amendment, 17 Colum. Hum. Rts. L. Rev. 11, 42-43 n.229 (1985).

19.   See Note, Group Defamation: Five Guiding Factors, 64 Tex. L. Rev. 591, 608-09 (1985). See also Note, A Communitarian Defense of Group Libel Laws, 101 Harv. L. Rev. 682, 691-92 n.69 (1988) (restricting the Note's defense of group libel laws to only those targeting potentially true or false statements of fact). In the international comparative context, see Kretzmer, Freedom of Speech and Racism, 8 Cardozo L. Rev. 445, 496 (1987).

20. See Hepps, 475 U.S. at 775-76.

21. See Arkes, Civility and the Restriction of Speech: Rediscovering the Defamation of Groups, 1974 Sup. Ct. Rev. 281, 301 (P. Kurland ed. 1975).

22. See Kretzmer, supra note 19, at 496.

23. See W. Keeton, D. Dobbs, R. Keeton & D. Owen, Prosser and Keeton On the Law of Torts § 116, at 840 (5th ed. 1984).

24. At least with regard to plaintiffs who are not public figures or public officials, the Supreme Court has not yet required the showing of a false claim of fact in cases brought on a theory of intentional infliction of severe emotional distress. For a contrary rule in the case of public figure plaintiffs, see Hustler Magazine v. Falwell, 108 S. Ct. 876 (1988). Whether Black Americans, for example, would count as a "public figure group" by the standards of Gertz v. Robert Welch, Inc., 418 U.S. 323 (1974) for purposes of the tort of intentional infliction of severe emotional distress has not yet been judicially resolved. See the discussion in Comment, Group Defamation and Individual Actions: A New Look at an Old Rule, 71 Calif. L. Rev. 1532, 1553 (1983).

25. See Comment, supra note 24, at 1545. In the context of actions brought on behalf of large religious groups, see Talal v. Fanning, 506 F. Supp. 186 (N.D. Cal. 1980).

26. See W. Keeton, supra note 23, § 112, at 788-95.

27. See id. at § 113; Note, supra note 15, at 309.

28. See W. Keeton, supra note 23, § 111, at 774.

29. See generally Delgado, supra note 6.

30. See Comment, supra note 24, at 1532.

31. See Note, supra note 15, at 311.

32. Note as well that criminal prosecution for attempts to incite racial hatred, or fear, or a breach of the peace may also be difficult if the language used can be shown to have instead had a natural and probable tendency under the circumstances to promote sympathy for the target group. See Cotterrell, supra note 11, at 379.

33.   See Restatement (Second) of Torts § 46 (1965).

34.   Comment, supra note 24, at 1550 (citation omitted).

35.   Dominguez v. Stone, 97 N.M. 211, 215, 638 P.2d 423, 427 (Ct. App. 1981).

36.   See, e.g., Contreras v. Crown Zellerbach Corp., 88 Wash. 2d 735, 565 P.2d 1173 (1977).

37.   See, e.g., Alcorn v. Anbro Eng'g, Inc., 2 Cal. 3d 493, 468 P.2d 216, 86 Cal. Rptr. 88 (1970) (en banc).

38.   See, e.g., id. at 498, 468 P.2d at 219, 86 Cal. Rptr. at 91.

39.   See id. at 498, 468 P.2d at 218-19, 86 Cal. Rptr. at 90-91. The en banc court held that "plaintiff's status as an employee should entitle him to a greater degree of protection from insult and outrage than if he were a stranger to defendants." Id. at 498 n.2, 468 P.2d at 218 n.2, 86 Cal. Rptr. at 90 n.2. This may reflect the employee's captive audience status, and his or her inability to ignore the employer. See Contreras, 88 Wash. 2d at 741, 565 P.2d at 1176.

40.   See, e.g., Lay v. Roux Laboratories, Inc., 379 So. 2d 451 (Fla. Dist. Ct. App. 1980).

41.   See Irving v. J.L. Marsh, Inc., 46 Ill. App. 3d 162, 167, 360 N.E.2d 983, 986 (1977); Dawson v. Zayre Dept. Stores, 346 Pa. Super. 357, 360, 499 A.2d 648, 649 (1985).

42.   See Dawson, 346 Pa. Super. at 360, 499 A.2d at 649.

43.   See id. The plaintiff in Dawson alleged, inter alia, that "she cried and was unable to gain her composure for one-half hour." Id.

44.   See id.

45.   See id.

46.   See Irving, 46 Ill. App. 3d at 167, 360 N.E.2d at 986.

47.   See Dawson, 346 Pa. Super. at 360, 499 A.2d at 649.

48.   See Alcorn, 2 Cal. 3d at 499 n.4, 468 P.2d at 219 n.4, 86 Cal. Rptr. at 91 n.4.

49. See id.

50. See generally Delgado, supra note 6.

51. See the defendant's contention in this regard, not definitively rejected on appeal, in Alcorn, 2 Cal. 3d at 499 n.4, 468 P.2d at 219 n.4, 86 Cal. Rptr. at 91 n.4.

52. See Dominguez v. Stone, 97 N.M. 211, 213, 638 P.2d 423, 425 (App. 1981).

53. See Delgado, supra note 6, at 136-37; Kretzmer, supra note 19, at 466. See also Thomas & Hughes, The Continuing Significance of Race: A Study of Race, Class, and Quality of Life in America, 1972-1985, 51 Am. Soc. Rev. 830 (1986) (blacks as scoring lower than whites on various measures of psychological well-being, even when social class is controlled for).

54. Cf. Dominguez, 97 N.M. at 215, 638 P.2d at 427.

55. See generally Cotterrell, supra note 11; Hadfield, The Prevention of Incitement to Religious Hatred, An Article of Faith?, 35 N. Ireland L.Q. 231 (1984); Hughes, Prohibiting Incitement to Racial Discrimination, 16 U. Toronto L.J. 161 (1987); Lederman & Tabory, Criminalization of Racial Incitement in Israel 24 Stan. J. Int'l L. 55 (1987); Leopold, Incitement to Hatred, The History of a Controversial Criminal Offense, 1977 Pub. L. 389.

56. See Comment, supra note 24, at 1547.

57. See Cotterrell, supra note 11, at 379.

58. See id.

59. See Hepps, 475 U.S. at 774-76.

60. See Lederman & Tabory, supra note 55, at 63.

61. Cf. Hughes, supra note 55, at 365.

62. See Whitney v. California, 274 U.S. 357, 378-79 (1027) (Brandeis, J., concurring).

63. See the discussion of this requirement in the international context in Kretzmer, supra note 19, at 502-3; Lederman & Tabory, supra note 55, at 64; Leopold, supra note 55, at 397.

64. See Kretzmer, supra note 19, at 502.

65. See Leopold, supra note 55, at 404.

66. See id.

67. See id. at 397-98; see also E. Barendt, Freedom of Speech 163 (1985) (discussing convictions of militant blacks).

68. Compare, e.g., Posner, The DeFunis Case and the Constitutionality of Preferential Treatment of Racial Minorities, 1974 Sup. Ct. Rev. 1, 25-26 (P. Kurland ed. 1975) and Van Alstyne, Rites of Passage: Race, The Supreme Court, and the Constitution, 46 U. Chi. L. Rev. 775, 809 (1979) (arguing against any differential treatment by government based on race) with Lempert, The Force of Irony: On the Morality of Affirmative Action and United Steelworkers v. Weber, 95 Ethics 86-89 (1984) (moral revulsion against anti-white alleged discrimination draws much of its moral force from centuries of racial oppression of relatively powerless blacks).

69. Bailey v. Binyon, 583 F. Supp. 923, 934 (N.D. Ill. 1984) (quoting Delgado, supra note 6, at 157).

70. Bradshaw v. Swagerty, 1 Kan. App. 2d 213, 215, 563 P.2d 511, 514 (1977).

71. P. Chevigny, More Speech 100 (1988). See also Lasson, supra note 18, at 33 (noting the possibility of construing racial defamation as nonspeech, akin to hard-core pornography).

72. See Lay v. Roux Laboratories, Inc., 379 So. 2d 451, 452 (Fla. Ct. App. 1980) (per curiam).

73. See Dawson v. Zayre Dept. Stores, 346 Pa. Super. 357, 359, 499 A.2d 648, 648 (1985).

74. See, e.g., Gaiters v. Lynn, 831 F.2d 51, 52 (4th Cir. 1987) (personally directed remark by singer during concert referring to plaintiff's appearance; remarks intended to be humorous).

75. See Bailey v. Binyon, 583 F. Supp. 923, 931 (N.D. Ill. 1984).

76. Cf. Irving v. J. L. Marsh, Inc., 46 Ill. App. 3d 162, 166, 360 N.E.2d 983, 985 (1977) ("[i]n arguing that [a particular racial epithet] implies that an

individual is generally lacking in the virtues of honesty, intelligence, or creativity, we believe plaintiff attributes a definition to the word that is far in excess of its meaning").

77. <u>See</u> <u>Sambo's of Ohio, Inc.</u>, 466 F. Supp. at 180; <u>see</u> <u>also</u> Heins, <u>supra</u> note 7, at 587-88.

78. <u>See</u> <u>Sambo's Restaurants, Inc.</u>, 663 F.2d at 698 n.4.

79. <u>Cf.</u> Lasson, <u>supra</u> note 18, at 39 ("[l]ittle, if any intellect is necessary to hurl racial epithets").

80. <u>Id</u>. at 45.

81. <u>See</u> Hughes, <u>supra</u> note 55, at 363.

82. <u>See</u> <u>id</u>.

83. <u>See</u> <u>Report of the Committee on Freedom of Expression at Yale</u>, <u>supra</u> note 6, at 374-75 (quoting Abrams v. United States, 250 U.S. 616, 630 (1919) (Holmes, J., dissenting)).

84. <u>See</u> Clarke v. Board of Educ., 215 Neb. 250, 256, 338 N.W.2d 272, 275 (1983).

85. <u>See</u> Delgado, <u>supra</u> note 6, at 136.

86. Note, <u>First Amendment Limits on Tort Liability for Words Intended to Inflict Severe Emotional Distress</u>, 85 <u>Colum</u>. <u>L</u>. <u>Rev</u>. 1749, 1755 (1985).

87. FCC v. Pacifica Found., 438 U.S. 726, 743 n.18 (1978) (opinion of Stevens, J., joined by Burger, C.J., and Rehnquist, J.).

88. <u>See</u> Virginia State Bd. of Pharmacy v. Virginia Citizens Consumer Council, 425 U.S. 748, 772 (1976) (citing Pittsburgh Press Co. v. Human Relations Comm., 413 U.S. 376 (1973)).

89. Delgado, <u>supra</u> note 6, at 171.

90. <u>See</u> <u>generally</u> Stone, <u>Content Regulation and the First Amendment</u>, 25 <u>Wm</u>. <u>&</u> <u>Mary</u> <u>L</u>. <u>Rev</u>. 189 (1983).

91. Delgado, <u>supra</u> note 6, at 167.

92. <u>See</u> <u>id</u>. Part I.

93. <u>Cf.</u> <u>id</u>. at 171.

94. See cf. Dominguez v. Stone, 97 N.M. 211, 215, 638 P.2d 423, 427 (App. 1981).

95. See Alcorn, 2 Cal. 3d at 499 n.4, 468 P.2d at 219 n.4, 86 Cal. Rptr. at 91 n.4.

96. See Contreras, 88 Wash. 2d at 741-43, 565 P.2d at 1177.

97. See, e.g., Kretzmer, supra note 19, at 456.

98. J. Tussman, Government and The Mind 91 (1977).

99. 315 U.S. 568 (1942).

100. Id. at 572.

101. Id.

102. See, e.g., Sambo's Restaurants, Inc. v. City of Ann Arbor, 663 F.2d 686, 694 (6th Cir. 1981) (citing Gooding v. Wilson, 405 U.S. 518, 524-27 (1972) and Lewis v. City of New Orleans, 415 U.S. 130, 143 (1974)). See also Note, supra note 86, at 1756 ("[w]hat constitutes 'fighting' words has been limited to utterances...likely to provoke an immediate violent response by the addressee"). But see Sambo's Restaurants, Inc., 663 F.2d at 697 n.1 (Keith, J., dissenting) (arguing for the continued viability of the infliction of injury by their very utterance prong of the "fighting words" doctrine).

103. See, e.g., Harbin v. State, 358 So. 2d 856 (Fla. Ct. App. 1978).

104. Arkes, supra note 21, at 323.

105. See Delgado, Can Science Be Inopportune? Constitutional Validity of Governmental Restrictions on Race, IQ Research, 31 UCLA L. Rev. 128, 185 (1983).

106. See T. Sowell, The Economics and Politics of Race 178 (1983).

107. But cf. the Dissenting Statement by Kenneth Barnes to the Report of the Committee on Freedom of Expression at Yale, supra note 6, at 390 ("[u]nder certain circumstances, free expression is outweighed by more pressing issues, including liberation of all oppressed people and equal opportunities for minority groups"). A narrower claim that the freedom of speech of majority groups, when used to propagate racist

sentiments generally, impairs the ability of minority groups to develop and exercise their own free speech rights and capacities does seem interesting and important.

108. See Loury, The Moral Quandary of the Black Community, 79 Pub. Int. 10, 16-19 (1985).

109. See generally Pettigrew, New Patterns of Racism: The Different Worlds of 1984 and 1964, 37 Rutgers L. Rev. 673 (1985). See also Crenshaw, Race, Reform and Retrenchment: Transformation and Legitimation in Antidiscrimination Law, 101 Harv. L. Rev. 1331, 1379-80 (1988).

110. See Pettigrew, supra note 109, at 686.

111. It has been observed in a broader context that "[q]uestions can be premature or belated, relevant or irrelevant, superficial or profound, helpful or destructive, pointed or distracting, proper or improper." J. Tussman, supra note 98, at 71. In a more specific context, see generally Delgado, supra note 105.

112. For an international example, see P. Bauer, Reality and Rhetoric: Studies in the Economics of Development 87 (1984).

113. P. Chevigny, supra note 71, at 103.

114. Id. Professor Chevigny concludes that "[c]ensorship, formal or informal, in every society where it is found, tends to spread over uncensored knowledge like a stain." Id.

115. See H. Schuman, C. Stech & L. Bobo, Racial Attitudes in America 206-7 (1985); Pettigrew, supra note 109, at 688.

116. For a sense of the stubbornness of attitudes and the lengths to which a society might be pressed in order to effectively change even erroneous beliefs, see G. Harman, Change in View 37-40 (1986).

117. See Kretzmer, supra note 19, at 486-87.

118. See Schwartz, The 1986 and 1987 Affirmative Action Cases: It's All Over But the Shouting, 86 Mich. L. Rev. 524, 525-26 & n.11 (1987) (enthusiastic response to affirmative action programs by the business community).

119. While the distinction between speech and conduct, including discriminatory conduct, is admittedly imperfect, it seems in most instances manageable. See generally United States v. O'Brien, 391 U.S. 367 (1968).

120. See Glass, Anti-Racism and Unlimited Freedom of Speech: An Untenable Dualism, 8 Can. J. Phil. 599 (1978).

121. Compare, e.g., Kluegel & Smith, Whites' Beliefs About Blacks' Opportunity, 47 Am. Soc. Rev. 518, 523 (1982) ("racial prejudice has markedly waned in the last three decases") with W. Wilson, The Declining Significance of Race 23 (1980) (holding open the possibility that racial conflict has not been substantially reduced historically, even though its nature and form have changed).

122. H. Schuman, C. Stech, & L. Bobo, supra note 115, at 135.

123. Thomas & Hughes, supra note 53, at 830.

124. Loury, "Matters of Color", Blacks and the Constitutional Order, 86 Pub. Int. 109, 114 (1987).

125. Kinder & Sears, Prejudice and Politics: Symbolic Racism Versus Racial Threats to the Good Life, 40 J. Pers. & Soc. Psychology 414, 416 (1981).

126. Pettigrew, supra note 109, at 674.

127. Frey & Gaertner, Helping and the Avoidance of Inappropriate Interracial Behavior: A Strategy That Perpetuates a Nonprejudiced Self-Image, 50 J. Pers. & Soc. Psychology 1083, 1083 (1986).

128. See Kinder & Sears, supra note 125, at 419.

129. See P. Sniderman, Race and Inequality: A Study in America 31 (1985).

130. See Jussim, Coleman & Lerch, The Nature of Stereotypes: A Comparison and Integration of Three Theories, 52 J. Pers. & Soc. Psychology 536, 544 (1987).

131. L. Bollinger, supra note 13.

132. See Collin v. Smith, 578 F.2d 1197 (7th Cir.), cert. denied, 439 U.S. 915 (1978); Village of Skokie v. National Socialist Party, 69 Ill. 2d 605, 373 N.E.2d 21 (1978).

133.   See L. Bollinger, supra note 13, at 14-15.

134.   See id. at 106-7.

135.   See id. at 12-25.

136.   Id. at 125.

137.   Id. at 121.

138.   See id. at 124.

139.   See A. Bloom, The Closing of the American Mind 25-43 (1987).

140.   See R. Goldfarb & L. Singer, After Conviction 182 (1973) (citing a figure of median time to parole of 45 months for first degree robbers).

141.   See The Republic book VIII, § 558.

4

Free Speech and the
Public School Student

INTRODUCTION

The judicial charter for the free speech rights of
minor children in public schools has been Tinker v.
Des Moines Independent Community School District,[1] in
which several youngsters were disciplined for
violating a newly promulgated school rule that
prohibited their wearing black armbands in school.
The Court held that a student in the position of the
petitioners "may express his opinions, even on
controversial subjects like the conflict in Vietnam,
if he does so without 'materially and substantially
interfer[ing] with the requirements of appropriate
discipline in the operation of the school' and without
colliding with the rights of others."[2] The Court did
little in Tinker to discourage the assumption that
both the "appropriate discipline" and "rights of
others" defenses to student speech claims would be
construed rather narrowly, but the Court in more
recent cases has sought to distinguish Tinker with
some aggressiveness.[3]

The Court's interest in placing its decisions in
this area in the context of broad free speech values
or purposes, or in confirming the correctness of its
analyses by means of linking its results to the
promoting of such values, has been limited. To the
extent that the Court has attempted this task, it has
resorted too quickly to rhetoric and to platitudes.
Our thesis in this regard is that in an ordinary
Tinker-type student speech case, and in a variety of
related cases, elected school officials or their
agents could reasonably feel that free speech goals or

values would not be subjected to a significant net
impairment by the most common and moderate sorts of
restrictions and sanctions imposed upon student
speech.

With respect to the free speech value of
individual self-fulfillment, Professor Emerson has
argued that "the proper end of man is the realization
of his character and potentialities as a human
being."[4] He has gone on to explain that "expression
is an integral part of the development of ideas, of
mental exploration and of the affirmation of self.
The power to realize his potentiality as a human being
begins at this point and must extend at least this far
if the whole nature of man is not to be thwarted."[5]
While this formulation is certainly broad enough to
implicate a variety of forms of student speech within
public schools, the difficulty is that just these
sorts of developmental and self-realization aims are a
major element of public school education itself, in
general, and of each of the constituents of its
ordered curriculum, however defined. At a minimum, a
public school could responsibly take such a view.

If so, why should an alleged free speech right of
students, insofar as it depends solely on a self-
fulfillment value argument, be thought to override the
school's authorized pursuit of just this value through
its broader curriculum and its individual components?
Individual capacity development through wearing a
politically expressive armband in math class might
well be thought, on some reasonable pedagogy, to
conflict with or distract full attention from the at
least equally important individual
capacity-developmental function of exploring the basic
principles of mathematics. If all are agreed on the
importance of free speech and its underlying values or
purposes, the federal courts do not appear to have any
clear comparative advantage over locally elected
decisionmakers in ascertaining the best mix of school
activities for promoting self-realization and
development.

The question has been posed: "Should the primary
goal of education be to enhance the self-realization
of the student or to mold the student to advance the
common goals of society?"[6] This apparent antinomy is,
at least for our purposes, resolvable. The approach
to student speech issues elaborated and defended below
would first require the minimal showing that the
challenged restriction promotes some legitimate
pedagogical goal sought by the relevant school
officials. It would also require a showing that the
challenged restriction is not crucially inconsistent
with or destructive of the broad development, growth,

and flourishing of the student's capacities for individual self-realization as a future adult possessed of mature and developed free speech capacities.

It is easy to suppose, and perhaps even correct, that "free speech plays an important role in the child's development...."[7] It may even play an indispensable role. But this is not to show that there must or should be a judicially enforceable right of the minor student to speak out on most or each of the particular occasions on which the student might seek to assert such a right. We should recognize instead, in the public school child, an enforceable free speech right prohibiting restrictions imposed by the school in such a way as to significantly impair, inhibit, or otherwise stunt the development of the student's future free speech-relevant capacities as an adult. But this right does not logically require that the child in effect be granted a constitutional right to participate in determining, unconstrainedly, the public school's broad curriculum in particular respects. Under our constitutional standard, a school generally is not barred from determining that students obtain ample practice and experience in speaking freely in non-school environments. It may even operate on the theory that certain sorts of regimentation, control, and hierarchical discipline within school may tend to produce graduates who are more generally free speech competent, in the sense that they have more fully, openly, and adaptably developed their capacities for logical thought for organized, persuasive presentation, based on a storehouse of arguably relevant information, than their peers educated along more permissive lines.

The availability of an option of intramural dissent or insurgency simply is not a necessary inference from an assumed value of individuality or distinctiveness.[8] A child can be different or unique in respects chosen by the child, and can display those qualities, on all or selected occasions, even if the classroom agenda-sharing option is foreclosed to the student. Not every broad rejection of Tinker logically implies totalitarianism. Being precluded from wearing a political armband in class does not preclude one from wearing such an armband elsewhere, thereby manifesting one's uniqueness, or from wearing one as an adult, after, if not before, the "due study and preparation" valued by John Stuart Mill.[9] Partisans of the value of individual self-realization or autonomy should recognize, as well, that such a value, however reasonably broadly conceived, may not do all the work expected of it in other respects.

Autonomy does not necessarily require a particularly broad ranging education, or exposure to a nearly infinite set of ideas, or the ability to think constructively within all such areas.[10]

Finally, it should be noted that a high percentage of the litigated cases, perhaps not surprisingly, fail to implicate significantly the value of individual autonomy for another reason. In Tinker, the petitioners were sixteen, fifteen, and thirteen years of age at the time of the political expression in question,[11] and apparently were, quite naturally and understandably, deeply influenced in this regard by their own highly motivated parents.[12] This is not to suggest that speech with clear causal motivations must be constitutionally trivial, but that merely reflecting, in some less developed, less articulate way, the convictions or example of one's parents is no more evidence of the child's individual autonomy than would be the child's acting, more or less reflectively, on the basis of lessons imparted or inculcated through school.

A similar analysis may be made of the separate value or purpose of the free speech clause that invokes the importance of democratic self-government and the participation in that process.[13] Given the range of curricular, extracurricular, and nonschool vehicles for a child's developing the social, cognitive, and forensic skills necessary to prepare the child in a minimally adequate way, the school system can easily argue that to effectuate this value it will virtually never be required to allow the child to unsolicitedly speak his or her mind on any particular current social issue. Ultimately, collective self-government is perhaps a crucial political aim of the public school education process.[14] This does not explain, however, why a court that ordinarily professes deference on matters of the practical soundness and efficacy of educational practices should assume, without constitutionally permitting local experimentation, that the best overall practical preparation for each child's future participation in self-government as an adult, must involve in some primitively analogous way, broad free speech rights as a school child.

There is certainly unassailable logic to the recognition that "'[i]t would be foolhardy to shield our children from political debate and issues until the eve of their first venture into the voting booth. Schools must play an essential role in preparing their students to think and analyze and to recognize the demagogue.'"[15] We may stipulate that parents, along with institutions other than schools, cannot discharge this burden alone, at least in certain respects. But it is simply not credible that a student's later-manifested ability as an adult to cast an intelligent vote, intelligently discharge the obligations of citizenship generally, or exercise reasonably fully and unconstrainedly what we have referred to as fully developed free speech capacities, depends upon the student's being granted the initiative and latitude implied by _Tinker_ and its progeny. Or so a school system might quite reasonably conclude. A school might reasonably determine that a student's future prowess in demagogue recognition, or in intelligent exercise of free speech rights generally, depends significantly not upon _Tinker_ type activities, but upon such mundane capacities as the ability to draw in an analytical, incisive way upon a reasonably rich storehouse of presumably basic historical and social factual knowledge, data, and theories.

Of course, freedom of speech is often thought to have underpinnings not only in the value of self-governance, but in its "truth detection" or "truth attainment" function.[16] In this regard, Justice Black urged that "[t]he original idea of schools, which I do not believe is yet abandoned as worthless or out of date, was that children had not yet reached the point of experience and wisdom which enabled them to teach all of their elders."[17] However curmudgeonly we may regard such pronouncements, it could reasonably be concluded that the wearing of armbands by the protestors in _Tinker_, aggregated across thousands or millions of sympathizers, would not have materially furthered our collective insight into the practical or moral dimensions of the Vietnam conflict, or otherwise given us access, potentially, to some truth about the conflict that we as a society did not already possess. This is partly because children tend not to be at the cutting edge of truth or insight into geopolitical issues, even of complex moral dimension, and partly because armbands, for example, tend, by virtue of their very nature, not to be very detailed, articulate, convincing, or insightful. Hence, they are severely limited as new truth-conveyance devices, or as articulate challenges to received wisdom. Much the same could be said of most of the other familiar media of symbolic political protest.

One writer, while conceding the normal immaturity of judgment of minor children, has maintained that "[g]uaranteeing the child's right of free speech...plays an instrumental role in advancing the search for knowledge and truth; the benefits do not accrue immediately, but neither can they be secured by sheltering the child until he is ready to join the adult community."[18] We have addressed the analogue of this argument in other contexts above, and we need not recast those arguments at this point. Suffice it to say that disagreeing with the result in cases like _Tinker_ does not commit anyone to relevantly ...sheltering... the student. The fallacy involved is in assuming the indispensability of the early and arguably superficial mimicry of a practice if the practice is ever to be later grasped as an adult. Our society does not mandate, for example, that because we want an ample supply of competent physicians in the future, we must now allow young schoolchildren to attempt or simulate simple actual diagnosis and treatment, perform fake or actual surgeries with appropriate safeguards, or prescribe (harmless) drugs, and so forth. Instead, we teach the young schoolchildren, who must in some proportion later become physicians, solely through basic education, acquisition of basic social skills, and through the authoritative inculcation of the principles of biology, chemistry, and so forth.

Thus, taken in this context, it is simply not true, or a reasonable democratically elected school system might well suppose it not to be true, that it is "crucial that the student learn by taking part in actual disputes that count for something."[19] Presumably, however, most defenders of broad free speech rights of public school students will have little general use for an "actually counting" standard; our natural impulse may be to say that many or most student elections that such persons would want to see broadly protected with respect to student speech do not actually "count for something" in any relevant sense.

In sum, it appears that the values underlying the free speech clause are, in this particular context, served at least equally well by nonschool experiences and by school experiences, including listening to and speaking with fellow students, not dependent upon the kinds of student speech rights argued for or extended in cases like _Tinker_. Even if this were not so, it remains true that because of age and immaturity, "[t]he ability of the child to influence the actions of the state through the political process and to reshape his own life as a result of information obtained through the first amendment is severely limited."[20] Nor is there necessarily an ounce of hypocrisy in a school board's acting on this truth.

TOWARD A SIGNIFICANT IMPAIRMENT OF RELEVANT CAPACITY STANDARD

While many of the student speech cases have been influenced by the metaphor of the classroom as peculiarly the "marketplace of ideas,"[21] we have seen that much or all of the value logic underlying that metaphor is not necessarily and significantly implicated by many litigated speech restrictions imposed on public school students. Moreover, free speech values can be as fully recognized and effectuated despite, or even because of, those restrictions.

We have thus far no reason to question the constitutionality of the view that "[t]he student and the student's parent should be able to feel that the schoolroom will not be bombarded by unsolicited and unplanned events, ideas, and activities."[22] While student speech, for example, asserting that a principal is a liar or a fool may, controversially, serve some useful educational function in certain respects, not all such speech acquires constitutional protection through its mere arguable utility, even if its utility bears upon recognized free speech values.[23] In our view, then, there may be merit to according recognition and weight to the possibilities of loss of civility or of non-physical disruption or distraction in a school or classroom.[24] Loss of authoritative control of the educational agenda, assuming a legitimate state interest in preventing such loss, need not be constitutionally mandated in Tinker type situations. But there must of course be limits, drawn from the free speech clause, to the authority of even democratically elected school officials to keep their students in blissful ignorance, to maliciously or complacently flout or ignore free speech values, or to impose a thoroughgoing tyranny within a public school system.

The logical standard to impose in public school speech cases involving minors stems from the conclusion that while the speech of minors in Tinker type cases does not significantly and uniquely implicate recognized free speech values, it is axiomatic that comparable sorts of general restrictions imposed on adults in general would clearly implicate such free speech values, and normally would be justifiably struck down on free speech grounds. As we will discuss at greater length below, there is plainly something constitutionally distinctive about adult status and adult activities pertaining to free speech. The free speech standard imposed within the public school should accommodate

that important difference. It should aim at
preserving, for the future adults that the young
students will eventually become, the range and depth
and value of the free speech rights that such future
adults might choose to exercise.

We thus argue for a "significant impairment of
relevant capacity" standard. By this we mean that
school officials should, under the free speech clause,
be liable in principle for the presumably rare
instances in which a school system, through action or
inaction, has the proximate effect of significantly
impairing or stunting a student's development, which
it is instead constitutionally bound to reasonably
assist. It is the school system's duty to further
such students' social, intellectual, forensic, and
other capacities necessary to or constitutive of the
overall capacity to make reasonably effective use of
an adult's free speech rights. Taken together, such
capacities can be referred to simply as a person's
"free speech capacities."

We require significant impairment partly to
reduce obvious measurement problems. We are
proposing, in effect, that a child be given a cause of
action for what he or she will be like several years
in the future, unless somehow perhaps rescued or
restored and reclaimed. For practical reasons, we
perhaps may want to toll the statute of limitations in
such cases at least until the plaintiff's adulthood.
These practical problems appear neither
insurmountable, nor without broad precedent in areas
such as personal injury tort law or the law of damages
measurement.

While "impairment" implies a relational standard,
or at least a comparison with some actual or
hypothetical unimpaired condition, recognition of
significant impairment in free speech capacities does
not seem deeply metaphysical or even unduly complex.
It is largely a matter of common sense and common
observation. In the case of otherwise normal, healthy
persons, unimpairment in our sense is essentially a
matter of some reasonable, and reasonably broad,
adaptable fluency and skill in the free speech
capacities. It is exemplified in such activities as
gathering information, reasoning, reflecting and
judging, and in forming and modifying principles and
conclusions, as well as in persuading others, as
compared with the level of comparable skills exhibited
in the real world or on test scores by the broad range
of one's peers, who have experienced the range of
contemporary public and private educational systems.
In the case of students who have been educated in more
than one school district, each district individually

should bear responsibility for not irresponsibly certifying the student for the next grade level in the absence of the student's having the free speech capacity skills minimally appropriate to the grade level in question.

We have not insisted, as constitutionally mandated, upon the public schools' maximization or optimization of the development of their students' free speech capacities manifested later as adults. The maximization standard would controversially exalt the free speech clause above other, arguably equally constitutionally fundamental values, and might require some unnerving costs and tradeoffs. The optimization standard, while in one respect unassailable as a matter of abstract logic, would seem practically unascertainable and unenforceable judicially. If we retreat to "rough optimization," we have returned to a zone-of-reasonableness standard.

Among the features and implications of this standard is its focus on effects, and not on the difficult to prove, and often irrelevant, motivation, intent, or purpose of the school in imposing its speech restraints. If the effect is one of relevant significant impairment, the school's purpose is of limited interest.[25] This follows not just from the language and logic of the free speech clause, but specifically from the fact that free speech values can be damagingly impaired in the absence of any sort of malice.

More importantly, this standard can presumably be met even though the school system, whether inevitably or maliciously, omits or otherwise suppresses classroom presentation or discussion of certain disfavored subjects or ideas. It is simply implausible to imagine that any student will necessarily suffer significant impairment in future free speech capacity because he or she was denied, until the age of majority, classroom exposure to some perspective on the New Deal, or fascism, or other issue, and where the student would not have suffered such capacity impairment had he or she been so exposed. Of course, certain content-based or viewpoint-based omissions or other curricular choices, for example, professions of racial supremacy, raise issues of independent constitutional rights, including that of equal protection of the laws for minority students. Similarly, we treat establishment clause and free exercise of religion questions as without significant impact on our major theses.

The questions of socialization and indoctrination, of value inculcation, and of coercion, are important in our context, and are discussed below.

It must be admitted at the outset, however, that our future capacity impairment test seems compatible with at least some limited attempt on the part of the school system to undertake the rightly constitutionally suspect goal of fostering a "homogeneous" people.[26] It is doubtful whether excessive homogeneity of thought and value currently genuinely looms as a particularly severe threat to American cultural integrity and progress. But there are limits to the school's authority, independent of any separate equal protection challenge. In our theory, the homogenization of minor public school students, whether intentional or inadvertent, may not take the form of, or lead to, significant future capacity impairment of the kind we have described.

Without delving immediately into the broader issues of coercion and indoctrination, it is possible to differentiate quickly our view from the theory that courts should interfere with public school officials' curricular or instructional choices "only in those rare instances when decisions of state and school officials are based upon narrow political, partisan, or religious considerations."[27] Religious issues aside, our focus would instead be on the possibility of significant future free speech capacity impairment in the absence of this sort of narrow partisanship. Such capacity impairment does not become constitutionally permissible merely because it reflects some neutral, even-handed inadequacy on the part of the schools.

On the other hand, it might be wondered whether all narrowly politically motivated instructional decisions should be vulnerable under the free speech clause if there is no relevant capacity impairment, no equal protection issues, and no religion clause problems. It should be noted that narrow indoctrination need not be practically effective, and even if temporarily effective, need not be permanently so, or leave some permanent detectable impact.[28] Effects of narrow classroom partisanship, other than generating undesired widespread skepticism and debate outside of class, may essentially "wash out" by the time of adulthood, the earliest time, in our theory, for full and independent free speech significance. If such effects do not so wash out by the constitutionally relevant moment, the analysis moves to that of considering whether any relevant capacity impairment is present.

This is not to suggest that the rights of students or parents under the religion or equal protection clauses never impinge upon a free speech analysis, in our theory. Were a public school to even covertly communicate an agenda of, say, racial hierarchism, this would be subject to objection not only on the basis of the fourteenth amendment's equal protection clause, but on grounds relevant to our free speech analysis.[29]   We might draw, in at least a loose way, on the judicial sociology of cases such as Brown v. Board of Education[30] for the proposition that such "teaching" may have the long-term effect, whether intended or not, of dampening or impairing the development of the future free speech capacities of disfavored and subordinated groups of students.

Similarly, it is intriguing to ask, the religion clauses utterly aside, about the free speech status of a public high school that, standing the case of Wisconsin v. Yoder on its head, insisted on teaching its students only in accord with the secular implications of Old Order Amish doctrine.[31]   There is at least some support in the descriptions of those tenets in Yoder for contrary views as to whether such a regime would violate a student's free speech rights on our relevant capacity impairment test.   No significant such impairment need follow if such a school were merely to emphasize self-reliance and manual work, and to deemphasize, as opposed to largely ignoring, "intellectual and scientific accomplishments, self-distinction, competitiveness, worldly success, and social life with other students."[32]   But plainly, to proceed too far in this direction, or to entirely "insulate" a broad range of public school students "from the modern world"[33] risks largely disabling students in relevant respects, and making their stance of aloofness and political silence an involuntary one.   To go this far is to fail the free speech test we have proposed.

THE NATURE OF CHILDHOOD EDUCATION AND CHILDREN'S SPEECH RIGHTS

While there are many questions yet unanswered, a tentative conclusion that may be drawn is that just as a parent's forcing or indoctrinating the minor child to wear a protest symbol to school would not, ordinarily, be significantly destructive of future free speech capacity,[34] neither, ordinarily, would a contrary requirement by the public school that the child not wear such a symbol to class.   Conclusions of this sort are best reconciled on the basis of the recognition, subscribed to by a majority of the Supreme Court in at least some contexts, that public school education is not simply a matter of the Romantic, spontaneous, unaided natural blossoming of latent abilities,   but is largely characterizable as a period of broad preparation and value transfer.[35]

Even in the _Tinker_ case itself, Justice Stewart in his concurring opinion sought to hold open the possibility of drawing crucial distinctions between adults and minor children.[36] He did so on the grounds of the permissibility of a state's determining that the latter are "not possessed of that full capacity for individual choice which is the presupposition of First Amendment guarantees."[37] This formulation is undoubtedly on the right track, but there is a certain unsatisfactoriness with it in that such schoolchildren are undeniably possessed of a full and richly developed capacity for vehement, if occasionally grossly immature and insensitive, choice and expression of preference.

Perhaps one social point in frustrating the preferences of schoolchildren to speak politically in class, at least on some occasions, is to ensure that there are first imparted important lessons in perspective, diplomacy and tact, dispassionateness in analysis, and the potential range and depth of relevant evidence when making political choices. This would include such matters as the admittedly non-disruptive, but potentially harmful, wounding effect of speech on some of one's fellow students, on emotional subjects, even if the speaker has not intended such an effect. It should be uncontroversial that "[w]ithout any formal schooling, children will be incapable of intelligently exercising their civil or political rights within our society."[38] Relatedly, "[c]hildren develop from incapacity toward capacity."[39] The practical order of things is one of childhood incapacity to exercise free speech rights until capacity is developed, as children "are not adults in miniature"[40] even for our purposes. The burden of showing impairment by the school, of otherwise potentially flourishing capacities, naturally rests on the claimant.

In our theory, minor students are in the relevant respects not finished products, but radically undeveloped.[41] This is not to suggest that children are not ends-in-themselves for ethical purposes. Even children may suffer unjustifiable affronts to their moral dignity. But childhood, particularly in the school context, is a stage of crucial preparation, with a sense of essential preliminariness. As we have seen, in matters of free speech, any rights of the student exist to point toward those of the future adult.

Of course, there is a certain roughness in choosing, as we have, either attaining the age of majority or graduation from high school as the

appropriate boundary markers.   But there is a clear
conceptual logic to these lines of demarcation, and we
may well not wish to pay exorbitant administrative
costs associated with more precise, individualized
determinations of the emotional, social, moral, and
intellectual development of student plaintiffs, or
potential plaintiffs.[42]   It is of course possible to
argue that there is some better dividing line, such as
entry into high school, or entry into one's senior
year in high school, even if it is recognized that the
privileged speech of persons in the more mature
category within the school may tend to unpredictably
affect younger people attending the same school.   The
argument has been made, as we noted above, that
"[r]ealistically, high school students are beyond the
point of being sheltered...."[43]
    Literally, the argument appears to be that high
school students are practically unshelterable.   This
is implausibly extreme.   A high school might well be
reasonably effective in banning the wearing of
offensive insignia.   If instead the argument concerns
the desirability of some degree of such sheltering,
then it repeats claims confronted throughout this
chapter.   If there is in fact a babel of voices, some
unruly and irresponsible, outside of school, it does
not follow, as a constitutional requirement, that a
public high school may not seek authoritatively to
achieve a somewhat different mix and range of voices
within its walls without defaulting on its obligation
to prepare students for the world outside.
    The alternative dividing line of senior status in
high school is suggested by the remark of Judge Rosenn
to the effect that

> A decision to limit the exposure of young
> adolescents, who have less developed
> critical skills, to works such as Mein
> Kampf, which express an ideology that school
> administrators find abhorrent, should
> normally remain undisturbed....The same
> would not be true if the students in
> question were high school seniors.[44]

This may be taken to recommend a dividing line between
eleventh and twelfth grades, even if we are not to
accord any unlimited exposure rights to the twelfth
graders.   The administrative burden on school
officials at this point may be large, however, even
assuming that the difference in the average level of
critical skills between eleventh- and twelfth-graders
is particularly significant, or that some particular
threshold is ordinarily not passed until entry into

twelfth grade.[45]

Precise boundary issues aside, the decisive relevance of age to the appropriate scope of liberty was recognized by John Stuart Mill in the context of his discussion of limiting governmental coercion to the prevention of harm to others: "It is, perhaps, hardly necessary to say that this doctrine is meant to apply only to human beings in the maturity of their faculties."[46] Mill continues to the effect that "[w]e are not speaking of children or of young persons below the age which the law may fix as that of manhood or womanhood."[47]

The developed ability to reason and exercise self-control is arguably essential to the broader system of political freedom generally.[48] Those abilities depend generally upon age and education, including certain educational or curricular restraints that may be necessary for the child's free speech capacities to develop. While the untutored and the intellectually undernourished person may indeed be free from many constraints to do many valued things, he or she must lack the presently reasonably developed capacity to exercise the range of skills that comprises the unconstrained exercise of freedom of speech.[49]

Public school children are in this respect relevantly differently situated from adults, whether the adults in question are at liberty or under constraint. Age matters in the ironic sense that even where we recognize that a given adult is dramatically impaired in free speech capacities, due perhaps to illiteracy, we do not compulsorily arrange for such an adult to be placed, against his or her will, in a position of taking more effective advantage of free speech rights.[50] This is undoubtedly true largely for a variety of practical reasons, but also in part because of respect for the dignity of choices made by a person of the requisite age.

It is certainly possible in some loose sense to spectacularly analogize the status of public school students to that of prisoners,[51] even if prisoners are restrained in their liberties all of the time, unlike students.[52] From our perspective, the crucial disanalogy is that schools are or ought to be constitutionally required, in our contexts, to give crucial weight to the future capacities of students and to their development, or to the students' future selves generally, in loose analogy to a constitutionally required focus on their rehabilitation or rescue from initial ignorance and lack of competence, whereas prisons can ordinarily, and constitutionally, focus more exclusively on the prisoner's own past, the retributive and vindictive functions, or on the present welfare of third parties, as where a prisoner may, if released, pose an immediate threat to the safety of particular persons, or of society in general.

THE CONSTITUTIONALLY LEGITIMATE FUNCTIONS OF THE PUBLIC SCHOOLS

There is an obvious, never fully resolvable constitutional tension between the public schools as an instrument in the process of intergenerational transmission of culture, the process of teaching, and the schools as potential sources of narrow, perhaps coercive, indoctrination causing negative effects that may continue into adulthood. Judicially, it has been maintained that "[t]here is no doubt as to the power of a State, having a high responsibility for education of its citizens, to impose reasonable regulations for the control and duration of basic education."[53] Similarly, the Court has concluded that "public schools are vitally important 'in the preparation of individuals for participation as citizens,' and as vehicles for 'inculcating fundamental values necessary to the maintenance of a democratic political system.'"[54] Apparently, that process need not be confined to values explicitly prescribed by the Constitution. In Pierce v. Society of Sisters,[55] the Court, though certainly in dicta at best, undoubtedly saw nothing constitutionally amiss with a state requirement that teachers be of "patriotic disposition."[56] Presumably such a disposition would often tend to reflect itself in one's teaching, and perhaps even in one's grading of students.

Constitutionally, the public school need not be essentially an extension of parental control in the value inculcation process. It has been sensibly argued that "the public school system is not merely a mechanism that translates the will of the parent into the upbringing of the individual child; it is also a mechanism that instills in the child the collective societal values of the community."[57] In our theory, of course, the schools constitutionally must do more, perhaps to the detriment of the above goals. The schools must, for example, work to provide students with the eventual capacity to do such things as defend or oppose many of those parental and collective societal values. Of course, none of this is to suggest that the formal learning process is of only instrumental value, or that education in a broad range of areas is not worthwhile for its own sake.[58]

There is judicial authorization as well for an

additional role for the schools. The Court has authorized value inculcation, at least within certain limits. We have argued for reading the free speech clause as mandating what might be called rights-exercise preparation. But relatedly, it has been contended that those who nurture and direct the destiny of the child have "the right, coupled with the high duty to recognize and prepare him for additional obligations."[59] We have not similarly emphasized any duty of preparation for future obligations, since our focus has not been on the possibility of overriding any prima facie speech rights of students by means of the school's showing an inconsistent compelling state interest not otherwise attainable. There is undoubtedly some overlap in concern, however, as it is doubtful that a person could discharge well the range of citizenship obligations if his or her schooling were such as to impair significantly the free speech capacities.

Our view thus falls between that adopted by two major contending camps. Those who accord relatively great latitude to school authorities have argued that "[t]he board, the principals, and the teachers may select a textbook favoring their own views and ideologies, and they might not permit alternatives."[60] This result may to some degree be simply unavoidable, but within the limits implied by our discussion above, it is permissible.

A variant of this latitudinarian approach argues for a constitutionally privileged status for inculcating "constitutionally recognized fundamental values while refusing to permit the study of beliefs contrary to those values."[61] Again, this may, up to a point, be permissible in our capacity impairment theory. But the practical and logical questions raised by this variant are intriguing. It can be argued, for example, that one unimpeachable constitutional value, in some sense, is the institutional process for the supersession and replacement of constitutional values, as in the supplanting of the equal protection values of Plessy v. Ferguson[62] with those of Brown v. Board of Education.[63] There is thus a paradox in pedagogically closing the class of constitutionally recognized values. If it is replied that both Plessy and Brown in fact uphold the same constitutional value, that of equal protection of the laws, then very little will count as a change in constitutional values.

In any of the latitudinarian theories, there must be some account of how one can clearly inculcate a particular favored value without simultaneously exposing the students to the value's opposite. The more serious problem for these theories, however, is posed by the other extreme to which our theory stands as a midpoint. The antithesis of the latitudinarian or inculcationist theories is constituted by writers who argue that "the courts have inadequately protected the interests of students in freedom of belief and have granted too much weight to government's claimed interest in inculcating and indoctrinating youth."[64]

This more restrictive approach is based on liberal principles and the observation that there are no uniformly acceptable political values.[65] In the absence of any universal current consensus on which values are genuinely fundamental democratic values, "to authorize government to inculcate 'fundamental democratic' values is to authorize those in power to pick and choose the versions of the values that serve their interests."[66] On this more restrictive approach, the courts should on principle bar any attempt by the public schools to impose on students any set of political ideas, values, attitudes, or beliefs.[67] The rationale underlying this approach is that a government that is to be subject to the genuine control of the electorate cannot have the authority to determine, partly through the public schools, the values and preferences of that electorate with respect to the government, lest democracy be merely a vicious circle.[68]

Rooted as such a conception is in one version of liberal individualism, one is tempted to respond to such restrictive approaches not on the level of its ethical soundness, but that of cultural anthropology. Is it not simply asking too much of any reasonably vital, self-assured, reasonably decent society that it be so remarkably diffident as to jeopardize its own perpetuation or its own continuity in even a general way by foreswearing an arguably vital means of political socialization? Will a society that is so scrupulously indifferent as to its advertisement to the succeeding generation not simply tend to be replaced on the world stage by societies less attractive by our own current majority's standards and most of our own received traditions? Particularly in light of a variety of private school options,[69] and in light of the relative uncontroversiality of certain basic political concepts, such as free speech for adults, the absence of an established church, broad civil tolerance, and opposition to explicit racism, we are naturally reluctant to grant a public school curricular veto to dissenters on such issues, beyond their ability to convince us of our error. On the strict logic of such a restrictive position, it cannot countenance the teaching, or "inculcation," if there is any difference, of the particular value of individual dignity. Not all persons subscribe to it. In our theory, such value inculcation is permissible, at least under the free speech clause, up until the point of significant future free speech capacity impairment.

There is, finally, for the restrictive approach to public school value transmission, the deeper practical problem of how a reflective citizen, reasonably open and unconstrained in his or her thinking, is actually produced. For an adult to be knowledgeable and critically insightful about society, it may be that some degree of value inculcation as a schoolchild is practically required. Professor Ackerman has assumed, quite plausibly, an infant's practical need for "cultural coherence."[70] Moreover, perhaps at some loss in obvious plausibility, it seems that a public school education in social matters that is simply an unordered, kaleidoscopic presentation of a succession of views, theories, and unendorsed value assertions, without any authoritative context, may tend to leave the student simply dismayed, without any coherent standpoint at all--not even a reflective, well-articulated relativism or skepticism. If so, it seems that the restrictive approach to value inculcation, which of course might also take the chimerical course of attempting to utterly exclude all values from the school, might itself be unconstitutional in our theory, as resulting in significant free speech capacity impairment. Relatedly, it should be noted that sanitizing the schools of all illicit value communication, even if this were possible, would for another reason not inevitably lead to an unquestionable enhancement of the child's autonomy and political freedom.[71] Certainly, some parents of public school children are themselves afflicted with something of the dictator's ambitions and lack of self-doubt.[72] To diminish the value enculturation aspects of public school education may be to dispose of a rival of and countervailing influence upon such would-be dictators.

The Supreme Court has recently shown signs of limited movement on the scope of the legitimate functions of the public schools. In <u>Bethel School District No. 403 v. Fraser</u>,[73] for example, the Court's majority was willing to itself characterize the respondent speaker's remarks at a school assembly as offensively lewd, indecent, and vulgar, even if not obscene.[74] The Court might, in a less judicially assertive moment, have relied more heavily on the reasonableness of such a characterization by school officials themselves, but it at least avoided the relativism with which it has, as we have seen, decided other free speech cases in the past. In _Fraser_, the majority, finding offensiveness along with an absence of political viewpoint discrimination, determined a sexually suggestive high school assembly speech to be constitutionally unprotected against the school officials' determination that such a speech would, or did in fact, "undermine the school's basic educational mission."[75]

The Court has also driven something of a wedge between the essentially physical "disruption" standard and the potentially broader "undermining of basic educational mission" language in _Fraser_. The ideal test case would involve nonlewd, nonindecent, nonvulgar speech or symbolic conduct that could reasonably be thought to detectably undermine the school's basic and legitimate educational mission, while at the same time not posing a substantial threat of an actual physical disruption. This would amount to a pure educational agenda control case. The recent case of _Hazelwood School District v. Kuhlmeier_[76] is probably the closest actual approach.

THE PRESERVATION OF FUTURE OPTIONS FOR THE CURRENT STUDENT

In a slightly different context it has been judicially observed that: "A State has a legitimate interest not only in seeking to develop the latent talents of its children but also in seeking to prepare them for the life style that they may later choose, or at least to provide them with an option other than the life they have led in the past."[77] Our focus, in the matter of option provision or non-preclusion, of course extends beyond recognizing such as merely a legitimate state interest and considers the extent to which option provision through education rises to a constitutional requirement derivable through the free speech clause.

In practice, there will be substantial overlap between a policy of providing future life style options for students and a policy of ensuring no significant impairment of future free speech capacities. These requirements are certainly not identical in principle, as we can envision a person who can assume a variety of less demanding life roles without being capable of deploying unconstrainedly a range of free speech-relevant capacities with reasonable fullness. Whether our capacity impairment standard is more demanding, overall, than a principle of preserving life style options is partly a matter of definition, and partly a matter of empirical investigation.

While it is similarly possible to assert that a high school graduate with a stunted, apparently permanently impaired free speech capacity is or may be a "good citizen,"[78] it is certainly possible to extend the notion of good citizenship to encompass more than merely not being a criminal, or voluntarily accepting a status as a public welfare burden,[79] by including a good citizenship requirement of at least preserving one's option for intelligent, adaptable political participation.[80]   Arguably, from the standpoint of society's interest in good citizenship, as well as from that of the individual student's own present and future interest in his or her future free speech capacities, "it is worse to restrict children's future opportunities against their will than it is to force them to keep their future options open."[81]   This follows in part from the relevant differences between schoolchildren and adults discussed above.

How far we extend the principle of option preservation depends, however, on whether we emphasize the societal interest or the individual rights interests of each particular student.   There is a lurking ambiguity in the claim that "[t]he value of a liberal democracy to its citizens is in large part contingent upon the ability of its citizens to exercise their political rights intelligently as well as to choose among alternative conceptions of the good life."[82]   A liberal democracy can function effectively, and confer value on all persons, as long as the percentage of well-educated persons does not fall below some minimum.   Various students may be deprived of their free speech rights, in view of their adult free speech incapacities, with the collective goal of liberal democracy still being realized, if in obviously imperfect measure.

Interpreted stringently, the individual child's "right to an open future"[83] is in some respects broader in its requirements than our interpretation of the free speech clause in terms of future free speech capacity impairment.   On a demanding interpretation, it is possible to assert that it is in some measure the responsibility of, for example, the El Paso public system that most El Paso public school students are never in a position, say, to take a particular major world religion like Shintoism seriously as a possible future life option.   This general sort of result is of course inevitable.   It remains possible to reconcile these standards either by interpreting the child's right to an open future less strictly, or by determining, implausibly, that the inadvertent practical inaccessibility of Shintoism, as one among a myriad of possible examples, must reflect a significant impairment in relevant free speech capacities.

COERCIVE INDOCTRINATION AND THE PUBLIC SCHOOLS

It follows from our theory, perhaps controversially, that a government may be guilty of an <u>attempt</u> to restrict a student's free speech rights impermissibly, without succeeding in the attempt, and therefore, despite all the malice in the world, not have violated the student's free speech rights. This is familiar in other contexts. That killing someone may amount to the crime of homicide does not in and of itself mean that an unsuccessful attempt to commit homicide must necessarily also be a crime, let alone the crime of homicide.

Similarly, on our theory, if the government has been sufficiently ineffective in its attempt to violate student free speech rights, or if its actions without such a suppressive intent are similarly inconsequential, there simply is no actionable free speech violation. Moreover, it becomes possible for a potential intended or unintended violation of a student's free speech rights to "turn out" to be not actionable because any immediate effects may become neutralized over time, leaving the student's free speech capacities unimpaired when he or she reaches adulthood.

This temporal dimension, in which putative free speech violations may dissolve, is also not unfamiliar. We do not charge someone who pays in advance for a future murder with any kind of homicide if, for some reason, the person he has paid to commit the murder is somehow prevented from carrying out the contract. But the analogy to "attempted" free speech violations, which may even appear "successful" temporarily, is often underrecognized. It has been urged, for example, that "the state may not attempt to coerce belief by the child, because it would thereby abridge future freedom of choice."[84] But on our theory, this would not necessarily follow, even if "attempt to" were omitted, and the focus only on successful attempts. Attempts to coerce belief may completely backfire, or otherwise go awry. They may also be merely partially or temporarily effective such that no significant impairment of free speech capacities is apparent once the child reaches the age of majority or leaves the school.

A coercively inculcated belief is therefore not necessarily a stable long-term or undislodgeable belief. This is significant because, on our theory, the free speech capacities of adults are far more constitutionally significant than those of the same adults as schoolchildren, and the first amendment forbids precisely the abridging of free speech rights, which literally excludes failed attempts to abridge those rights from the scope of its coverage.[85]

Unless one simply defines coercive inculcation of beliefs in terms of future option closing, a uniform objection against all such coercion by the public schools raises difficult empirical questions.[86] Is it even possible for a vital society to resist the understandable temptation to simply implant basic beliefs or attitudes within the minds of its public schoolchildren, bypassing or simply not waiting for the critical reflective capacities of such children? Is it perhaps true that some or all children in fact require some minimal anchoring in basic beliefs not fully critically examined if they are to develop a reasonably effective critical intelligence? Is there perhaps some trade-off between minimal coerced inculcation of belief as a child and later resistance as an adult to propagandizing? More exotically, is it possible that one coercive childhood experience may "offset," or be offset by, another such experience?[87]

In any event, it seems clear from casual observation that persons may be both reasonably free speech competent as adults and yet have been subject to evidently permanent, coercive, reason-bypassing indoctrination as a schoolchild. Any normative theory to the effect that any nonrational indoctrination of schoolchildren violates the free speech clause[88] should confront not only the empirical issues raised immediately above, but the limited relevance of autonomy concerns to schoolchildren as schoolchildren, in light of their undeveloped capacities, and their dependence in any event on deep socialization by parents. Not entirely frivolously, it might be asked why compulsory public school courses in mathematics do not tend to coercively inculcate values associated with "mere linear rationality" that may well not be shared uniformly among parents of public school students.

Our view of the legitimate role of educational coercion might also be contrasted with the broader view espoused by Professor Ackerman, who argues that adults may coercively inculcate certain adult norms if such inculcation is necessary to minimize the probability or severity of criminal law restraints being required to control the child later.[89] This broader view, despite its undoubted libertarian intent, might of course in principle be used to justify an unexpected degree of consequentialist state intervention into matters such as, for example, the

viewing of television violence. Our focus is narrower
in that preventing future criminality by even the
least intrusive means may license more intrusive
restraints than our requirement of the preservation of
future free speech capacities.

Judicially, there have been attempts to
distinguish between a school's instilling values
through "choice of emphasis" on the one hand, and by
"shielding" students from disfavored ideas on the
other.[90]   Alternatively, it has been urged that
"[s]chool boards may establish their curriculum in
such a way as to transmit community values...but...may
not deny access to ideas in a way that prescribes an
orthodoxy in matters of opinion."[91]   Tests such as
these may have some sorting power, but they quickly
become merely alternative favorable and unfavorable
ways of characterizing essentially the same phenomenon
or educational technique.   Under our capacity
impairment test, as we have seen, some degree of
"shielding" may be permissible under the free speech
clause, while it is possible that broad and extreme
"emphasis" may sometimes not.   Such characterizations
are therefore of limited utility.

The Court has also found some attraction in an
argument in the following terms: "That [the schools]
are educating the young for citizenship is reason for
scrupulous protection of constitutional freedoms of
the individual, if we are not to strangle the free
mind at its source and teach youth to discount
important principles of our government as mere
platitudes."[92]   At least the last clause of this
sentence is supported by Dean Levin, who argues that
"if the educational institution is wholly
undemocratic, students are likely to get mixed signals
with regard to the democratic values needed to
function as citizens in our society: The way in which
school administrators operate schools may have a more
powerful influence on students than the lessons in
their civic textbooks."[93]   This argument of course
minimizes the relevant differences between children
and adults.   Our society has, overall, probably been
moving in that direction for some time.

The strangulation argument, at least at a literal
level, overlooks the possibility that a school may
reasonably presume that despite the absence of
governmental hinderance or constraint, an untutored,
undeveloped mind is essentially not yet a politically
free mind in the relevant sense.   A young student
eventually may take most significant advantage of free
speech rights as an adult only if he or she is subject
to broad, reasonable restrictions on present
inclinations as a child to do such things as engage in

political protest, or its semblance, during class. In the meantime, a young student may, quite incorrectly, get mixed signals about our commitment to democracy precisely because the student, in virtue of his or her immaturity, underrecognizes the significance of the difference between maturity and immaturity.

Similarly, while we obviously do not want to preach the value of free speech and political democracy to children while hypocritically violating those principles in our classroom dealings with them, we must not simply beg the issue by assuming that free speech in the schoolroom should be analyzed along the lines of free speech in the union hall, or on the picket line, or that democracy in a classroom must extend as far as it might in other institutional contexts. We must discern the scope of children's free speech rights, the point at issue, before knowing whether we are setting a bad example, or simply adhering sensibly to the purpose-driven legitimate scope of those principles. There may be relevant distinctions to be drawn between minor children in a public school and adults generally, whether children perceive such distinctions or not.

THE SCOPE OF THE STUDENT'S RIGHT TO KNOW PARTICULAR THINGS

Our theory includes some free speech clause limitations on the unwillingness of schools to instruct. But it is reasonable to ask whether a particular student could ever have a free speech right that certain identifiable facts, principles, theories, or values be taught. One possible answer is that "[t]he right to know should not impose an affirmative obligation on the state to provide specific information; the better role for free speech is to restrict attempts by the state to coerce belief or to forbid the acquisition of knowledge. Affirmative provision of information seems better left to parents."[94]

The analysis is a bit different, however, under our theory. It seems correct that there is no general constitutional right of public school students under the free speech clause to specific, identifiable bits of information or perspectives. But there is an obvious free speech basis, under our free speech capacity impairment test, for requiring the school to impart some broadly content-variable irreducible minimum quantity and variety of arguably basic information, theories, and viewpoints. The school must not simply assume that this minimum nutrition for developing free speech capacities is coming from some other source, such as the family.

There may, as an empirical matter, be some particular ideas that seem so fundamental and inescapable that the school's failure to in any way present them, even briefly, may be most plausibly explained on the basis of the school's desire to impair, or its indifference toward the impairment of, free speech capacity development.[95] The idea of the very existence of the United States as a nation state or the idea of political participation would seem to fall into this category. Another such individually necessary particular idea may be that adult Americans are widely thought to hold, descriptively or normatively, some defensible free speech rights. It is difficult to imagine some set of different ideas which, if conveyed to the student, would sufficiently compensate for the absence of the above ideas. Under our theory, therefore, there is probably some limit to the undeniably large legitimate variability of the sets of basic ideas which when imparted to the student will suffice to avoid the relevant capacity impairment. This supplies in turn a principled limitation on the scope of the student's free speech right to know particular things.[96]

It is possible to seek to expand the student's free speech right to know particular things by appealing to the fact that motivation enhances learning, and that some matters, such as sex in general, are of greater intrinsic interest to schoolchildren than other matters.[97] But as fascinating as such subjects may be, as indicated by the ample time devoted to them by adolescents outside of class, it may be difficult to show significant future free speech capacity impairment because of the exclusion of such particular matters from the curriculum. An individual school might plausibly maintain that it prefers to impart the lessons that interests and tastes in conversational subject matter need not be brute, but can be cultivated. Or it may teach that classroom discussion of such matters undermines the assumed importance of developing dispassionate, impersonal analytical and expository skills that draw upon statistical, rather than anecdotal or introspective evidence. It is far from clear, as we shall discuss further below, that the federal courts should be in the business of simply second-guessing such pedagogy in the absence of other legal considerations.

An interesting variant of the particular item of knowledge problem concerns the permissibility of a school system's entirely closing or failing to furnish, for reasons other than an actual lack of

resources, any sort of school library or close
substitute therefor. To some, such an action by the
school board would be entirely unproblematic. Chief
Justice Burger, for example, wrote that "[o]f course,
it is perfectly clear that, unwise as it would be, the
board could wholly dispense with the school library,
so far as the first amendment is concerned."[98]

Under our theory, however, we must at least hold
open the admittedly unlikely possibility that such a
board decision, perhaps in conjunction with other
decisions, could have the effect, whether intended or
not, of causing significant relevant capacity
impairment. The absence of any sort of school library
or its equivalent puts at least some strain on the
classroom teaching component of the development of
free speech capacities. While our focus is on
effects, rather than the school board's intentions, we
may wish to trace actual effects through intended
effects, and we are properly constitutionally curious
about, for example, a school with ample space and
resources for at least an informal library that
refuses all donations.[99]

THE ROLE OF JUDICIAL DEFERENCE AND EXPERTISE

Proper resolution of student speech cases is unlikely
on a consistent basis unless some care is taken in
attending to the precise relative advantages and
competencies of judges, local and national experts of
various sorts, and democratically elected school
officials and their agents. It will not suffice to
characterize the crucial issue as "whether local
schools are to be administered by elected school
boards, or by federal judges and teenage
pupils...."[100] There is doubtless merit, within its
proper scope, to the judicial tradition of deference
to the management discretion of local school
authorities, who may be both popularly elected and
particularly familiar with the values and preferences
of the local community, in addition to having
familiarity with the operation of local pedagogical
practices.[101] But, while under our theory judicial
intervention into student speech issues will
presumably be rare, the logic of deference is an
incomplete and misleading explanation for this result.

To begin with, while "American public education
has always been under local political control...,"[102]
the scope, applicability, and infringement of free
speech rights are matters that are intended precisely
not to be subject to local majoritarian control.
Under our theory, the significant impairment of
students' future free speech capacities cannot be

justified by any mere preferences and insights of
local officials, or local values, no matter how
popular or otherwise reasonable. The presumed
advantage in understanding first amendment law must go
to the federal courts, even if one assumes that the
compatibility of local federal judges' values with
those of the populace in general played no role in
their selection. Of course, matters of educational
pedagogy, and the actual impact of a given school
curriculum on local students, may be crucial under our
theory in deciding a given case.

It is doubtful, however, whether a member of even
a distant United States Supreme Court, being well-
briefed and benefitting from the views of local as
well as leading national experts, in the record or via
the briefs filed, and with an opportunity to pose
questions on oral argument, is really at a
disadvantage compared to local political decision
makers on matters even of educational theory,
psychology, and cognitive development. It may be
unrealistic to assume that local officials understood
the impact of their curricular policies on their
students in a way that is simply not communicable to
the justices who must decide the case. With or
without such mechanisms as amicus briefs, the
judiciary may be in at least as good a position to
draw upon and comprehend the range of relevant
national expertise as were the local decision makers
at the time of their decision.[103] Even if we assume
infinite conscientiousness on the part of local
decision makers, even the most distinctively nonlegal
issues may not be particularly local in nature.

Even if these considerations were of no effect,
it would still be important to note that our approach
to student speech tends to minimize the risks of
inappropriate judicial intrusion. It is plausible to
argue that a distant judiciary may "miss" some subtle
classroom distraction or interference with the
classroom learning process.[104] It is less plausible
to maintain that the distant judiciary will tend to
commit the opposite error, of hallucinating some
imagined significant free speech capacity impairment
that is not really present, for reasons understood by
local officials but incomprehensible to the judiciary.
If the students cannot, at graduation, describe the
American political process, for example, in any
rudimentary way, the judiciary may rightly be
impatient of esoteric explanations by school officials
of why this is inevitable. The date of graduation is
referred to here simply to indicate roughly the first
point at which a legally cognizable injury to the
student will ordinarily be said to have arisen.

There are thus insufficient grounds for concluding that "courts should apply only a limited standard of review to local school administration action: the minimum rationality standard currently used to review government activity that does not implicate fundamental rights."[105] Fundamental rights, though of a limited scope, are indeed involved. While "contemporary community standards"[106] have an established role to play in first amendment adjudication, there is not much point to constitutional protection if they are invariably decisive,[107] or if any minimal legitimate public purpose trumps the free speech right.

It should be noted that our cases differ in a number of respects from the due process cases the Court has confronted in which, for example, a student has been dismissed from college or professional school for reasons of alleged deficiencies in academic or professional performance.[108] Even if the right to remain in medical school except for legitimate reasons were of the same constitutional moment as the right to freedom of speech, we would expect greater judicial deference to the conscientious efforts of colleges of medicine to sort out marginal doctors than we would in the more accessibly common-sensical inquiries our free speech rule would typically require.

Finally, despite the expressions of deference to the discretion of local political decision makers, the courts have at least occasionally been willing, in small cases and great, to in effect overrule the pedagogical judgment of local officials in the context of a significant rights violation. In Meyer v. Nebraska,[109] for example, the Court, without citation to the record or to any authority, concluded, contrary to the evident determination of Nebraska authorities, that "[i]t is well known that proficiency in a foreign language seldom comes to one not instructed at an early age, and experience shows that this is not injurious to the health, morals or understanding of the ordinary child."[110] The Court in effect constitutionally overrode a collective decision by the State to allow the study of languages such as Greek and Latin, but not German and French, during the early grades, despite whatever pedagogical arguments the school might have mustered. More importantly, it is possible to interpret the landmark case of Brown v. Board of Education[111] as implying a judicial willingness to implicitly overrule the determination by local school officials that the quality of education for black children, and this could be translated into terms of the significant impairment of the general future capacities of current black students, was not being significantly impaired in a constitutionally suspect way under the established school system.[112]

The case for only limited intervention by the courts into the operations of the public schools in student speech cases thus need not rely heavily on considerations of deference and comparative expertise. Overruling the judgment of the relevant Topeka officials on the largely empirical matter of the development of the educational capacities of black students was not by itself thought to be hopelessly complex or illegitimate in <u>Brown</u>. It is not the commands of judicial deference, but the narrow legitimate scope of the free speech rights of public schoolchildren, that best justifies only infrequent judicial intervention in public school decisions regarding the rights of juveniles under the free speech clause. Under our substantial future free speech capacity impairment test, as outlined above, the courts may intervene to vindicate genuine deprivations of student free speech rights, while respecting the proper scope of discretion of democratically elected local educational authorities.

NOTES

1. 393 U.S. 503 (1969).

2. <u>Id</u>. at 513 (quoting Burnside v. Byars, 363 F.2d 744, 749 (5th Cir. 1966)) (brackets in <u>Tinker</u>).

3. The Court's most recent examinations of these broad issues have come in Bethel School Dist. No. 403 v. Fraser, 478 U.S. 675 (1986) and in Hazelwood School Dist. v. Kuhlmeier, 108 S. Ct. 562 (1988).

4. Emerson, <u>Toward A General Theory of the First Amendment</u>, 72 <u>Yale</u> <u>L.J</u>. 877, 879 (1963).

5. <u>Id</u>.

6. Levin, <u>Educating Youth for Citizenship: The Conflict Between Authority and Individual Rights in the Public School</u>, 95 <u>Yale</u> <u>L.J</u>. 1647, 1649 (1986).

7. Garvey, <u>Children and the First Amendment</u>, 57 <u>Tex</u>. <u>L</u>. <u>Rev</u>. 321, 338 (1979).

8. <u>Cf</u>. <u>id</u>. at 347 (seeking to tie individuality to the possibility of defiance of authority).

9. <u>J.S</u>. <u>Mill</u>, <u>On Liberty</u> 275 (B. Wishy ed. 1959).

10.   *See* Gardner, *Liberty and Compulsory Education*, in *Of Liberty* 109, 126 (A.P. Griffiths ed. 1983).

11.   *Tinker*, 393 U.S. at 504.

12.   *See* *id*. at 516 (Black, J., dissenting).

13.   *See*, *e.g.*, Garvey, *supra* note 7, at 338.

14.   *See*, *e.g.*, *Fraser*, 478 U.S. at 681.

15.   Seyfried v. Walton, 668 F.2d 214, 220 (3d Cir. 1981) (Rosenn, J., concurring) (quoting James v. Board of Educ., 461 F.2d 566, 574 (2d Cir.), *cert*. *denied*, 409 U.S. 1042 (1972)).

16.   *See*, *e.g.*, Emerson, *supra* note 4, at 878-79.

17.   *Tinker*, 393 U.S. at 522 (Black, J., dissenting).

18.   Garvey, *supra* note 7, at 344.

19.   *Id*. at 361.

20.   Diamond, *The First Amendment and Public Schools: The Case Against Judicial Intervention*, 59 *Tex*. *L*. *Rev*. 477, 488-89 (1981).

21.   *See*, *e.g.*, Keyishian v. Board of Regents, 385 U.S. 589, 603 (1967).

22.   Diamond, *supra* note 20, at 493.

23.   *See* Nahmod, *Beyond Tinker: The High School As An Educational Public Forum*, 5 *Harv*. *C.R.-C.L*. *L*. *Rev*. 278, 287 (1970); *but* *cf*. Poling v. Murphy, 872 F.2d 757, 758 (6th Cir. 1989) (discussing civility as apparently recognizable and as a legitimate pedagogical concern).

24.   Note the analysis of the case facts in *Tinker*, 393 U.S. at 517-18 (Black, J., dissenting).

25.   *Cf*.   Justice Blackmun's concurrence in the library book removal case of Board of Educ., Island Trees Union Free School Dist. No. 26 v. Pico, 457 U.S. 853, 879-82 (1982) (focusing on the school authorities' intent in removing the books).

26.   *Cf*. *Tinker*, 393 U.S. at 511 (repudiating such a policy goal). *See* *also* Diamond, *supra* note 20, at 481.

27. Freeman, _The Supreme Court and First Amendment Rights of Students in the Public School Classroom: A Proposed Model of Analysis_, 12 _Hastings Const_. _L.Q_. 1, 49 (1984).

28. _Cf_. _id_. at 52   (recognizing the dangers of indoctrination, but not discussing the possibility of the fading or superseding of such influence over time).

29. _Cf_. _id_. at 55 (discussing the inculcation of doctrines of racial hierarchism).

30.   347 U.S. 482 (1954).

31.   406 U.S. 205 (1972).

32.   _Id_. at 211.

33.   _Id_. at 210.

34. _Cf_. Hafen, _Children's Liberation and the New Egalitarianism: Some Reservations About Abandoning Youth to Their "Rights,"_ 1976 _B.Y.U_. _L_. _Rev_. 605, 646 (discussing the rights of parents to exercise control in this respect over their children).

35. _See_ _e.g._, _Fraser_, 478 U.S. at 681.

36. Professor Tushnet maintains that, with specified qualifications, "[t]he first amendment rights of young adults in schools are, according to _Tinker_, exactly the same as those of adults." Tushnet, _Free Expression and the Young Adult: A Constitutional Framework_, 1976 _Ill_. _L_. _Forum_ 746, 760.

37. _Tinker_, 393 U.S. at 515 (Stewart, J., concurring) (quoting Ginsberg v. New York, 390 U.S. 629, 649-50 (1968) (Stewart, J., concurring in result)).

38. Gutmann, _Children, Paternalism, and Education: A Liberal Argument_, 9 _Phil_. _&_ _Pub_. _Aff_. 338, 349 (1980).

39.   Hafen, _supra_ note 34, at 648.

40. _Id_. at 651 (quoting _J_. _Goldstein_, _A_. _Freud_, _&_ _A_. _Solnit_, _Beyond The Best Interests of The Child_ 13 (1973)).

41. _Cf_. _Fraser_, 478 U.S. at 683 (discussing the need for appropriate examples and role models for children in schools).

42.   See Tushnet, supra note 36, at 750.

43.   Fraser, 755 F.2d at 1363, rev'd, 478 U.S. 675 (1986).

44.   Seyfried, 668 F.2d at 220 (Rosenn, J., concurring).

45.   For a possible distinction in a somewhat
different context between the first amendment rights
of "older" versus "younger" minors or juveniles, see
American Booksellers Ass'n v. Commonwealth of Va., 792
F.2d 1261, 1264 n.7 (4th Cir. 1986), vacated and
remanded, 109 S. Ct. 254 (1988).

46.   J.S. Mill, supra note 9, at 251; Gardner, supra
note 10, at 117.

47.   J.S. Mill, supra note 9, at 251. See also Hafen,
supra note 34, at 612.

48.   See Gardner, supra note 10, at 112.

49.   See id. at 114.

50.   See id. at 109.

51.   See Diamond, supra note 20, at 517 n.181.

52.   See id.

53.   Wisconsin v. Yoder, 406 U.S. 205, 213 (1972).

54.   Pico, 457 U.S. at 864 (1982) (plurality opinion)
(quoting Ambach v. Norwick, 441 U.S. 68, 76-77 (1979)).

55.   268 U.S. 510 (1925).

56.   Id. at 534.

57.   Diamond, supra note 20, at 494 n.86.   For a
discussion of the moral rights of children with
respect particularly to their parents, see D.
Phillips, Toward A Just Social Order 159-83 (1986).

58.   Cf. Gardner, supra note 10, at 127.

59.   Pierce v. Society of Sisters, 268 U.S. 510, 535
(1925), quoted in Hafen, supra note 34, at 620.

60.   Diamond, supra note 20, at 497.

61.   Freeman, supra note 27, at 56.

62.   163 U.S. 537 (1896).

63.   347 U.S. 483 (1954).

64.   VanGeel, The Search for Constitutional Limits on Government Authority to Inculcate Youth, 62 Tex. L. Rev. 197, 203 (1983).

65.   See Kamenshine, The First Amendment's Implied Political Establishment Clause, 67 Calif. L. Rev. 1104, 1134 (1979).

66.   VanGeel, supra note 64, at 250.

67.   See id. at 239.

68.   See id. at 249-50.

69.   Professor VanGeel cites a figure of 11% private school attendance as of 1983. Id. at 283 n.386.

70.   B. Ackerman, Social Justice in The Liberal State 141 (1980).

71.   See Hafen, supra note 34, at 650.

72.   See B. Ackerman, supra note 70, at 156.

73.   478 U.S. 675 (1986).

74.   See id. at 685.

75.   Id.

76.   108 S. Ct. 562 (1988).   For a more recent case with substantial agenda-control features, see Burch v. Barker, 861 F.2d 1149 (9th Cir. 1988) (endorsing broad control by the school of "official" or "curricular" materials).

77.   Wisconsin v. Yoder, 406 U.S. 205, 240 (1972) (White, J., concurring).

78.   Cf. id. at 212 (discussing desire of Amish to be good citizens, though at a level compatible with modest education).

79.   Cf. id. at 224-25 (noting absence of evidence of any Amish tendency to become social burdens).

80. *Cf*. *id*. at 221 (discussing Jefferson's linkage of political participation and good citizenship). It has been argued that the educational standards set by in *Yoder* may be too low to promote later "meaningful choice." *See* Gutmann, *supra* note 38, at 356.

81. Gutmann, *supra* note 38, at 355.

82. *Id*. at 350.

83. VanGeel, *supra* note 64, at 261.

84. Garvey, *supra* note 7, at 350.

85. It might be argued that a government that once, or repeatedly, sought unsuccessfully to abridge a person's free speech rights, at some cost to that person, was violating the person's right to equal protection of the laws.

86. *See* VanGeel, *supra* note 64, at 253, 261.

87. *See* **B**. *Ackerman*, *supra* note 70, at 159, for a discussion of the possibility of what might be called countervailing intolerances.

88. *See* VanGeel, *supra* note 64, at 261; Garvey, *supra* note 7, at 327.

89. *See* **B**. *Ackerman*, *supra* note 70, at 147-48.

90. *Pico*, 457 U.S. at 882 (Blackmun, J., concurring in part and concurring in the judgment).

91. Bell v. U-32 Bd. of Educ., 630 F. Supp. 939, 944 (D. Vt. 1986).

92. *Tinker*, 393 U.S. at 507.

93. Levin, *supra* note 6, at 1649.

94. Garvey, *supra* note 7, at 374.

95. *Cf*. Levin, *supra* note 6, at 1660, 1666 (discussing limitations on the discretion of teachers in selecting ideas to be presented).

96. *Cf*. Freeman, *supra* note 27, at 44 (maintaining the illimitability in principle of any such right).

97. *See* Garvey, *supra* note 7, at 348.

98. _Pico_, 457 U.S. at 887 n.3 (Burger, C.J., dissenting). _See also_ Diamond, _supra_ note 20, at 511 n.145.

99. _Cf_. Levin, _supra_ note 6, at 1659 (discussing the absence of any constitutional mandate for any school library at all).

100. _Pico_, 457 U.S. at 885 (Burger, C.J., dissenting).

101. _See_ Diamond, _supra_ note 20, at 482, 498-500; Freeman, _supra_ note 27, at 69-70.

102. Diamond, _supra_ note 20, at 498.

103. _But cf_. Tushnet, _supra_ note 36, at 754 (inevitability of judicial reliance upon professionals in areas where social science evidence is important).

104. _See_ Diamond, _supra_ note 20, at 497.

105. _See id_. at 477.

106. See Miller v. California, 413 U.S. 15 (1973).

107. _Cf_. Diamond, _supra_ note 20, at 50-58 (discussing conflicting roles of community standards and nonmajoritarianism in first amendment adjudication).

108. _See, e.g._, Board of Curators v. Horowitz, 435 U.S. 78 (1978) (no violation of due process when respondent was fully informed of faculty dissatisfaction with her academic performance prior to dismissal).

109. 262 U.S. 390 (1923).

110. _Id_. at 403. _See also_ Garvey, _supra_ note 7, at 343.

111. 347 U.S. 483 (1954).

112. _Cf_. Diamond, _supra_ note 20, at 507-9 (emphasizing the considerations favoring greater judicial deference toward local school board determinations generally).

5

Fowler v. Board of Education:
**A Case Study in the Scope of Public
School Teachers' Free Speech Rights**

INTRODUCTION

On its distinctive facts, <u>Fowler v. Board of Education
of Lincoln County, Kentucky</u>[1] is ideally suited for
examining some of the deeper issues associated with
the in-school speech of public high school teachers in
particular and with free speech law in general. In
light of its facts and the prior case law, it is
hardly surprising that <u>Fowler</u> evoked three separate
and distinct responses from the Sixth Circuit panel
deciding the case. This chapter, through a shift in
the formulation of the precise issues presented,
presents a fourth approach. The justification for
this apparently perverse multiplication of complexity
is simply that it allows us to see the virtues and
limitations of each of the three approaches taken by
the Sixth Circuit.

To begin by temporarily oversimplifying, <u>Fowler</u>
involved a tenured public high school teacher who was
subjected to the sanction of dismissal after a school
board hearing because she had shown a popular "R"
rated movie on a noninstructional day to her morning
and afternoon class of fourteen-to seventeen-year-old
students, while exercising only desultory attempts to
edit the video portion of the movie.[2]

At the federal court trial on her wrongful
discharge claim, the teacher, Jacqueline Fowler, was
awarded reinstatement and money damages.[3] On appeal
to the Sixth Circuit, her judgment was vacated and her
claim dismissed.[4] No single approach commanded a
majority of the Sixth Circuit panel. To oversimplify
the law as much as the facts, Judge Milburn concluded

that Fowler had not engaged in speech containing the expressive or communicative elements necessary to invoke the protection of the free speech clause.[5] Judge Peck, while concurring in the majority result, reasoned that Ms. Fowler had engaged in constitutionally protected speech, and had shown that her protected speech was a substantial and motivating factor in the school board's decision to discharge her. However, in his view, the board had then met its burden of showing that it would have dismissed her for her conduct and poor judgment anyway. That is, Judge Peck concluded that the court had not premised its decision upon those aspects of her speech or conduct that were constitutionally protected, nor upon any motivation on the part of the board to impose sanctions attributable to such protected activity.[6] Judge Merritt dissented. In his view, at least some protected speech, either in the category of instruction or entertainment, was present. In contrast to Judge Peck, he concluded that the board had failed to prove that Fowler's speech was severable into protected "substance," or messages, or meanings on the one hand, and unprotected means, or "form," featuring violence, sexuality, and vulgarity on the other. In his view, the board did not meet its burden of showing that it would have terminated Fowler for reasons other than its admitted disagreement with the substance and presumed messages of the film.[7]

THE MILBURN OPINION: THE ALLEGED ABSENCE OF PROTECTED SPEECH

Most, but not all, of the facts underlying the Fowler case were not in serious dispute. It is more generally the constitutional significance of the underlying facts that guides the case's resolution. Judge Milburn's opinion recites most of the relevant facts, including those already briefly alluded to. The underlying activity at issue was Ms. Fowler's apparently unilateral decision to show the "R" rated movie, Pink Floyd, The Wall, to her ninth-through eleventh-grade public high school classes on the last day of the 1983, 84 school year. This was a "noninstructional" day during which teachers devoted their attention to completing report cards. A "noninstructional" school day, an institution bespeaking remarkable complacency in the face of the apparent gradual deterioration of American public school educational standards, evidently involves, depending upon one's choice of metaphor, the babysitting or warehousing of students, who remain in the physical custody of their teachers, without there necessarily being any effort made to educate them. While there may be some sort of low-level pedagogy involved, for example, techniques of collectively coping with enforced time-wasting, the day is apparently best described as noncurricular, or as a hybrid school-nonschool day.

The particular circumstances in which alleged speech, or allegedly protected speech, may be evaluated on a noninstructional day may be of legal benefit to a plaintiff teacher in Ms. Fowler's situation. The teacher may be able to construct a valid argument that balances the interests of the public or the school in efficiently attaining its reasonable pedagogical objectives against her interests as a teacher in freely speaking on arguably relevant subjects.[8] She could plausibly argue that the state's interest is reduced, if not utterly waived, implicitly, by the very character of a noninstructional custodial school day. The discussion below will simply assume that Ms. Fowler's ordinary day-to-day subject matter teaching responsibilities encompassed what she assumed to be the themes or import of the movie in question.

The movie in question was apparently one with which Ms. Fowler was unfamiliar.[9] The students themselves had suggested bringing it in. Despite some reservations, Ms. Fowler had made arrangements to accommodate their request, with Ms. Fowler apparently motivated by a desire to keep them occupied and entertained as she concentrated on the task of posting grades.[10] She had deputized one of her students, age fifteen, to exercise censorial editing authority over the video portion of the movie, arming him with a file folder for his use in screening out unsuitable scenes.[11] The student had evidently been left effectively in charge on those several occasions on which Ms. Fowler left the room for unspecified lengths of time.[12] At trial, Ms. Fowler testified that she believed in her designated student editor's statement that he had faithfully continued to edit the visual portion of the movie while she was out of the room. It is unclear whether the 15-year-old student editor was chosen for his ability to heroically resist peer pressure, or for his ability to edit while averting his own underage eyes from the screen. She had consulted several persons, including students, on the propriety of showing the film,[13] but did not herself preview it.[14] No one suggests that a less potentially objectionable movie could not have been selected.

It is possible to question the relevance of Ms. Fowler's failure to screen the film for classroom suitability in advance. For example, a teacher may well have a legitimate expectation of free speech protection if under appropriate circumstances she were to assign an acknowledged classic work on her own authorized initiative, based on the strength of its general cultural reputation, intending to impart or convey some sort of broad social idea, whether she wishes to affirmatively endorse such an idea or not. The availability of such protection would not depend upon her screening of the work in advance, even if it turned out to contain passages arguably unsuitable for the audience in question. The teacher in this situation could be regarded as having constitutionally "spoken" through the partially unfamiliar words of another.

On the other hand, Ms. Fowler's failure to preview a movie, the contents of which were unknown to her, for whatever reasons, seems to indicate her intent merely to occupy and entertain her students, rather than to convey, even if merely for purposes of reflection or discussion, any sort of rudimentary social idea to them. What she knew, or could reasonably be charged with knowing, at the time of her initial decision to show the movie, was its apparent popularity, its "R" rating, any rumors of its controversial scenes which may have reached her, and the ages of both her intended audience and of her chosen student censoring agent. As it turns out, her student monitor's editing attempts, however effective, were arguably irrelevant, except insofar as the inherent insufficiency of the method chosen reflected on Ms. Fowler's judgment and sense of responsibility. The audio portion of the movie by itself apparently "contained enough offensive language to mandate an automatic 'R' rating under motion picture industry standards,"[15] and it had been played uninterruptedly.[16] Ms. Fowler presumably would have been aware of this at the very latest by the time of her second afternoon screening of the movie.

A reasonable public could find Ms. Fowler's conduct and decisions to be excessively casual and ill-considered. Such a public attitude would, of course, not suffice to deprive otherwise constitutionally permissible conduct of its protection. But such an attitude could reinforce a broad public determination to insure that to the greatest extent possible, and otherwise consistently with the free speech clause, decisions as to curriculum, materials, and teaching methods should be left to he more direct, more politically responsible agents of the democratic electorate, the school board, and, in turn, its most directly responsible subordinates or agents, the superintendents and

principals, rather than to individual classroom
teachers.   In effect, a reasonable democratic
electorate could determine, based on its assessment of
the level of skill and judgment that it might expect
or that it wished to pay for, among the range of
individual classroom teachers, that teacher contracts
should be drafted and interpreted to reasonably
minimize the level of judgment and discretion
authorized at their level.

Judge Milburn concluded that two of the factual
findings of the district court were clearly erroneous.
These findings had dealt with the degree of actual
success achieved by the student monitor armed with the
file folder in editing the visual portion of the movie
at both showings and on whether Ms. Fowler had formed
an opinion as to the significance or value of the film
at some point during the morning showing.[17] At least
arguably, though, Judge Milburn's findings of clear
error on the part of the trial court were not
necessary to reach his result.   If the school board's
case otherwise fell into place, the mere fact that Ms.
Fowler had shown the film with unedited "R"-rated
audio in the afternoon session, after having been made
aware of its character during the morning screening
could, by itself, supply sufficient grounds for
sanctions.   Similarly, her opinion as to the
significance of the film (despite the imperfect
attention she gave to this evaluation) is at least
arguably irrelevant to any alleged improprieties
visited upon her captive, if eager, student audience
prior to the point at which she formed this opinion.

There are two sticking points for Ms. Fowler's
case at this juncture.   The first, less significant
problem is that strictly speaking, the mere forming of
an opinion as to the movie's significance, whether
such an opinion was formed or crystallized during or
after the screening of the movie, is not precisely the
same thing as developing an intent, general or
specific, that the film be shown to communicate some
sort of broad social idea.   In a word, a teacher's
estimation or appreciation of a movie is not
equivalent to her intent to convey what is held in
estimation, even if without endorsement or approval.

The second and more significant sticking point,
already alluded to, is that intent to convey an idea
does not operate retroactively. A fair reading of the
testimony establishes that there was some period of
time, at least during the morning showing of the
movie, in which Ms. Fowler intended that it be shown,
for whatever reasons, but did not apparently intend to
convey, with or without endorsement, any particular,
even rudimentary, sort of broad social idea. Judge

Milburn's opinion can be read as asserting that if something like this intent to convey a social idea is not present, constitutionally protected speech is also not present. On this view, Ms. Fowler could raise no free speech defense against allegations based on or stemming from those segments of time preceding the point at which she formed the requisite intent. Of course, while such an assertion is quite sensible on many counts, it suffers the defect of not being one to which the Supreme Court has proved willing to subscribe.[18]   While a teacher might claim to be vindicating the free speech or freedom-to-hear rights of her student audience, it is doubtful that, on the merits, any violation of student free speech rights can be asserted under the facts of Fowler.[19]

To the extent that the contemporaneous intent of a putative speaker was decisive on the issue of whether speech in the relevant sense was present, the other factors discussed by Judge Milburn would not be decisive, or even relevant. If it were to be found that Ms. Fowler had the requisite intent to broach or convey some sort of broad social idea, it would be immaterial, on the issue of speech vel non, that she had not previously screened the movie, that her attention had been otherwise occupied, that she had been absent from the room for periods of time, and even that she had not attempted to explain or discuss the film before or after either screening.[20] It would seem perfectly possible, for example, to have both the requisite idea-conveyance intent about, say, the movie Shoah, or Richard Attenborough's Gandhi, and yet to otherwise detach oneself from the showing of the film, as Ms. Fowler did. Perhaps more controversially, it may be true that nothing can take the place of the requisite intent. At least arguably, the free speech clause should not, at least considering the putative speaker's interest alone, protect a school teacher who distributes copies of War and Peace to students under the bizarre misapprehension that the books are only paperweights, intended as useful gifts. This would be so even if the teacher later discovers the mistake and decides, in retrospect, that it was a splendid thing that the students were exposed to the broad social ideas conveyed through the novel.

To the extent that she merely formed, eventually, a considered opinion that "the movie contained important, socially valuable messages,"[21] the problem of her contemporaneous intent remains. Of course, to the extent that the precise issue is that of speech vel non, courts are, and should be, reluctant to inquire into or independently assess the speaker's claim that the speech or material involved is really important, or valuable. The kind of contemporaneous intent that a speaker must evidence varies, however, with the way in which the legal problem is conceived. There is more than one way to conceptualize Ms. Fowler's legal circumstances. First, one might reasonably view what transpired as essentially outside the established school curriculum, but still involving an issue of free speech in the context of a public high school, with a teacher as the putative speaker. In this view the case would represent a teacher speech analogue to student speech cases such as Bethel School District No. 403 v. Fraser[22] and Tinker v. Des Moines Independent Community School District.[23] This was the predominant view taken, and the line of cases principally emphasized, by Judge Milburn.[24]

An alternative view, and one which may be preferable because of its greater concreteness and specificity, would be to consider Ms. Fowler's case as one involving the dismissal of a public employee for exercising free speech rights in the course of her employment. In this conception, the most useful authority would then be cases such as Connick v. Myers[25] and Pickering v. Board of Education.[26] This alternative view was touched upon, but not logically pressed, by Judge Milburn.[27]

Which of these two distinct lines of cases is applied will determine whether one finds Judge Milburn's result justifiable or not. The thrust of the judge's rationale is that for speech to qualify as constitutionally protected, a speaker must, at a minimum, have a contemporaneous, expressive or communicative[28] intent to convey a "particularized message"[29] in circumstances indicating a great likelihood that it "would be understood by those who viewed it."[30] But in light of at least some Supreme Court case law in the general area of free speech, these alleged minimum requirements do not reflect the law in all free speech contexts.

This should not be surprising, despite the obvious logic in some of Judge Milburn's rationale. It is difficult to believe that the law would recognize as protected speech a college course assignment of Kahil Gibran's The Prophet, in view of its likely comprehensibility, but that it would deny protection to an otherwise similar assignment of Heidegger's Being and Time, on grounds that it would have a low probability of being understood by the students, any ambition and optimism of the assigning professor aside. The apt gridiron simile would be that "speech" is more like "a pass" than "a completed pass." And as we have seen, the Supreme Court has

seen fit to extend at least some measure of free
speech protection to activities that, it is fair to
say, do not invariably involve an intent to convey a
particularized message.   An example would be
commercial nude dancing which does not pretend to
communicate anything other than an entertaining visual
stimulus.

It is, therefore, perfectly possible to
c h a r a c t e r i z e   t h e   _Fowler_   c a s e   a s   a n
entertainment-speech, teacher speech analogue   to the
political-speech, student speech case of _Tinker_.
Since neither teachers nor students shed their free
speech rights at the schoolhouse gate,[31] and since
"entertainment" speech, devoid of any particularized
message, may be constitutionally protectable, Judge
Milburn's opinion offers no direct rebuttal to this
characterization.   His rebuttal is really more a
matter of perspective, a perspective which drives his
selection of the "appropriate" precedent.[32]

Accordingly, viewing _Fowler_ as a public employee
dismissal case in which the dismissal is alleged to
violate the employee's free speech rights, one reaches
a result more consistent with that of Judge Milburn.
This is because it has been clearly established in the
speech-based dismissal cases that it is necessary for
a terminated employee to show not merely that she
"spoke," but that her speech "may be 'fairly
characterized as constituting speech on a matter of
public concern.'"[33] This is an inquiry of law, rather
than of fact,[34] and is determined by reference to the
content, form, and context of the utterance as gleaned
from the entire record.[35] The best that can be said
about the speech fairly attributable to Ms. Fowler is
that it does not easily fit within the presumed
antithesis of speech on a matter of public interest or
concern, speech on matters of merely private or
personal concern.   Ms. Fowler was not merely airing
some narrow personalized grievance.

On the other hand, what Ms. Fowler sought to
"say" via the offending film, at the time of the first
showing, at least, was essentially that her audience
should be merely entertained and occupied.   This was
not speech on a matter or subject of general public
interest or concern.   The speech, therefore, intended
only as unambitious entertainment, would not be
constitutionally protected.   This is because speech
intended to entertain is protected only in an
appropriate context (e.g., nude dancing is protected
expression in a barroom but not a school room).   Nude
dancing as entertainment does not qualify as
expression addressing matters of public interest or
concern.   It is protected on a completely different

basis. Therefore, in the context of a public employee
discharge, Fowler's free speech challenge would fail,
without any need for interest balancing or any
motivation analysis of the school board's decision.[36]

It should be noted, however, that such
distinctions are, in practice, a bit less tidy than
this.   The Supreme Court has, for whatever reasons,
insisted that even where a public employee's speech
does not address matters of public concern, such
speech is not "'totally beyond the protection of the
First Amendment.'"[37]   It is tempting to suggest in
response that if the speech in question does not
address a matter of public interest or concern, the
values or aims underlying the free speech clause are
presumably no more strongly implicated than they would
be in a variety of obviously nonspeech contexts.   In
any event, the Court has concluded that "absent the
most unusual circumstances, a federal court is not the
appropriate forum in which to review the wisdom of a
personnel decision taken by a public agency in
reaction to the employee's behavior,"[38] at least in
the absence of speech addressing matters of public
interest and concern.

Now, a person in the position of Ms. Fowler would
no doubt feel a strong temptation to argue that her
speech had in fact addressed matters of public
interest.   It would certainly be possible to interpret
Pink Floyd, The Wall as addressing broad and important
social issues of alienation, educational repression,
and general authoritarianism.[39]   But the issue is not
whether it is possible in the abstract to find social
value in the movie, but rather whether the speaker
intended some idea partially embodying that value to
be conveyed at the time the movie was shown.   It is
clear that, at least for a time, Ms. Fowler intended
only to entertain and occupy her students.   She was
unaware during this time of the film's content.
Consequently, the film was not even a subject of
speech, let alone a subject of general community
interest or concern.

This result need not be intellectually
disquieting.   A speaker has only a limited practical
interest, at best, in things not intended to be
conveyed at the time of speaking.   This is clear from
a broader perspective.   It would seem unlikely, for
example, that a society would be enthusiastic about
fighting and dying on foreign battle fields to protect
a free speech right to say things utterly
unintentionally.   Accordingly, it is unlikely that
constitutional drafters and ratifiers would have
intended to give special protection to such a right.

Of course, it is also possible to argue that

showing an edited version of a movie rumored to be
sexually suggestive is itself some sort of a statement
on a matter of public interest. In this view, the
editing itself is seen to be a statement as to the
propriety of showing such movies to persons under
seventeen, quite apart from any other message that
might be derived through the film's thematic content
or implications. The problem with this argument,
assuming that Ms. Fowler was disciplined for precisely
this statement, is simply that, in its looseness, the
argument proves too much. Every act of insider
trading, or euthanasia, or of drinking and driving, in
some sense implies a speaker who in effect says
something like "I approve of, or am willing to
tolerate, insider trading/euthanasia/drinking and
driving under at least some circumstances." The
framers and ratifiers of the Constitution did not
intend to convert every controversial act into a
constitutionally protected statement on the rationale
that the act addressed a matter of public interest
because it implicitly challenged established public
policy.

Focusing on the appropriate precedents, then, it
would be perfectly reasonable to dismiss Ms. Fowler's
free speech claim without any balancing of interest or
analysis of the board's motivation, though not
precisely along the lines adopted by Judge Milburn.
Seeking to blunt the effect of precedent such as the
Schad[40] commercial nude dancing case, Judge Milburn
correctly notes that the Supreme Court
"has...indicated that in determining whether a given
type of entertainment is protected by the First
Amendment, it will look to the kind of entertainment
involved and the appropriateness of the entertainment
under the circumstances such as the time and place
where offered."[41] The Court has applied this
rationale even in speech-based dismissal cases, but
only at that stage of analysis at which it seeks to
determine whether the public employee's interest in
the speech, and that of the public, outweighs the
employer's and the public's interest in the efficient,
unjudicialized operation, at a reasonable level of
morale, of the public office in question.[42] At such a
stage, the time, place, and manner of the speech at
issue becomes relevant. But this inquiry is
undertaken only after it is first determined that
speech itself, and further, speech addressing a matter
of public interest, is present.[43]

This should not be a surprising result. It is
hardly obvious why the question as to whether an
utterance or an act is speech at all should depend
upon whether a school board (or a trial or reviewing

court) finds it to be appropriate under the circumstances. This logic concludes that inappropriate speech is not only unprotected, but a contradiction in terms. Inevitably, one must distinguish the threshold question: "Is this speech in the constitutional sense?" from the follow-up question, "If it is, do we want to protect this speech under these circumstances from the sanction at issue?"[44] Judge Milburn's response to Schad may mark this distinction insufficiently.

With the speech issue behind him, Judge Milburn then briefly addressed Ms. Fowler's claims that the operative Kentucky statute, which permits dismissal for "conduct unbecoming a teacher,"[45] is unconstitutionally vague, that it did not provide her with adequate notice of the likelihood of discipline for her conduct, and that her conduct did not fall within the intended or established scope of its provisions. Judge Milburn rejected all of these contentions.[46]

Ms. Fowler's vagueness challenge to the statutory language of "conduct unbecoming a teacher" implicated the classic due process principle which bars application of a statute that "either forbids or requires the doing of an act in terms so vague that men of common intelligence must necessarily guess at its meaning and differ as to its application."[47] An inevitable tension arises in "vagueness" analysis when courts attempt to decide whether the language of the statute, in fact, makes it difficult to apply in common borderline cases, or whether the plaintiff is simply asserting "vagueness" as a means of evading compliance with its literal terms.

The phrase "conduct unbecoming a teacher" is, unless judicially or administratively narrowed or refined, hopelessly vague in borderline cases. Reasonable minds could differ as to its intended scope in at least some common cases, even if not in Ms. Fowler's case itself. Yet, it must be said that whether hers was a borderline case or not, Ms. Fowler sped recklessly past clear, particularized warning signs. In showing an unpreviewed "R"-rated movie to students known to be, in some cases, at least two years below the age normally allowed admittance to such movies, with only a desultory attempt at editing and supervision, and in apparently not exploring the students' reactions to the film at all, Ms. Fowler engaged in conduct that could be objected to in almost quantitative terms.[48] The risks of such conduct were predictable by her at the time.

What might, to an outsider, seem less predictable was the severity of the school board in imposing on a

tenured, fourteen-year veteran teacher the sanction of
permanent dismissal as a penalty for such conduct.
While some might infer an attitude of defiance from
Ms. Fowler's statement that she would show the film
again if given the chance,[49] her attitude appears more
precisely to have been only that "she would show an
edited version of the movie again if given the
opportunity to explain it."[50]

Less sympathetically, it might be said that due
process does not require reasonable predictability by
the grievant of the imposition of the most severe but
otherwise permissible sanction.   More broadly, the
school board's interpretation of, or resort to, a
statute, and even the terms of the statute itself in
the long run, are no less bargainable by teachers'
unions than any other noneconomic issue.   In
principle, it should be possible for those who bargain
on behalf of teachers to extract a policy of
moderation in this regard from the school boards in
exchange, perhaps, for modest concessions by the
teachers in other areas.[51] To the extent that public
school teachers have focused in their contract
bargaining solely upon issues unrelated to teacher
discipline, they deserve no more and no less sympathy
than we would ordinarily give to other competent
adults who knowingly choose to accept risks in
exchange for other benefits.

In deciding the final issue as to whether the
conduct of Ms. Fowler fell, as a matter of statutory
interpretation, within the scope of "conduct
unbecoming a teacher," Judge Milburn relied upon two
recent Kentucky cases involving conduct that would
ordinarily be regarded as more egregious than that
engaged in by Ms. Fowler.   In Board of Education v.
Wood,[52] two teachers had committed the criminal act of
smoking marijuana in their apartment with two fifteen-
year-old students.   In Board of Education v.
McCollum,[53] a teacher was discharged under the
"conduct unbecoming a teacher" provision for filing
false sick leave affidavits and lying about time spent
on a special home instruction program.   The latter
case at least involved wilful, insubordinate rule
violation, as compared to Ms. Fowler's mere lack of
judgment and general irresponsibility.

The Kentucky Supreme Court in Wood explained that

> The purpose of teacher tenure laws is to
> promote good order in the school system by
> preventing the arbitrary removal of capable
> and experienced teachers by political or
> personal whim....A teacher is held to a
> standard of personal conduct which does not

permit the commission of immoral or criminal
acts because of the harmful impression made
on the students.   The school teacher has
traditionally   been   regarded   as   a   moral
example for the students.[54]

Both sides in the _Fowler_ case could have reasonably
drawn some comfort from this generalized judicial
statement of statutory purpose.   Ms. Fowler could
reasonably have called her discharge "political" in a
broad sense of the term, but not in a narrow, partisan
sense.   Her actions were, it is true, not immoral in
precisely the egregious sense at issue in _Wood_.   In
that   case,   students   had   been   encouraged   to
intentionally violate the criminal law.   However, a
reasonable board of education could nevertheless refer
to Ms. Fowler's conduct as immoral without speaking
eccentrically.   Arguably, she did not on this occasion
set a moral example for her students.
    If general statements of statutory purpose such
as those expounded in _Wood_ do not satisfactorily
resolve the applicability of the statute to Ms.
Fowler's conduct, then the resolution might be found
in the legal principle that encourages federal courts
to   defer   to   reasonable   interpretations   of   state
statutes made by local administrative agencies.   The
principle is well established that if a statute does
not by its own terms unambiguously compel a particular
interpretation, the courts are still not authorized to
substitute their own interpretation for a reasonable
one made by the local factfinder.[55]   It would seem, in
this   regard,   excessive   to   categorize   the
interpretation and application of the statutory
standard made by the school board in the _Fowler_ case
as unreasonable, even if reasonable minds could differ
on the result.
    Of course, it is possible to question whether
this degree of judicial deference is due in this case.
Fowler   does   not   involve   a   highly   technical
interpretation by a centralized administrative agency
based on special accumulated expertise,[56] at least in
any rigorous sense, nor does it involve any formally
promulgated prior interpretation by the agency.[57]
Nevertheless, once all constitutional issues are set
aside, it seems clear that due sensitivity to the
values of localized democratic decision making and
institutional   legitimacy   demands   deference   by
unelected federal courts to the reasonable
interpretations of a state statute, implicating local
social values, made by a local politically responsible
body.

THE PECK OPINION: A JUSTIFIED DISMISSAL DESPITE THE PRESENCE OF SPEECH

Judge Peck concurred in the result with Judge Milburn.[58] He would have conceded that Ms. Fowler's conduct involved constitutionally protected speech, but would have gone on to conclude that the school board could have legitimately dismissed Ms. Fowler if its decision had been based on or motivated by constitutionally permissible grounds exclusively.[59]

Judge Peck began by correctly noting that much of the authority relied upon by Judge Milburn to conclude that speech in a constitutional sense was not present in Fowler had principally dealt with symbolic conduct. Those cases, he pointed out, which had addressed the circumstances under which symbolic conduct could constitute protected speech, "do not lend themselves to the reverse purpose of defining what kind of communication cannot be expressive."[60] We have seen, however, that while Judge Milburn's particular approach to the issue of speech vel non is suspect, his result may be defensible on other grounds. Judge Peck did not discuss the threshold[61] issue of whether, under the Pickering-Connick line of cases, Ms. Fowler's speech rose to the level of speech addressing a matter of public interest or concern.[62] Instead, Judge Peck would have held that the trial court "erred in its finding that, but for Ms. Fowler's constitutionally protected activity of communicating various ideas and political thoughts to her students, she would not have been fired."[63]

Under the Mount Healthy employer mixed motive test, a plaintiff employee must show that her constitutionally protected conduct or speech was a substantial or motivating factor in the board's decision to dismiss her, but the board must then be given the opportunity to show that it would have reached the same decision if it had considered only her unprotected conduct.[64]

In a manner consistent with the Mount Healthy approach, Judge Peck sought to distinguish between permissible and impermissible motivations affecting the Board's decision to discharge Ms. Fowler. He reasoned that since courts were required to give deference to reasonable school board decisions, it was appropriate for the Fowler court to find that the Board in that case had relied only upon permissible considerations in its decision to dismiss Ms. Fowler. In making this argument, Judge Peck refers to the "intertwining" of permissible and impermissible grounds affecting the board's decision to dismiss Ms. Fowler,[65] and he is criticized for this by Judge

Merritt in dissent.[66] However, Judge Peck's choice of terms is misleading. If permissible and impermissible motivations were in fact inseparably, inextricably intertwined, the board could hardly have discharged its burden of showing that the impermissible motivations were not a but-for cause of the discipline.[67]

It is, therefore, crucial to Judge Peck's analysis that permissible and impermissible board motivations be distinguishable. To a degree, this seems to have been possible in the instant case. Ms. Fowler's poor judgment in not previewing the "R"-rated film and her casualness in providing only an underage, partially unsupervised student monitor armed with a file folder to edit out objectionable segments seem to constitute permissible considerations that the board might have relied upon to dismiss her. These seem as severable from impermissible board considerations, such as mere ideological disagreement, as circumstances are commonly likely to admit.

But, more controversially, Judge Peck also seeks to distinguish between "improper" considerations (such as perceived anti-establishment or anti-authoritarian political or social themes or messages in the film) and "proper" considerations (including vulgarity, violence, sexuality, and general unsuitability for the age group involved).[68] His opinion gives us no reason to believe that there is any surgical distinction between such impermissible and permissible motivations, beyond the roughest approximation. At least where the speaker has intended to endorse, or at least raise for consideration, a message of liberation and anti-authoritarianism, and is disciplined for doing so, it is entirely open to her to argue that such punishment, allegedly based on vulgarity, in effect requires her to send a different "message." While this observation can, as we have argued, be overdrawn, one can readily imagine a less vulgar readily available alternative formulation being both more articulate and more powerful, it evidently has some force, at least as regards certain of the considerations that are allegedly constitutionally permissible in Judge Peck's analysis.[69]

THE MERRITT OPINION: AN UNJUSTIFIED DISMISSAL BASED ON SPEECH

At least by inference, the essential thrust of Judge Merritt's dissenting opinion has been discussed above. In brief, Judge Merritt determined that the movie in question presented a message warning of the adverse consequences of excessive authoritarianism.[70] He observed with undeniable factual acumen that what may strike one federal judge as "gross and bizarre"[71] may seem to another to be "mild and not very 'sexually suggestive.'"[72]   In this, Judge Merritt echoed the aesthetic relativism embodied in Justice Harlan's classic observation that "it is...often true that one man's vulgarity is another's lyric."[73]

Judge Merritt was able to deploy the commercial nude dancing case of <u>Schad v. Borough of Mount Ephraim</u>[74] against Judge Milburn's apparent claim that pure entertainment could not fall within the scope of constitutionally protected speech, but as we have seen, this ambitious premise was unnecessary to Judge Milburn's central argument.   However, his position is less clear with respect to Judge Peck's argument that the Court should be deferential in determining that the board relied upon a constitutionally permissible basis, such as the vulgarity and unsuitability of the film, to dismiss Ms. Fowler, even though it was possible that impermissible motivations, such as an ideological distaste for the message of the film, may have been intertwined.   He simply concludes that "I do not believe an argument based on intertwining [of permissible and impermissible motives] can be used to suppress protected speech; vulgarity should not be allowed to subsume that which is protected."[75]

As discussed above, however, Judge Peck's argument in fact relies not on any intertwining of motive, but on the at least partial separability of permissible and impermissible motives.[76]   Judge Merritt does not explicitly challenge such a premise. His conclusion also seems too categorical, if it is taken literally.   Especially in a public school context, it seems clear that at some point, even vulgarity or violence that is considered essential to the intended message, or to its full impact, could legitimately be viewed as unacceptably extreme.   It should be borne in mind that the major thrust of the argument against pedagogical vulgarity is not that the students have never seen vulgar, violent, or sexual materials outside of class, and will be stunned by first encountering them in the school, but rather that vulgarity ought not to be practically legitimized through its use in the public school context.   One could, for example, undoubtedly make a coherent point about social alienation to a captive or noncaptive audience of ten-year-olds by exposing them to the most gruesome sort of graphically filmed violence. Presumably, an extreme of vulgarity is no more sacrosanct than an extreme of violence.   But it is probable that Judge Merritt himself believes that some such limits to free speech are appropriate and can be imposed, at least in extreme cases.

CONCLUSION

The problem of the scope and limits of public school teacher speech is manageable in the abstract, but difficult at the level of the concrete case. All three opinions in <u>Fowler</u> enjoy substantial plausibility, but all can be seen as ultimately flawed, at least at some level of detail. Accordingly, <u>Fowler</u> reflects the fact that "the decided cases fail to provide any comprehensive scheme for delineating the role of the Constitution in resolving curricular and pedagogical conflicts."[77] The decided cases often seem fact-sensitive in this regard, so that no single case tends to have much controlling power.[78] If there is any mainstream position on this general range of issues, it is perhaps best expressed by the view that while "[t]he first amendment does not give to the teacher autonomy to determine either what or how he shall teach,"[79] this general rule is subject to some range of exceptions.[80]

It has been properly observed that "cases involving restrictions on teachers' rights of curricular control are often erroneously viewed as censorship cases when the real issue is who should make curricular choices given the fact that someone has to make [them]."[81] Such an observation gets the analysis off to a sensible start, but in this fact-sensitive area of the law, it cannot contribute much to the resolution of a particular case. If one adds to this the relevant idiosyncracies of the <u>Fowler</u> case, including the absence at least in part of a genuinely relevant intent to speak, in a constitutional sense, on the part of Ms. Fowler, the non-instructional character of the school day, the dubious attempts at delegated editing, and the apparent severity of the punishment imposed, one despairs of resolving a case like <u>Fowler</u> on the basis of any mechanical application of broad principles.

On the analysis recommended in this chapter, it is decisive in resolving <u>Fowler</u> that there was an absence of any speech addressing a matter of public interest or concern at some relevant times. The plaintiff's failure to meet that threshold requirement is fatal to her free speech case insofar as her dismissal was based upon actions or speech lacking the requisite speech intent.[82] While it is, of course, possible to deny the legitimacy of imposing such a requirement, doing so is consistent with the scope of the broad run of values and purposes widely thought to underlie the free speech clause in the first place.

NOTES

1. 819 F.2d 657 (6th Cir.),cert. denied, 108 S. Ct. 502 (1987).

2. Id. at 658-59.

3. Id. at 658, 660.

4. Id. at 658.

5. Id. at 664.

6. Id. at 667-68 (Peck, J., concurring in result).

7. Id. at 668-70 (Merritt, J., dissenting).

8. See Pickering v. Board of Educ., 391 U.S. 563, 568 (1968).

9. Fowler, 819 F.2d at 658.

10. Id. at 664 n.8, 665-66; id. at 669-70 (Merritt, J., dissenting).

11. Id. at 658.

12. Id. at 659.

13. Id. at 658.

14. Id.

15. Id. at 659.

16. Id.

17. Id. at 659 n.1.

18. See, e.g., Schad v. Borough of Mount Ephraim, 452 U.S. 61, 65-66 (1981) (extending some measure of free speech protection, of indeterminate strength, to ordinary commercial live nude dancing).

19. See generally supra Chapter 4.

20. See Fowler, 819 F.2d at 659-60.

21. Id. at 660.

22. 478 U.S. 675 (1986).

23. 393 U.S. 503 (1969).

24. See in particular Fowler, 819 F.2d at 661.

25. 461 U.S. 138 (1983).

26. 391 U.S. 563 (1968).   See also Rankin v. McPherson, 107 S. Ct. 2891 (1987) (clerical employee in county constable's office not dismissable under the circumstances for orally endorsing to a coworker a hypothetical future assassination of President Reagan).

27. See Fowler, 819 F.2d at 662.

28. See id. at 664.

29. See id. at 662.

30. Id. at 663.

31. Tinker v. Des Moines Ind. Community School Dist., 393 U.S. 503, 506 (1969).

32. See generally Schauer, Precedent, 39 Stan. L. Rev. 571 (1987).

33. Rankin v. McPherson, 107 S. Ct. 2891, 2897 (1987) (quoting Connick v. Myers, 461 U.S. 138, 146 (1983)).

34. See Connick, 461 U.S. at 148 n.7, 150 n.10.

35. See Rankin, 107 S. Ct. at 2897.

36. See the burden-shifting process required under Mount Healthy City Bd. of Educ. v. Doyle, 429 U.S. 274 (1977), once the threshold speech on matters of public concern test is met.

37. Rankin, 107 S. Ct. at 2897 n.7 (quoting Connick, 461 U.S. at 147).

38. Id.

39. See the reported testimony of Ms. Fowler, Fowler, 819 F.2d at 659, and the assessment of Judge Merritt, id. at 668, 669 (Merritt, J., dissenting).

40. See 452 U.S. at 65-66.

41. _Fowler_, 819 F.2d at 664 n.8.

42. _See_ _Connick v. Myers_, 461 U.S. 138 (1983); Pickering v. Board of Educ., 391 U.S. 563 (1968).

43. _See_ _Connick_, 461 U.S. at 149-54.

44. _See_ _F. Schauer_, _Free Speech: A Philosophical Enquiry_ 89-92 (1982) (distinguishing between the "coverage" and "protection" of a right).

45. _Ky. Rev. Stat. Ann._ § 161.790(1)(b) (Baldwin 1986).

46. _See_ _Fowler_, 819 F.2d at 664, 666.

47. _Id._ at 664 (quoting Connally v. General Const. Co., 269 U.S. 385, 391 (1926)).

48. _Id._

49. _Id._ at 660-61.

50. _Id._ at 659-60.

51. _See generally_ Wright, _A Contractual Theory of Due Process_, 21 _Val. U.L. Rev._ 527 (1987).

52. 717 S.W.2d 837 (Ky. 1986).

53. 721 S.W.2d 703 (Ky. 1986).

54. 717 S.W.2d at 839.

55. _See_ Chevron U.S.A., Inc. v. NRDC, 467 U.S. 837, 843 (1984).

56. _See_ _id._ at 844.

57. _See_ _id._ at 843-44.

58. _Fowler_, 819 F.2d at 666-68 (Peck, J., concurring in result).

59. _Id._ at 668 (Peck, J., concurring in result).

60. _Id._ at 667 (Peck, J., concurring in result).

61. _See, e.g._, Mings v. Dep't of Justice, 813 F.2d 384, 387 (Fed. Cir. 1987).

62. That one intends to apply a _Mount Healthy_ mixed-employer motive inquiry does not obviate the prior need to show speech on a matter of public interest. See Wren v. Spurlock, 798 F.2d 1313, 1317 (10th Cir. 1986); Ferrara v. Mills, 781 F.2d 1508, 1512 (11th Cir. 1986).

63. _Fowler_, 819 F.2d at 667-68 (Peck, J., concurring in result).

64. See _Mount Healthy_, 429 U.S. at 287.

65. _Fowler_, 819 F.2d at 668 (Peck, J., concurring).

66. _Id_. at 669, 670 (Merritt, J., dissenting).

67. See _Mount Healthy_, 429 U.S. at 287.

68. _Fowler_, 819 F.2d at 668 (Peck, J., concurring).

69. Judge Peck additionally sought to bolster his argument for judicial deference in this context by citing Bethel School Dist. No. 403 v. Fraser, 478 U.S. 675 (1986), but it should be noted that _Fraser_ involved more disruption of the classroom educational process than _Fowler_. See _id_. at 678.

70. _Fowler_, 819 F.2d at 669 (Merritt, J., dissenting).

71. _Id_. at 666.

72. _Id_. at 669 (Merritt, J., dissenting).

73. Cohen v. California, 403 U.S. 15, 25 (1971), quoted in _Fowler_, 819 F.2d at 670 (Merritt, J., dissenting). Courts have often quoted this passage without the qualifying language of "oftenness," as a flat relativist principle. See, e.g., State v. Authelet, 120 R.I. 42, 385 A.2d 642, 648 (1978). But cf. Lewis v. City of New Orleans, 415 U.S. 130, 140 (1974) (Blackmun, J., dissenting) (referring to "the easy and imagined self-assurance that 'one man's vulgarity is another's lyric.'"). For philosophical background, see, e.g., _Rationality and Relativism_ (J. Hollis & S. Lukes eds. 1983).

74. 452 U.S. 61, 65-66 (1981).

75. _Fowler_, 819 F.2d at 670 (Merritt, J., dissenting).

76. Judge Merritt again referred to the "conflation of vulgarity and anti-establishment ideas set forth by Judge Peck." Id. (Merritt, J., dissenting).

77. Hunter, Curriculum, Pedagogy, and the Constitutional Rights of Teachers in Secondary Schools, 25 Wm. & Mary L. Rev. 1, 54 (1983).

78. Among the lower court cases not extensively discussed in Fowler are Zykan v. Warsaw Community School Corp., 631 F.2d 1300 (7th Cir. 1980); Brubaker v. Board of Educ., 502 F.2d 973 (7th Cir. 1974); Clark v. Holmes, 474 F.2d 928 (7th Cir. 1972); Keefe v. Geanakos, 418 F.2d 359 (1st Cir. 1969); Cary v. Board of Educ., 427 F. Supp. 945 (D. Colo. 1977), aff'd, 598 F.2d 535 (10th Cir. 1979); Wilson v. Chancellor, 418 F. Supp. 1358 (D. Or. 1976); Mailloux v. Kiley, 323 F. Supp. 1387 (D. Mass.), aff'd per curiam, 448 F.2d 1242 (1st Cir. 1971); Parducci v. Rutland, 316 F. Supp. 352 (M.D. Ala. 1970).

79. Nahmod, First Amendment Protection for Learning and Teaching: The Scope of Judicial Review, 18 Wayne L. Rev. 1479, 1503 (1972).

80. See id.

81. Goldstein, The Asserted Constitutional Right of Public School Teachers to Determine What they Teach, 124 U. Pa. L. Rev. 1293, 1356 (1976).

82. For a recent judicial recognition of the necessity of communicative intent, see Redgrave v. Boston Symphony Orchestra, Inc., 855 F.2d 888, 895 (1st Cir. 1988), cert. denied, 109 S. Ct. 869 (1989).

6

Defining Obscenity:
The Criterion of Value

INTRODUCTION

The government is constitutionally permitted to restrict or prohibit the sale of sexually explicit materials, at least within narrow limits. Despite judicial permissiveness in the area of what it is almost euphemistic to call sexually explicit materials, obscenity cases are still being brought in substantial numbers. The most significant limitation on the government's restrictive power is that material cannot be condemned as obscene if the material is found by the trier of fact to possess value of a certain kind. It is the purpose of this chapter to sort out and seek to resolve the outstanding problems associated with value standards. If such problems can be satisfactorily resolved, this would provide a reason not to decriminalize all otherwise obscene materials out of sheer jurisprudential frustration, rather than conviction. The standards advocated below would not constitutionally protect some materials, but would remain faithful to the underlying value logic of the free speech and free press clauses.

The Supreme Court majority in Miller v. California[1] imposed as a constitutional requirement that if a state is to convict a criminal defendant in an obscenity case, it must show that the allegedly obscene work "taken as a whole, lacks serious literary, artistic, political, or scientific value."[2] The Court explicitly superseded the prior test of Memoirs v. Massachusetts[3] which required a showing that the work be "utterly without redeeming social value."[4] The Court's revised formulation of this

requirement in <u>Miller</u> was undeniably thoughtfully
undertaken. This chapter examines whether the <u>Miller</u>
formulation was constitutionally or otherwise optimal.
Indisputably, virtually every word of the <u>Miller</u> test
regarding the work's value raises litigable issues of
interpretation, some of a profound sort. The Court
referred to its overall obscenity standard as one of
"basic guidelines" to orient the finder of fact. It
has continued, however, to adhere to, if not require,
this precise formulation with unswerving fidelity.[5]

TAKING THE VALUE OF THE WORK AS A WHOLE

Working through the value element of the <u>Miller</u> test,
the first requirement is that the value inquiry
consider the work "as a whole."[6] The Court's intent
in focusing on the work as a whole is evidently to
discourage excesses of both suppression and
permissiveness. However the test for value is
otherwise formulated, a work of acknowledged value
should not be condemned on the basis of isolated,
incidental, meretricious passages.[7] Neither, though,
should an otherwise obscene work be protected merely
because it is modestly adorned with an intellectually
invigorating quotation from Voltaire on the flyleaf,
or in the introductory credits.[8]

    Just as the whole may be greater than the sum of
the parts, so the value of a work, taken as a whole,
may be greater or less than the value of the sum of
its parts. The value of a work as a whole cannot
reliably be said to reflect the value, or lack
thereof, of even a clear majority of its pages,
sections, chapters, or frames. This is for two major
reasons. First, a theme or aspect of a work may be
recognizably the primary or predominant theme of the
work even though a page count reveals that most pages
are not directly linked to that theme. By way of
analogy, a ring may be mostly setting in a physical
sense, but if it has a gemstone, the ring's value will
more crucially reflect that of the gem. Second, and
by way of contrast, it is plausible to argue that a
work may be subject to prohibition even though it is
mostly or preeminently constituted by valuable, or at
least unobjectionable, material. This possibility
reflects the recognition that parts of a whole may do
more than lie in proximity to one another. They may
be detectably organically related to one another.
Alternatively, they may be only arbitrarily or
gratuitously placed together.

    A reasonable trier of fact in a given case may
therefore conclude that the bulk of a work is of the
requisite value, but that some remaining portion, say

20 percent, is utterly devoid of any value of any sort
and is therefore itself potentially obscene. If there
is no traceable organic relationship between these two
portions of the work, it is not unreasonable under the
Miller standard to put the author or publisher to the
choice between suppression of the whole work as
presented, or the severance of the offending from the
larger, unoffending segments.   By hypothesis, the
severance would not impair the work's organic unity.
In brief, if a short work is deemed to be obscene
under Miller, it does not become protected merely
because a distributor sells it glued to The Brothers
Karamazov. Nor does the cause of freedom of speech
and press suffer cognizably if the entire
glued-together mélange is duly suppressed, despite the
classic status of the greater component of this
compound work.

"LACK" AND THE VALUE DETERMINATION

Assuming, then, a focus on the work as a whole, the
task becomes that of interpreting how the state is to
show a lack of some sort of value. The nature of this
showing is only partially elucidated by the
recognition that it is serious value of some sort, a
lack of which the state is to show.   The language
following "lacks" cannot, by its nature, solve all
interpretive problems.   A work might utterly lack
serious value of a given sort, or it might only
substantially lack serious value of such a sort while
demonstrating "some" serious value or at least a
"scintilla" of serious value.
     The literal meaning of "lack" is probably closer
to "utterly lack," or an absolute lack. This literal
interpretation of "lack" would seem inconsistent,
however, with the logic of the Miller court in
rejecting the Memoirs requirement of showing that the
material at issue is "utterly without redeeming social
value,"[9] on the theory that such a burden on the state
was "virtually impossible to discharge under our
criminal standards of proof."[10]
     In an effort to determine whether the Miller
formulation is a significant improvement in light of
the Court's own purposes, this Chapter considers the
relationship between the Memoirs and Miller tests in
further detail below. In the meantime, just as we
cannot fully clarify lacks by looking ahead to serious
value, we cannot fully clarify the term "lacks" by
looking backward to the requirement of taking the work
as a whole. The courts can and must look everywhere
in the work, or to its preeminent theme, in context,
in the light of the relationship of the parts of the

work to one another, or the absence of such
relationships, when looking for value, or showing lack
of value. This does not tell us whether finding, say,
a scintilla of (serious) value of the proper sort will
bar an otherwise valid obscenity conviction,
considering the work as a whole.

The notion of serious value itself raises
problems both of interpretation and of normative
appropriateness. Is there such a thing, for example,
as "mere" value of the relevant sort, as opposed to
"serious" value of the relevant sort? It is often
supposed that there is such a thing as "mere" value,
as, for example, in one reviewing court's
determination, in evaluating the films at issue, that
"each film is devoid of any value, let alone any
serious value, aside from its intended commercial
purpose to cater to a prurient interest in sex."[11]

"SERIOUS" VALUE AND "IMPORTANT" VALUE

Pursuing the nature of the distinction between value
and serious value as a matter of the magnitude or
character of the value, courts have sometimes
suggested that serious value implies, if it is not
synonymous with, "important value."[12] At least as a
rough approximation, however, serious value would seem
easier to show, or less restrictive, than important
value. Certainly a work could be "serious" without
rising to the level of being "important." This may be
partly because of the greater selectivity implied by
the notion of important value, and partly because
seriousness, even of value, seems to partake more of
the author's intent than does the intent-independent
concept of a work's importance. "Important" implies
"successful," at least more than does "serious."

One distinguished commentator has maintained in
this connection that the Court's message is:

> If you plan to write a novel that contains
> explicitly sexual scenes that an average
> person in a remote community would judge to
> be titillating or shocking, you had better
> make sure that it has important literary
> value; if it turns out to be merely mediocre
> on literary grounds, your publisher may end
> up in jail.[13]

This is doubtless too demanding a formulation of the
Court's intent. The Court's requirements need hardly
be read as so rigorous. A book may still be a work
that has at least some serious literary value even
though it is not in any sense important because it is

universally recognized as of only average or ordinary
quality in all respects and is incontestably "merely
mediocre on literary grounds."[14] Such a work may even
possess not merely some serious value, but a
substantial amount of serious value, if the latter
standard is thought to be both higher and
constitutionally required.

Even slight departures from language recommended
broadly by the Supreme Court may be argued to
constitute deviations prejudicial to the free speech
rights of obscenity defendants. For example, it may
seem inconsequential to formulate the issue as whether
the allegedly obscene materials "are presented in a
sufficiently 'serious' manner to warrant invocation of
the first amendment."[15] Error can credibly be
predicated upon a jury instruction taking this form,
though, because the Supreme Court has more precisely
indicated that what counts is not the seriousness of
the manner of presentation, or even the seriousness of
the work's content or message, but the seriousness of
the work's value.

SERIOUS IDEAS AND SERIOUS VALUE

An even more subtle, but readily litigable, departure
from a plain reading of the Supreme Court's
formulation is exemplified by the language from the
Texas case of Andrews v. State.[16] The Court in
Andrews characterized the relevant test as "whether
the material advocates or communicates any ideas or
opinions concerning serious literary, artistic,
political, or scientific values."[17] Setting aside any
concern for the categories of values themselves,
courts must decide whether there must be ideas
concerning serious values, or whether the ideas
themselves must be serious, or themselves have serious
value. Clearly, there is a potential difference. One
might seek to communicate a not-particularly-serious
idea, or a frivolous idea or opinion, about a serious
value or subject.

It is arguable that the Andrews formulation is in
fact a superior formulation. This is because it may
well be that there is a broader, more nearly
objectively based consensus as to what sorts of values
or subjects are serious than there is about whether a
given particular idea itself is serious. Government
monetary policy is by consensus a serious subject or
"value." Statements about such policy, or that
communicate or convey some rudimentary idea or message
relating to such policy, could be securely protected
under the Andrews formulation. If the test is instead
a matter of the seriousness of the particular idea,

for example, that monetary policy is in fact dictated by some nefarious international cabal based in Zurich, courts may have to decide cases not only on more of a case-by-case basis, but on a basis giving broad scope to the expression of mere jury prejudice against unpopular ideas.   The _Andrews_ formulation, perhaps inadvertently, enhances predictability and fairness in free speech adjudication, while still faithfully serving the acknowledged broad purposes of the free speech clause.

VALUE AND USE

The question then arises whether, in making the serious value determination, courts are to consider the work in itself, on its own merits, or, instead, in some particular context.   That courts are to consider the work as a whole means that they must consider the internal context of an allegedly obscene passage or illustration.   For example, this may be helpful in rescuing explicit illustrations in medical school anatomy text.   There are external contexts as well. The Washington statute at issue in _Brockett v. Spokane Arcades_[18] spoke, for example, of considering the value of the work "in the context in which it is used...."[19]
    It seems realistic and fair to allow the defendant to place the allegedly obscene work in context.   There may be some difference, however, between the context in which the work is ordinarily used, the context in which it was actually used in a given case, and the context in which the author genuinely intended the work to be used.   Control over the use of a work, even by those with the legal right to control, may be imperfect.[20]   A work intended for use by one sort of audience may be foreseeably or unforeseeably "intercepted" in another context, such as retail display, by another audience, perhaps of juveniles.[21]   _Miller_ is best interpreted to protect the author of an otherwise serious work that is unforeseeably used in some depraved, frivolous context, while permitting the suppression of a work that might be of value in some conceivable context, but which is, to the author's knowledge, uniformly used in circumstances that render the use of the work without the constitutionally requisite value.

VALUE, COMMUNITY, AND EXPERTISE

Of course, a local community within which a work is disseminated may also be said to be a context within which the work is used.   The Court has loosely approved the application of divergent community standards in obscenity cases, despite constitutional objections.[22] It is easy to argue, though, that if a work is of value for the nation as a whole, or in a national context, it is unjustifiable, if not incoherent, to claim that it is not of value within the particular community in which the obscenity trial is being held. Certainly, a work may be of broad or national interest, but not interest anyone in a local area. While lack of local interest may imply that the work is not locally valued, a work clearly can be valuable even it if is not subjectively valued by a given community. On the most common accounts, a local community can, subjectively, fail to perceive the value in a work that is by consensus detectable by recognized experts or those widely regarded as well-tutored in the subject matter.[23]

This argument does not require as a premise that the serious literary value, for example, of a work be objective in the sense of some quality or property that is invariant or incontestable, or precisely measurable and independent of any observer. Value, whether recognized or not, is unavoidably value for some person or group, or broader society, in the sense of bearing upon their recognized or unrecognized interests, aims, or desires.[24] Value may also be interpreted as only value according to, or in the opinion of, or as recognized by at least one observer, based on a range of standards and kinds of evidence.

If the recognized literary critics, then, unanimously find serious literary value in a work, the Miller test is reasonably interpretable as permitting a judge, at trial or on appeal, to effectively overrule a local jury on the precise issue of serious literary value. There is no disputing Judge Posner's observation that "evaluation of a work of (purported) art [may be relatively] difficult and uncertain,"[25] and that "the values, experiences, and preconceptions of the adjudicator" may play a significant role.[26] The same is true, to at least some degree, of medical diagnosis. But courts would not be unduly reluctant to overrule a jury's untutored collective medical diagnosis, especially if not all available relevant evidence were presented to them, if the consensually recognized expert medical community demurred for reasons that the jury would not necessarily be assumed to have considered or comprehended. The detection of literary merit in a work at least falls between the process of medical diagnosis and a purely arbitrary expression of equal-status personal tastes and preferences, where evidence, reason, and insight play no role.

It is true as well, as Justice Douglas argued,

that "what may be trash to me may be prized by others."[27]   It is more pertinent to observe that we do not distribute art professorships, or museum curatorships, on a random basis, even if we are a bit nervous about the objectivity of our precise rankings of the artistic merits of the great masters.   The connoisseur's studied determination that a Turner is of greater serious aesthetic value than a painting of the pool-playing dogs is not the same kind of determination as a preference for chocolate to vanilla, even if the ice-cream evaluator offers sensible reasons for the preference.

In the realm of social policy, the point has been made in the following terms:

> In supposing, for example, that the elimination of racism has intersubjective value, we suppose that racists do not simply differ with us in taste, but that they are <u>blinded</u> to the impersonally apprehensible evils of racism, either by a refusal to consider them impersonally or by an incapacity to appreciate what they apprehend.   If, we think, the blinders of privilege, self-interest, and ignorance were to be stripped away in a situation that allowed full impersonal attention, they too would share our impersonal preference.[28]

It goes without saying that the jury selection and judicial trial process generally, in the obscenity context and elsewhere, does not guarantee the latter transformation.   Particularly if no evidence on the matter is introduced other than the allegedly obscene works themselves, the jury may conceivably be blind to value that may require assistance or expertise to discover.   The court on appellate review may, with some degree of reliability, detect such blindness.

VALUE AND THE NECESSARY PRESENCE OF AN IDEA

If there must be a direct response to the relativistic logjam feared by Justice Douglas, what may be trash to some may be prized by others, it should perhaps be that the others may be right, and the material they champion should be protected under the <u>Miller</u> test if they can articulate or otherwise establish the presence and communication of some sort of "idea" falling within the categories of value stipulated by <u>Miller</u>, such as, literary, artistic, political, and scientific.   While the idea intended to be conveyed need not be some crudely literal message, so that, for

example, we protect the Beethoven Fifth Symphony only
if we determine that it is somehow about the nobility
of struggling against fate, there must be an intent to
communicate some rudimentary, not necessarily
intellectualized, sort of idea falling within the
Miller categories.

Interpreting the Miller serious value requirement
to demand no more than some rudimentary idea of a sort
falling within the Miller categories draws some of the
sting of Justice Brennan's objection that "[t]he
Court's approach necessarily assumes that some works
will be deemed obscene, even though they clearly have
some social[29] value, because the State was able to
prove that the value, measured by some unspecified
standard, was not sufficiently serious to warrant
constitutional protection."[30]   In our interpretation
of Miller, the Court need not make the exceptionally
subjective determination of the "seriousness" of the
work or idea itself.   The potential for judicial
arbitrariness or abuse of such a nebulous standard,
particularly during stressful or uneasy historical
periods, is clear.[31]   In our interpretation, the
courts need make only the occasionally difficult, but
at least minimally logic-bounded, inquiry into the
intended presence of an idea of the proper sort,
whether or not that intended idea was understood or
received by its audience.   An idea might be of a
constitutionally sufficient sort if it is a literary
idea, or an artistic idea, or a political idea, or a
scientific idea, independent of any judgment of the
seriousness of the idea.   There is no need to assume
under Miller that the word "idea" functions precisely
the same in each of these contexts.   An idea in the
realm of artistic communication may be utterly unlike
an idea in the realm of scientific communication.   But
this need be of no constitutional consequence.

Of course, terms such as "artistic" and
"political" can be employed in narrower or broader
senses.[32]   The Miller formulation itself suggests,
however, that while the courts should be sensitive to
important broadly encompassing understandings of the
realm of the political, for example, they are not to
assume that every articulated interpersonal dispute is
inevitably a matter of political expression in the
sense intended in Miller.   Perhaps every truly
voluntary, noncompulsive, fully informed transaction
in allegedly obscene goods between competent buyers
and sellers in at least some sense enhances the
subjective welfare of both, else it would not be
agreed upon and undertaken.   It is value-enhancing in
this sense, but the value involved need not inevitably
be described as including the communication of a

political idea. A less disingenuous way of describing at least some such transactions would advert to a simple market exchange of money, or financial value, for a particular psychological or psychosomatic effect, or for erotic value of one sort or another. The value conferred by the supplier of such materials may be essentially private or personal to the buyer, "autobiographical," in a way not intended by the Miller Court to be encompassed within the admittedly broad realm of the political, or of political ideas. Euphoria induction is not necessarily a sufficient idea.

Such a line of demarcation would hardly be irrational. One can readily imagine a set of rational Framers seeking to constitutionally protect the political idea-communicative elements of market transactions, while countenancing the government's regulating the financial, autobiographically erotic, or other transaction-motivating values that may be characterized as political only in an extended sense upon the showing merely that the regulation promotes some significant governmental interest. It is perfectly conceivable that to the Framers, unencumbered discussion and debate on broadly public issues was more worth fighting and dying on the battlefield for than unencumbered consumer choice among an inconceivable variety of erotic stimulants.

There is as well an independent argument, grounded in the value of political stability, in favor of interpreting Miller to require a showing of not merely an absence of genuinely serious value, but an absence of any intended even rudimentary idea falling within one of the specified categories. The latter standard, which requires less judicial "grading" of the idea at issue, is more consonant with the valuable civic virtues of mutual political restraint and mutual political compromise.[33] It avoids the greater suppression of a demanding serious value standard, while taking seriously the claim that some allegedly obscene materials are still in many communities both deeply and widely offensive and do not even purport to significantly implicate any of the range of values or aims that distinctively underlie the doctrine of freedom of speech. In order for "distaste for the content of the speech" to be an impermissible basis for government regulation,[34] the "speech" at issue must first be speech for constitutional purposes. The literal or figurative speech attendant upon some allegedly obscene works may simply not be speech in the requisite sense if core free speech values and, as well, attributes such as discussion, reflection, issues, information, and debate are only tangentially implicated.

The judicial task, on the theory outlined above, in some cases admittedly may not be simple. Just as the court should not infer the absence of the requisite kind of idea from the racy promotion or advertising of the work, so the court need not take at face value implausible post-hoc assertions of defense counsel as to the true nature of the work. Applied as intended, though, the above interpretation minimizes the risk that works will be struck down because of government disapproval of the ideas expressed.[35] If the defendant can show government disapproval, or any other attitude, toward the ideas expressed in the work, the work is presumably protected by the free speech clause. In sum, then, a professed desire to "rely on the capacity of the free marketplace of ideas to distinguish that which is useful or beautiful from that which is ugly or worthless"[36] is not, by its terms, a purely libertarian standard; to qualify, there must be an idea of a cognizable sort.

"REDEEMING" VALUE

Confusion is further reduced if courts set aside the idea that the work's value must be redeeming value. The language of "redeeming" value is a holdover from Memoirs v. Massachusetts,[37] in which the Court's plurality imposed the requirement that the allegedly obscene material be "utterly without redeeming social value."[38] While the Court in Miller repudiated the terminology of "social value"[39] and apparently objected to the "utterly" language as impossibly requiring the state to prove a negative,[40] it did not explicitly disavow the idea that value was to be "redeeming," even though such language does not appear in the Miller "serious value" formulation.

While other approaches are possible, it seems best to assume that all value of the proper sort is (some amount of) serious value, and that the work's value, as somehow quantitatively determined, need not be found to be of a magnitude sufficient to somehow outweigh the work's less attractive qualities. The language of "redeeming value" retains some current vitality in Supreme Court[41] and other[42] opinions construing federal and state obscenity statutes. However, such language is either unnecessary or misleading in suggesting a balancing of judicially determined positive value against the egregiousness of the work, as though a particularly offensive work could perhaps only be "redeemed" by some sort of proportionately great perceived value. Balancing the precise degree of offensiveness of a work against its precise degree of, for example, literary merit, should be a daunting task.

Taking the formulations as a whole, it is clear that the Court assumed that the <u>Miller</u> "serious value" of a specified category standard would be easier for the government to meet than the <u>Memoirs</u> "utterly without redeeming social value" standard.[43] Despite the consensus on the correctness of this assumption, it has been rightly observed that since the <u>Miller</u> formulation took effect, the country witnessed no substantial reduction in the quantity or explicitness of sexual materials,[44] and apparently "neither the total number of obscenity prosecutions nor the nationwide conviction rate in cases actually brought has substantially changed since the [<u>Miller</u>] decision was rendered."[45] It has been found, contrary to expectations, "that the conviction rate under the old standard was fairly high and that <u>Miller</u> did not materially affect it."[46]

Assuming the accuracy of such empirical findings, there may be numerous contributing causes of various sorts. One step toward an explanation is the recognition that a jury might well not find the <u>Memoirs</u> and <u>Miller</u> standards substantially different, or not find the latter to be significantly laxer. <u>Memoirs</u> requires an "utter absence," but a jury might interpret <u>Miller</u> to require an "utter absence" as well, on the theory that absence or lack means "utter" absence. While a jury under <u>Miller</u> might ask whether the value of the work is "serious," a jury under <u>Memoirs</u> might ask whether the work is truly "redeeming" or not. Moreover, a jury under <u>Miller</u> might tend to assume that all genuine value is "serious" value. It is even possible that a jury that finds literary or artistic value under <u>Miller</u> might narrowly interpret the term "social," and fail to find "social" value in the work under <u>Memoirs</u>.

IDEAS AND ARTISTIC EXPRESSION

The range of interpretive questions raised by the <u>Miller</u> value formulation is nearly inexhaustible. Many of the most important can be resolved along the lines suggested above. It is still possible to argue, however, that the emphasis on "ideas," even in the literary and artistic realms, is insensitive to the nature of art and artistic expression, and that our approach in this respect in fact amounts to "the constitutional canonization of sheer philistinism."[47]

Professor Finnis observes that

Aesthetics contains a welter of conflicting

doctrines, but there is universal agreement
that artistic work does not derive its
<u>artistic</u> value from any "message" which it
may happen to convey and which could be
presented in the form of ordinary discursive
thinking.   Aesthetic attention is not
looking at something in order to <u>find out
about</u> something.[48]

However, the approach endorsed above does not commit
the courts to protect artistic works only to the
extent that the work constitutes a kind of tract in
which an otherwise plainly articulable message is
distortedly expressed in translation through art.   As
we have suggested above, an idea for, say, scientific
purposes need not be the same kind of thing as an idea
for aesthetic purposes.   An idea, and its expression
in the artistic realm, need not be purely
intellectualized or essentially propositional.[49]

Potential disagreement in this regard falls away
when it is recognized that

What makes art art is not that it stimulates
feelings, which any family picture album can
do, but that it expresses them symbolically.
To be more precise, art expresses <u>ideas</u> of
feeling, and it does this by embodying these
ideas in the more or less conventional
symbolic forms of music, painting,
sculpture, architecture, poetry, drama, and
prose.[50]

On Professor Finnis' own emphasis, art necessarily
involves the expression of ideas of one sort or
another.   One may, of course, wish to question whether
the emphasis on "feeling" is always satisfactory, a
Beethoven Trio might appeal as much to the intellect
as to the senses, or emotions, or to "feelings", but
this does not affect our argument.   One may simply
adopt a preferred substitute conception to fill in the
blank left by "ideas of _____," however one likes.

Courts must not become too cavalier, though, in
conferring free speech protection on art merely
because art may express something, in some sense.
Minimally, an idea of the sort described above must be
present.   Courts should not take too sweepingly
Professor Feinberg's remark that "when the only
'conduct' involved is the expression of some
proposition, attitude, or feeling in speech or
writing, or of whatever it is that gets 'expressed' in
art, music, drama, or film, then restrictive
legislation would seem to contravene the explicit

guarantees of the first amendment."[51] If a particular
work of art expresses nothing more than, say, the
craftsmanship or prideful attention to detail that
might be "expressed" by a skilled bricklayer in
virtually all of the bricklayer's work, it is not
clear why the artist should be able to invoke the
protection of the free speech clause any more than the
bricklayer, because we will have been given no reason
to relevantly distinguish the alleged artistic
expression from ordinary, unpretentious bricklaying.

PORNOGRAPHIC VALUE

Even if it is agreed that mere invocation of the
honorific title of art does not necessarily confer
free speech protection, it may be argued that the
alleged value of some or all pornographic works
transcends the category of artistic or literary value.
Some or, perhaps more disquietingly, all pornography
has been defended on independent value grounds. In
one case, "the district court noted that the
behavioral psychologist, B. F. Skinner, had recently
cited with approval the theologian Paul Tillich for
his defense of pornography as 'extending sexuality
into old age.'"[52]
     This value-defense of pornography would seem to
apply to at least some degree to all pornography,
without distinction.   On this approach, all
pornography is valuable, if not of serious value.
This implication itself may give us pause. The more
significant issue, however, is the relationship
between the value of extending sexuality into old age,
on the assumption that this cannot be accomplished
without materials that would otherwise be legally
obscene, and the value categories listed in Miller.
The hedonic or sensuality value involved would appear
not to fit readily within the categories of literary,
artistic, political, or scientific value except in
some controversially attenuated sense.   So much the
worse it may be thought, for the unduly restrictive
Miller categories.   But the Miller value categories
should not be viewed as an obviously failed attempt by
the Court to sum up all possible kinds of value in the
world into four categories. Some or all pornography
may be of hedonic value. Some or all pornography may
be of commercial value.   These sorts of value,
however, simply do not count, in the context of
obscenity determinations, because they have no
substantial relation to the range of purposes or
values underlying our common desire to specially
protect a realm of free speech.
     A fair reading of even the great champion of

freedom of speech, John Stuart Mill, or of any of his historical predecessors in this regard, leaves the door open to reasonable state suppression of materials that even the _Miller_ test itself is normally thought to protect. It is clear that "Mill did not consider...public displays of 'dirty pictures,' and the like, to be forms of 'symbolic speech,' or expressions of _opinion_ of any kind."[53] Professor Feinberg goes on to observe, in accord with the broad values underlying our devotion to the special protection accorded speech, that "[t]he presumption in favor of liberty is much weaker in the case of conduct that does not have the 'redeeming social importance' peculiar to assertion, criticism, advocacy, and debate; and hence, even 'mere offensiveness' in the absence of harm may be a valid ground for suppressing it."[54]

Similar responses could be made to other formulations of the values arguably deriving from some or all pornography or deriving in greater measure from otherwise constitutionally unprotected material. Material is occasionally held obscene despite expert psychiatric testimony that the materials at issue at least "had some educational value."[55] It is possible, however, to educate oneself about, or by means of, matters of only tangential first amendment concern. It is equally possible, allegedly, to educate oneself, or to derive educational value, through the voluntary ingestion of hallucinogenic substances. That educational value may be allegedly derived from an activity does not convert that activity into speech, let alone protected speech.

It is possible, however, to rationalize pornographic activity through the allegation that pornography at least implicitly sends a cognizable message, or conveys an arguably important idea. It has thus been argued, for example, that "[i]n opposition to the sorrowing Catholic dismissal of sexuality as an unfortunate and spiritually superficial concomitant of propagation, pornography affords the alternative idea of the independent status of sexuality as a profound and shattering ecstasy."[56] Alternatively, Professor Dworkin has argued that in this context, "[r]estricted publication leaves a certain hypothesis entirely unmade: the hypothesis that sex should enter all levels of public culture on the same standing as soap opera romance or movie trivia. . . ."[57]

These sorts of ideas may qualify as sufficiently implicating political value under _Miller_. What seems more dubious is whether, in a given transaction

involving allegedly obscene materials, any such
message or idea would have been genuinely intended by
the sender or seller of the material, or even whether
any such message would actually have been received by
the purchaser. No one doubts that such transactions
may be rationalized by acute, uninvolved third parties
who may seek to invest with political value a
transaction otherwise devoid of such value.
Similarly, diligent criminal defense attorneys should
be able to incorporate such intellectualizations, post
hoc, into their theory of the case. In a given case,
however, a reasonable juror might well conclude that
none of this Olympian discourse was any sufficient
part of the intent of the seller, or of either buyer
or seller, and the law might reasonably hold that this
fact matters for free speech purposes. After all,
virtually any observable event may inspire articulate
political reflections in a sufficiently sensitive
observer. This does not make whatever the stimulus
was into an act of protected speech, independent of
the actual intent of any actor.

As to Professor Dworkin's "unmade hypothesis"
argument,[58] it seems clear that such an argument
confuses the expression of a given hypothesis with its
realization in practice. Why, on Professor Dworkin's
hypothesis, could one not argue that a misdemeanor
restriction on the act of littering itself leaves
entirely unmade the hypothesis that littered and
unlittered landscapes should be treated as on a par?
One can argue for the positive value or
appropriateness of littering, or make that hypothesis,
without engaging in the activity of littering itself.
One can just as easily make a passionate, articulate,
comprehensive defense of pornography and its value
without buying or selling the materials themselves.
Defending pornography is not the same as selling it,
just as advocating the burning of one's draft card is
not the same as burning it in protest.[59] Contrary to
Dworkin, the defense, or the advocacy, itself makes
the hypothesis.

The process of rescuing or not rescuing allegedly
obscene works on value grounds is not entirely devoid
of irony. Professor Kalven distinguished between
pornography that was "at best" unrelated to any
serious human concerns, and that was "at worst" a
depiction of "a degrading, hostile, alien view of the
sexual experience."[60] Surprisingly, it may be
pornography "at its worst" that has a better claim to
free speech protection than pornography "at its best"
in this sense. Pornography at its "best," devoid of
any reference to serious human concerns, may simply
not implicate the _Miller_ value categories. At least

some pornography at its "worst," in taking a degrading "view" of the sexual experience, may claim protection precisely in virtue of taking, more or less intentionally, a coherent, articulate, if unpopular "view" of serious matters. Thus the double edge of the feminist critique of some or all pornography as expressing a disfavored repressive male ideology.[61]

If, on the other hand, it is possible to treat some or all alleged obscenity as not intending to convey an ideological or political point, it becomes possible for the prosecution to more readily and uncontroversially meet the "value" absence criterion of Miller. Perhaps "[t]he pornographic item is a sexual surrogate. It takes pictorial or linguistic form only because some individuals achieve sexual gratification in that way."[62] To the extent this characterization is an accurate depiction of at least some pornography, such materials should present easy cases under the Miller value criterion as interpreted above.

THE ROLES OF EXPERTS AND JURIES

This chapter's approach to the Miller value criterion admittedly may require limitations on some lines of analysis that have found favor with the Court. As seen above, value may be attributable to a work, or a coherent impersonal idea may have been evidently intended by a work, without a jury necessarily perceiving such value, or such an idea, without assistance. In the detection of value in a work, a consensual expert may be able to convincingly make manifest, to the jury's satisfaction, literary value that the jury might otherwise not have perceived. While evaluating books or films is not categorically beyond the ken of ordinary persons, expert opinion may well, in a particular case, aid the jury's understanding of the relevant value considerations.

In the context of value determinations, therefore, courts should be reluctant to extend the Supreme Court's observation that the allegedly obscene materials themselves "are the best evidence of what they represent,"[63] and that placing the materials themselves in evidence therefore supplants the need for expert testimony. While in some respects, even "hard core pornography...can and does speak for itself,"[64] our society has not yet reached the point at which without qualms it can invariably assume that the opinion, on artistic value, of the curator of the local museum is no better or worse than the untutored reactions of the local jury. In some sense, James Joyce's Ulysses is the best evidence of its own literary value, but an expert witness may appreciably aid the jury in mediating the confrontation between text and jury. In certain respects, then, it is not true that "[s]tudying the material for hours doesn't tell a judge any more about its obscene character than he knew when he first looked at it."[65] The difficult, even insoluble, issues center instead on the precise deference to be given to jury verdicts that are inconsistent with some portion of the expert testimony, or all of the expert testimony, introduced on the issue of the work's value. The obscenity cases have been read by at least one commentator to imply that "[t]o prevail on appeal, the defendant would have to show that as a matter of law the material was so clearly meritorious that the jury should not have been allowed to find it otherwise."[66] This is a demanding standard in the free speech area, particularly in conjunction with the settled principle that the jury is "not bound to accept the opinion of any expert in weighing the evidence of obscenity...."[67]

    While it is easy to imagine a reasonable jury ignoring the self-serving, overblown claims of agenda-pushing professional experts in favor of the patent vacuousness of the allegedly obscene materials themselves, it is also possible to imagine a jury's ignoring the disinterested, credible testimony of distinguished, mainstream scholars, on the grounds that the jury believes that sexually explicit, deeply offensive materials may be proscribed regardless of any literary value. This approach, however attractive to a particular jury, would plainly not be consistent with Miller. The appellate courts should not be reluctant, on appropriate occasions, and on appropriate issues, to exercise their power "to conduct an independent review of constitutional claims...."[68]

    The courts should on the other hand be extremely reluctant to, in effect, inform local juries that they were incontrovertibly mistaken in finding the particular materials at issue to have been patently offensive to their own local community standards.[69] It is neither especially undignified, however, nor institutionally burdensome,[70] nor a matter of presumptuous judicial overreaching, for the courts to review on appeal a staid amicus brief discoursing on the unsuspected literary value of the work in question. It is worth reflecting on the possibility that it is inherently prejudicial to the defendant, at least in a loose sense, to ask the jury to pass on the question of the work's literary value just after the same jury has determined that the work appeals to the prurient interest in sex and portrays sex in a

patently offensive way according to community
standards.[71] As a matter of individual psychology,
more than group dynamics, it may be asking a lot to
expect a jury to stay its hand by finding the
necessary value after it has found patent
offensiveness. Searching, even aggressive appellate
review on the value element may compensate for such a
tendency on the part of the jury. If the court on
review finds sufficient value of the proper sort, it
should not be reluctant to intervene to save the
material.

THE UNNECESSARY COMPLEXITY OF THE MILLER STANDARD

An intriguing question, however, is that of the
constitutionally permissible consequences of the
finding by a jury and reviewing court that the
material does not meet the value standard established
by _Miller_. One virtue of this chapter's
interpretation of the value requirement is that
problems of vagueness, notice, and due process aside,
it becomes insignificant from the standpoint of the
free speech clause what the remaining elements of the
obscenity test are, once the material is determined to
lack serious value in the sense of not seeking to
convey an idea within the _Miller_ value categories. If
no such idea conveyance is intended, the remainder of
the obscenity test becomes irrelevant for free speech
purposes, because the values or purposes underlying
the free speech clause are, by hypothesis, not
significantly implicated.

To put the point concretely, consider the
constitutional role of the prurient interest element
under _Miller_. Under this element, the trier of fact
is to determine whether an average person in the
appropriate community, applying those community
standards, and taking the work as a whole, would find
that the work appeals to a prurient interest in sex.[72]
Obviously, a number of practical and interpretive
problems lurk in this element. The Supreme Court has
taken it upon itself to discourse at length on the
nature of the concept of prurience, and to
authoritatively draw a remarkably non-relativistic
distinction between normal sexual desires and those
that are excessive or morbid.[73] However, it should
simply not be necessary, as far as the free speech
clause is concerned, to fret about the nature of
prurience, or any related issue. Again, assuming fair
notice, and the absence of vagueness or due process
problems, and assuming no extraneous constitutional
issues are involved, such as equal protection, the
courts should be able to enforce a statutory ban on

material that is without free speech value and that is
patently offensive under the second element of the
Miller test.   If a work seeks to convey no idea, on
the view elaborated above, and the work "depicts or
describes in a patently offensive way, sexual conduct
specifically defined by the applicable state
law...,"[74] why should it be constitutionally
protected, all else equal?   Why should the state be
constitutionally required to show that the sexual
interest was, on someone's or anyone's standards,
excessive, or shameful, or morbid?

It follows _a fortiori_ that most partial
revisions, simplifications, and reinterpretations of
the prurient interest requirement would be
permissible, under the free speech clause, as this
chapter has interpreted the "serious value"
requirement.   And a parallel argument can easily be
made for simplifying, if not utterly dispensing with,
the patent offense requirement.   If a work fails this
Chapter's conception of the "value" requirement, thus
not significantly implicating free speech values, and
if it is found to appeal to a prurient interest in
sex, on some reasonable test, then why, all else
equal, should the state also be required to separately
show anything like the current patent offensiveness
element?

This chapter's reinterpretation of the Court's
"serious value" criterion may well be attractive on
its own merits.   Even if not, it possesses the
practical advantage of allowing a substantial
simplification of the other elements of the _Miller_
test, allowing the courts to bypass such intractable
issues as that of the constitutionally permissible
scope of the community that may be selected when
applying community standards on the prurient interest
and patent offensiveness elements.   While the Court
itself has not adopted the recommended approach in
either letter or practice, it has occasionally at
least verbally accepted portions of the underlying
logic of such a view.   Even in a case contemporaneous
with _Miller_, the Court recognized that "[w]here
communication of ideas, protected by the First
Amendment, is not involved,...the mere fact...some
human 'utterances' or 'thoughts' may be incidentally
affected does not bar the State from acting to protect
legitimate state interests."[75]   If the communication
of the requisite ideas is not involved in a given
case, there is little point in imposing numerous,
specific additional substantive and evidentiary
burdens on the state, at least in the name of the
First Amendment.

OBSCENITY AND THE POSSIBILITY OF DECADENCE

It is certainly possible to link all sorts of sexually explicit speech to the concept of value in a much broader way. For the libertarian, there is the sense that progressively rolling back the frontiers of, or progressively emptying the category of, the obscene is inherently of value. In such a view, the judicial task is not so much to define and protect some appropriately limited, circumscribed range of freedom of speech as to expand the boundaries of protected speech whenever feasible. In light of the values of pluralism, tolerance, and diversity, freedom of speech is a good thing, and expanded freedom of speech is a better thing.

There is some reason in history and theory, however, to suspect that such a perpetual expansionist project may also be describable in less self-congratulatory terms. Both the proliferation of increasingly extreme sexually explicit speech, the prior unenvisionability of which renders the pornography of another era merely quaint by comparison, and the judicial reaction thereto may, less happily, constitute aspects of the phenomenon of societal decadence.[76]

For our purposes, decadence may be thought of as "the valuing of experience for its own sake, irrespective of the quality of the experience, the object of the experience, that upon which the experience is, as it were, directed being left out of account."[77] In a decadent era, "[t]he success of our lives will...be judged not by the degree to which they realize an end, achieve a goal, fulfill a purpose or conform to a standard which we have recognized as authoritative, but by the extent to which they contrive to embody a series of significant experiences."[78] Decadence is therefore thought to be associated with generalized subjectivism, with epicurianism and hedonism in the realm of conduct, with skepticism in matters of belief,[79] and with factors such as loss of cultural self-confidence,[80] with lack of "an animating vision of an ideal state of affairs,"[81] with lack of self-discipline and "a very high tolerance of incompatible standards and codes of behavior,"[82] and with irreverence for its own sake.[83]

Of course, neither the pornographer nor the accommodating judge need feel immediately compelled to acknowledge the relevance of decadence. What to the decadence theorist looks like long-term gradual disintegration and fragmentation of putatively objective standards will, with at least some temporary plausibility, be seen by many as so many stages in the extension of pluralism, diversity, and tolerance in a legal milieu increasingly dubious about the availability of objective standards of judgment. Both camps can, for a time, account for such phenomena as the increasingly extreme character of commercial pornography. The decadence theorist will point factors such as the inherent self-exacerbating quality of irreverence for its own sake: as less is revered, or is less revered, irreverence must presumably become increasingly extreme in order to provoke much of a psychological effect. The accommodationists will doubtless view the same phenomenon as reflecting the exploration of uncharted aesthetic and hedonic possibilities in which the bonds of societal repression and gratuitous inhibition are gradually cast off. But then, we would not expect decadence to persist unless it were almost indefinitely rationalizable.

Some of the underlying logic of the project of accommodating the arguably obscene was recently articulated by Justices Brennan, Marshall, and Blackmun in an entirely different context. Those Justices joined in expressing the view that "[w]e are not an assimilative, homogenous society, but a facilitative, pluralistic one, in which we must be willing to abide someone else's unfamiliar or even repellant practices because the same tolerant impulses protect our own idiosyncracies."[84] On the issue of assessing the value of allegedly obscene materials itself, Justice Scalia has forthrightly, if question-beggingly, concluded that in the absence of ascertainable standards of objective value in at least this realm, there is no point in disputing over, let alone attempting to litigate, matters of taste.[85]

At the state court level, the Oregon Supreme Court case of State v. Henry[86] represents a logical extension of developing trends in the area of offensive, vulgar, or obscene speech. The court in Henry held broadly that allegedly obscene speech is generally protected by the free speech provision of the Oregon Constitution. The Oregon Supreme Court concluded that

> [A]lthough Oregon's pioneers brought with them a diversity of highly moral as well as irreverent views, we perceive that most members of the Constitutional Convention of 1857 were rugged and robust individuals dedicated to founding a free society unfettered by the governmental imposition of some people's views of morality on the free expression of others.[87]

This quotation helps to illustrate how phenomena often associated with social decline can be converted to objects of pride through a combination of creative characterization and some sort of loose, de facto ethical relativism. This creative characterization is the court's response to the nagging fear that pornography may be "out of control" in the sense of being more pervasive and extreme now than formerly, with the pervasiveness and extremity of the materials exceeding what is thought desirable by most adults, or even by many consumers of pornography. Even the complete demise of any standards at all can be characterized as evidence of "robustness," of "nonprudishness," of "ruggedness," or as reflecting pluralism and diversity.

Unfortunately, if a society is in fact in the process of fragmenting, praising it as diverse, open, and pluralistic may not be sufficient to restore it to health. A society in which the depth and breadth of common values are decreasing may be in the process of losing collective confidence and declining, even while we celebrate the society's pluralism. There may be some self-delusion in deciding simply to choose the more favorable characterization. Certainly, our greatest liberal writers, such as John Stuart Mill, have emphasized the values of pluralism and diversity. But not without limits. It has been rightly observed that "[n]either Mill nor others like him have ever argued for a society pluralist to its roots. Indeed, the liberty they plead for only makes sense within a society that strives after the highest ideals of the West; within a society, that is, committed to rational enquiry..."[88]

Of course, the Oregon Supreme Court in _Henry_ at no point explicitly adopts any sort of technical moral relativism. Instead, the Court in _Henry_ seems to assume that the abolition of obscenity laws should follow the observable fact that people's views of morality differ, together with the premise that rugged individualism characterized Oregon's constitutional Framers and is itself a desirable quality. It appears unwarranted, then, to permit "governmental imposition of some people's views of morality on the free expression of others."[89]

The Oregon Supreme Court's _de facto_ ethical relativism is neither extreme nor unusual. Perhaps the most familiar kindred statement is that of Justice Harlan for the Court in _Cohen v. California_. In the context of adjudicating the status of the "distasteful" antidraft slogan emblazoned on Cohen's jacket, Justice Harlan declared that "it is...often true that one man's vulgarity is another's lyric."[90]

Similarly, Justice Harlan concluded, "governmental officials cannot make principled distinctions in this area..."[91]   Justice Harlan apparently viewed the underlying issue as a matter of "taste and style."[92]

Justice Harlan's language is in fact often cited in a more extreme version, without his qualification as to what is "often true," resulting in the flat, if perhaps ultimately self-contradictory, relativism that "one man's vulgarity is another's lyric."[93]   Echoes of Justice Harlan's approach can be heard in Justice Douglas's observation that "what may be trash to me may be prized by others"[94] and in the Court's more general formulation that "[w]hat seems to one to be trash may have for others fleeting or even enduring values."[95]   At least one court, in an alleged indecent public language case, has explicitly interpreted the Cohen analysis as viewing "obscenity" as "subjective, a relative matter."[96]

As we have seen, some sorts of relativism and subjectivism are often thought to be associated with societal decadence.   But if the courts make no such connection between relativism and decadence, their response to an increase over time in arguably offensive public language or to obscenity is likely to encourage or tacitly promote such phenomena through an implied legitimization.   A court attuned to the possibility of decadence is likely to view a perceived historical increase in offensive language or obscenity with some concern.   But to a relativist-minded court, not attuned to the possibility of decadence, an increase over time in arguably offensive public language or obscenity takes on a self-validating quality.

The Fifth Circuit, for example, in Bazaar v. Fortune[97] referred to the arguably objectionable language at issue as "no longer really that unusual,"[98] perceived a trend toward its use, and observed, without endorsing the language at issue, that "things considered horribly 'indecent' a few years ago are quite commonplace today."[99]   To a decadence theorist, this state of affairs might be cause for concern.   To a relativist, the same state of affairs shows most crucially the increasingly broad popularity, or at least acceptance, of the language at issue.   For a relativist court, the step from popular acceptance to judicial acceptability is hardly noticeable.

It is possible to seek to allay the fears of the decadence theorist in this regard by assuming that the use of language predictably offensive to some of one's audience is simply to be expected to increase in an era of sustained political and social conflict.   But this does not seem a particularly convincing explanation for the more frequent use of intentionally offensive language. The language for which persons such as the defendant in Cohen have been prosecuted has been technically available throughout the course of the virtually unceasing political and social conflict endemic to American political history. Further, in view of the increased stakes, it is not obvious why an increase in political and social conflict should not tend to drive out intentionally or predictably offensive language in favor or more cogent or otherwise persuasive language. More importantly, however, it should not be assumed that the typical offensive language case at the appellate level is deeply imbued with political and social issues, at least in any direct sense. As we have seen, most such cases are not.

Instead, the more convincing explanation for the historical increase in offensive language, or of the use of particular profanities, as well as for cases such as Henry, may lie in the "erosion of the Protestant ethic and the Puritan temper,"[100] which were ordinarily thought of as "codes that emphasized work, sobriety, frugality, [and] sexual restraint...."[101] The increasing doubts about the judicial imposition of such values may be simply one more respect in which "the typical bourgeoise is rapidly losing faith in his own creed."[102]

With the partial demise of traditional rigorous systems of public morals in these areas, the Supreme Court has naturally tended to minimize consideration of the most abstract, ephemeral kinds of alleged injuries. The Court has tended to exclude "claims of harms to 'sensibilities' as a justification for suppression of offensive language. It has recognized as a valid state interest only the prevention of violent reactive conduct and has been willing to assume the likelihood of such behavior only in the narrow case of fighting words."[103] If the courts are not particularly attuned to the possibility of gradual, long-term societal decline, they will quite naturally tend to focus on the risk of only the most tangible, immediate, concrete sorts of harms. Even under the broadest analysis, if the courts see no risk of promoting societal decline, they will not pause to balance any risks of contribution to societal decline against even a very slight perceived risk of legislative or judicial oppression. If no tangible harm can be shown to befall the immediate parties, the courts are likely to feel that the only alternative grounds for failing to protect the challenged conduct must be some moral code that is not universally shared.[104]

But the possibility of gradual, long-term societal decline, or such matters as the gradual loss of a sense of community in particular, is neither concrete, nor tangible, nor immediate, nor clear cut and unequivocal. One person's loss of community is another person's enhanced pluralism. Such sorts of alleged harms certainly do not fit within the kind of clear-and-present-danger analysis with which we are most comfortable in the general free speech area.[105] While it seems undeniable that there can be such a thing as a moral climate or moral environment, however amorphous, and that such things can be culturally important, and can change arguably for the worse, such considerations may be too ineffable for a judiciary to systematically manage. To the extent that our social life is organized "legalistically," the problems of offensive or obscene speech may simply not be soluble in the long run.[106]

NOTES

1.   413 U.S. 15 (1973).

2.   _Id_. at 24. The Supreme Court's latest, and less than entirely felicitous, essay into value determinations in obscenity cases is Pope v. Illinois, 107 S. Ct. 1918 (1987).

3.   383 U.S. 413 (1966).

4.   413 U.S. at 24 (quoting _Memoirs_, 383 U.S. at 419 (emphasis in _Miller_)).

5.   _See, e.g._, Smith v. United States, 431 U.S. 291, 300 (1977); Brockett v. Spokane Arcades, Inc., 472 U.S. 491 (1985).

6.   413 U.S. at 24.

7.   _See_ Penthouse Int'l, Ltd. v. McAuliffe, 610 F.2d 1353 (11th Cir.), _cert_. _dismissed_, 447 U.S. 931 (1980).

8.   _See_ Kois v. Wisconsin, 408 U.S. 229, 231 (1972).

9.   413 U.S. at 22 (citing _Memoirs_, 383 U.S. at 418) (emphasis in _Miller_)).

10.   _Id_.

11.   United States v. Bagnell, 679 F.2d 826, 837 (11th Cir. 1982).

12. See, e.g., Andrews v. State, 652 S.W.2d 370, 389 (Tex. Crim. App. 1983) (en banc).

13. Feinberg, Pornography and the Criminal Law, 40 U. Pitt. L. Rev. 567, 602 (1979).

14. Id.

15. Leventhal, An Empirical Inquiry into the Effects of Miller v. California On the Control of Obscenity, 52 N.Y.U. L. Rev. 810, 930 (1977).

16. 652 S.W.2d 370 (Tex. Crim. App. 1983) (en banc).

17. Id. at 384.

18. See 472 U.S. 492 (1985).

19. Id. at 494.

20. See, e.g., United States v. 12 200-Ft. Reels of Super 8mm. Film, 413 U.S. 123, 129 (1973).

21. See, e.g., American Booksellers Ass'n v. Virginia, 792 F.2d 1261 (4th Cir. 1986), vacated and remanded, 109 S. Ct. 254 (1988).

22. See, e.g., Hamling v. United States, 418 U.S. 87, 106 (1974).

23. Cf. Finnis, "Reason and Passion": The Constitutional Dialectic of Free Speech and Obscenity, 116 U. Pa. L. Rev. 222, 240-41 (1967) (seeking to protect the "classics" as implicitly part of, rather than offenders against, current community standards).

24. See E.J. Bond, Reason and Value 57-58, 84 (1983).

25. Posner, Free Speech in an Economic Perspective, 20 Suffolk U.L. Rev. 1, 25 (1986).

26. Id.

27. United States v. 12 200-Ft. Reels of Super 8mm. Film, 413 U.S. 123, 137 (Douglas, J., dissenting); cf. Cohen v. California, 403 U.S. 15, 25 (1971) ("it is...often true that one man's vulgarity is another man's lyric").

28. S. Darwall, Impartial Reason 141 (1983) (emphasis in the original).

29. Actually, the Court in Miller had explicitly rejected the allegedly ambiguous concept of "social importance" as a value category. See Miller, 413 U.S. at 25 n.7.   The categories of literary, artistic, political, and scientific value presumably replace the more readily abused notion of "social" value.

30.   Paris Adult Theatre I v. Slaton, 413 U.S. 49, 97 (1973) (Brennan, J., dissenting) (emphasis in original).

31.   See generally Blasi, The Pathological Perspective and the First Amendment, 85 Colum. L. Rev. 449 (1985).

32.   For an example of the use of "political" in a particularly broad sense in the context of free speech debate, see Perry, Freedom of Expression: An Essay on Theory and Doctrine, 78 Nw. U.L. Rev. 1137 (1983).

33.   For discussion of the mutual restraint value, see Rawls, The Idea of an Overlapping Consensus, 7 Oxford J. Legal Studies 1, 21 (1987).

34.   See Note, Community Standards and Federal Obscenity Prosecutions, 55 S. Cal. L. Rev. 693, 703 (1982).

35.   See id. at 723.

36.   See Smith v. United States, 431 U.S. 291, 321 (1977) (Stevens, J., dissenting) (citing Justice Holmes' "test of truth" of ideas rationale set forth in his dissenting opinion in Abrams v. United States, 250 U.S. 616, 630 (1919)).

37.   383 U.S. 413 (1966).

38.   Id. at 418, 419.

39.   See Miller, 413 U.S. at 25 n.7.

40.   See id. at 22.   Of course, the state still arguably was required under Miller to "prove a negative," that the material did not have serious value of the right sort.   See Paris Adult Theatre I, 413 U.S. at 98 (Brennan, J., dissenting).

41.   See Brockett v. Spokane Arcades, Inc., 472 U.S. 491 (1985).

42.   See, e.g., Red Bluff Drive-In, Inc. v. Vance, 648 F.2d 1020, 1027 (5th Cir. 1981) ("serious redeeming value" standard allegedly under Miller), cert. denied sub nom. Theatres West, Inc. v. Holmes, 455 U.S. 913

(1982).

43. See the explicit comparison drawn in Hamling v. United States, 418 U.S. 87, 116 (1974). See also Richards, Free Speech and Obscenity Law: Toward a Moral Theory of the First Amendment, 123 U. Pa. L. Rev. 45, 71 (1974) (lighter burden on prosecution under Miller than under Memoirs); Leventhal, supra note 15, at 811, 929; J. Choper, Judicial Review and the National Political Process 126 (1980).

44. See Leventhal, supra note 15, at 930. See also United States v. Various Articles of Obscene Merchandise, Schedule No. 2102, 709 F.2d 136 (2d Cir. 1983) (Meskill, J., concurring in result) (raising the possibility that if the materials at issue are as a matter of law not patently offensive by contemporary New York standards, nothing is obscene in New York).

45. Leventhal, supra note 15, at 928.

46. Id. at 929.

47. Finnis, supra note 23, at 231.

48. Id. (emphasis in original).

49. Cf. Richards, supra note 43, (interpreting Miller as protecting nonpropositional artistic "expression").

50. Finnis, supra note 23, at 232-33 (citations omitted) (emphasis in original).

51. Feinberg, supra note 13, at 576.

52. See United States v. Various Articles of Obscene Merchandise, Schedule No. 2102, 709 F.2d 132, 134 (2d Cir. 1983) (citing district court opinion).

53. J. Feinberg, Rights, Justice, and the Bounds of Liberty 71 (1980) (emphasis in the original).

54. Id.

55. People v. Sequoia Books, Inc., 146 Ill. App. 3d 1, 3, 496 N.E.2d 740, 741 (1986).

56. Richards, supra note 43, at 81.

57. R. Dworkin, A Matter of Principle 342 (1985).

58. Id.

59.   See United States v. O'Brien, 391 U.S. 367 (1968).

60.   Kalven, The Metaphysics of the Law of Obscenity, 1960 Sup. Ct. Rev. 1, 13 (P. Kurland ed. 1960).

61.   See American Booksellers' Ass'n v. Hudnut, 771 F.2d 323 (7th Cir. 1985), aff'd mem., 475 U.S. 1001 (1986); MacKinnon, Pornography as Sex Discrimination, 4 Law & Inequality 38 (1986); Stone, Anti-Pornography Legislation as Viewpoint Discrimination, 9 Harv. J.L. & Pol'y 461 (1986); Sunstein, Pornography and the First Amendment, 1986 Duke L.J. 589.

62.   F. Schauer, Freedom of Speech: A Philosophical Enquiry 181 (1982).

63.   Paris Adult Theatre I v. Slaton, 413 U.S. 49, 56 (1973).

64.   Id. at 56 n.6.

65.   Kalven, supra note 60, at 44.   Cf. Feinberg, supra note 13, at 588 ("Pure pornography is easy to recognize; what are hard to spot are the 'redeeming' units or aspects of expression in such impure admixtures as artfully pornographic films and erotic realism in novels.").

66.   O'Neil, Federalism and Obscenity, 9 U. Tol. L. Rev. 731, 751 (1978).

67.   Hamling v. United States, 418 U.S. 87, 100 (1974).

68.   Jenkins v. Georgia, 418 U.S. 153, 160 (1974).

69.   But cf. id. at 161 (holding that the film at issue "could not, as a matter of constitutional law, be found to depict sexual conduct in a patently offensive way....").

70.   See Paris Adult Theatre I, 413 U.S. at 91-93 (Brennan, J., dissenting).

71.   See Miller, 413 U.S. at 24.

72.   See id.

73.   See Brockett v. Spokane Arcades, 472 U.S. 491 (1985).

74.   See Miller, 413 U.S. at 24.

75.   Paris Adult Theatre I, 413 U.S. at 67.

76.   For a broader discussion of this phenomenon, see Wright, Judicial Responses to Long-Term Societal Decline, 30 Ariz. L. Rev. 271 (1988).

77.   C. Joad, Decadence: A Philosophical Inquiry 54 (1948).

78.   Id. at 101.

79.   Id. at 100.

80.   See P. Sorokin, The Crisis of Our Age 252 (1941).

81.   L. Haworth, Decadence and Objectivity 3 (1977).

82.   White, On Properties and Decadence in Society, 87 Ethics 352, 354 (1977).

83.   See Molnar, On Decadence and Decline, 21 Modern Age 395, 401 (1977).

84.   Michael H. v. Gerald D., 109 S. Ct. 2333, 2351 (1989).

85.   See Pope v. Illinois, 107 S. Ct. 1918, 1923 (Scalia, J., concurring).

86.   302 Or. 510, 732 P.2d 9 (1987).

87.   Id. at 523, 732 P.2d at 16.

88.   White, supra note 82, at 360-61.

89.   Henry, 302 Or. at 523, 732 P.2d at 17.

90.   403 U.S. 15, 25 (1971).

91.   Id.   See also Rutzick, Offensive Language and the Evolution of First Amendment Protection, 9 Harv. C.R.-C.L. Rev. 1, 20 (1974).

92.   Cohen, 403 U.S. at 25.

93.   See, e.g., State v. Authelet, 120 R.I. 42, 54, 385 A.2d 642, 648 (1978).

94.   United States v. 12 200-Ft. Reels of Super 8mm. Film, 413 U.S. 123, 137 (1973) (Douglas, J., dissenting).

95.   Hannegan v. Esquire, Inc. 327 U.S. 146, 157-58 (1946) quoted in Pope v. Illinois, 107 S. Ct. 1918, 1927 (1987) (Stevens, J., dissenting) ("what one judge

sees as 'gross and bizarre,' another may find...mild and not very 'sexually suggestive'").

96. People v. Klein, 67 Mich. App. 556, 557, 242 N.W.2d 436, 437 (1976) (per curiam). See also Farber, Civilizing Public Discourse: An Essay on Professor Bickel, Justice Harlan, and the Enduring Significance of Cohen v. California, 1980 Duke L.J. 283, 299 (distinction between "vulgarity" and "lyric" as "subjective" in nature).

97. 476 F.2d 570 (5th Cir. 1973), aff'd as modified, 489 F.2d 255 (4th Cir.) (en banc), cert. denied, 416 U.S. 995 (1974).

98. Id. at 580.

99. Id.

100. D. Bell, The Cultural Contradictions of Capitalism 55 (1976).

101. Id.

102. J. Schumpeter, Capitalism, Socialism and Democracy 161 (3d ed. 1962).

103. Rutzick, supra note 91, at 27.

104. See, e.g., Justice Tobriner's argument in Crownover v. Musick, 9 Cal. 3d 405, 441, 509 P.2d 497, 521-22, 107 Cal. Rptr. 681, 705-6 (1973) (en banc) (Tobriner, J., dissenting), overruled, Morris v. Municipal Court, 32 Cal. 3d 553, 651 P.2d 51, 186 Cal. Rptr. 494 (1982) (per curiam). Justice Richardson, in turn dissenting in Morris, sought unsuccessfully to have the Court consider the risk to an already "declining sense of community" posed by overruling Crownover. Id. at 576, 652 P.2d at 65, 186 Cal. Rptr. at 508 (Richardson, J., dissenting).

105. See Brandenburg v. Ohio, 395 U.S. 444 (1969) (per curiam); A. Bickel, The Morality of Consent 73 (1975).

106. See A. Solzhenitsyn, A World Split Apart 21 (1978).

7

How to Decide Close Cases:
An Illustration

INTRODUCTION

Some of the most difficult problems in legal analysis
involve concepts that are slippery and amorphous but
indispensible to the adjudication of cases. The
distinction between speech on matters of public
interest or concern and speech that is not is one such
concept. This vital distinction has proven difficult
to apply on a consistent, noncontroversial basis. The
concept may even qualify, under the logic of W. B.
Gallie's classic article,[1] as an essentially contested
concept. The distinction between public, general
interest speech and other speech is especially vital
when courts are deciding cases that may involve
important social interests and fundamental
constitutional rights. The focus of this chapter will
be on the judicial use of the distinction between
speech that is on a matter of public or general
interest or concern and speech that is not, as a means
to illustrate how a broad range of close free speech
cases may be rationally resolved. Courts sometimes
blur this distinction by focusing on the general
subject of the speech rather than on the speech
itself.[2] For the sake of convenience, the distinction
will be referred to as one between speech on matters
of public interest or concern (MOPIC) and speech that
is not (non-MOPIC). These abbreviations are merely
for the sake of convenience, and are not intended to
beg any interesting questions.
    While the MOPIC versus non-MOPIC distinction was
important to the classic Warren and Brandeis
discussion of privacy rights,[3] only recently has it

become central to the law of defamation and to the law of public employee discharge or other disciplinary actions allegedly based on the employee's protected speech. The central case in the defamation area is <u>Dun & Bradstreet, Inc. v. Greenmoss Builders, Inc.</u>[4] and <u>Connick v. Myers</u>[5] is the central case in the employee discharge area. Of course, the public interest or public concern nature of public employee speech does not dictate a favorable result for the employee. The employee might have been terminated anyway for independent reasons. There must also be, under <u>Connick</u>, a balancing of legitimate free speech interests and the general interests of the employer in workplace discipline and efficiency.[6]

In <u>Greenmoss</u>, the plaintiff sued Dun & Bradstreet for distributing an inaccurate credit report to the plaintiff's creditors. The plurality opinion in <u>Greenmoss</u> referred to public or to individual "matter[s]"[7] and "issue[s]"[8] but concluded by declaring that the award of presumed or punitive damages in the absence of any "actual malice" on the part of the libel defendant is not a violation of the First Amendment so long as the speech does not involve matters of public concern.[9] In order to determine whether the allegedly libelous speech addresses a matter of public concern, the court must examine the speech's "content, form, and context...as revealed by the whole record."[10]

The dissent in <u>Greenmoss</u> disagreed with the plurality's characterization of the Dun & Bradstreet credit report on Greenmoss Builders as not being a matter of public concern.[11] More importantly, however, the dissent observed that the plurality had offered "almost no guidance as to what constitutes a protected 'matter of public concern.'"[12]

In the area of libel law, judicial reactions to the Court's MOPIC versus non-MOPIC distinction range from conceding its difficulty in application[13] to the more despairing characterization of the distinction as "amorphous and undefinable."[14] In the area of public employee dismissal, the reaction has been similar. No clear definition of public concern has been established,[15] and the courts have had substantial difficulty in determining when speech involves an issue of public concern.[16] More importantly, the distinction, or its underdevelopment, has resulted in substantial numbers of inconsistent, irreconcilable decisions in the frequently litigated public employee speech-based dismissal cases.[17]

Determining whether or not speech is on a matter of public interest is unavoidably problematic. The distinction invites an unusually high percentage of subjective and arbitrary judicial decisions within a wide border zone of close cases dividing the categories. The litigated cases tend to cluster in this wide indeterminate "close case" area separating MOPICs from non-MOPICs, resulting in large numbers of unpredictable case outcomes. Unfortunately, this difficulty cannot be the sole consideration in deciding whether to modify or dispense with the distinction between public interest and nonpublic interest speech.

Particularly in sensitive areas involving important free speech rights, there is a reluctance to accept easier-to-use substitutes for these speech categories, even if the categories of MOPIC and non-MOPIC speech are themselves difficult to apply. In addition, there exists a reluctance to trade off validity or accuracy of a distinction for greater consistency or reliability. The MOPIC versus non-MOPIC distinction appears to be indispensable. Given our basic consensus with regard to the underlying values and purposes of the free speech clause, it is a logically central distinction, for which there are no good substitutes.

The Supreme Court has long held that not all kinds of speech are equal in constitutional importance because not all kinds of speech implicate with equal depth the central values thought to underlie the First Amendment.[18] While speech on matters of purely private concern is not thought to be utterly outside the scope of the First Amendment,[19] MOPIC speech is thought to be at the heart of the First Amendment and receives the most stringent constitutional protection.[20] The Supreme Court has stated that "speech concerning public affairs is more than self-expression; it is the essence of self-government."[21] Non-MOPIC speech is not so central and accordingly receives less protection.[22]

The MOPIC versus non-MOPIC distinction thus reflects consensual judgments as to the scope and purposes of and values underlying the free speech clause. Most obvious possible substitutes for this distinction can be rejected on grounds such as ideological bias and susceptibility to partisan abuse. The distinction cannot be dispensed with in favor or of a more convenient, less controversial distinction which does not so directly address fundamental free speech value concerns.

This is not to suggest that applying the MOPIC versus non-MOPIC speech distinction is invariably difficult in practice. Some cases can be easily resolved.[23] The obvious cases, those which clearly involve MOPIC or non-MOPIC speech, can be resolved on just about any reasonable rationale of the distinction involved. With regard to those clear cases, there is no need, therefore, to compare and rank alternative conceptions of how the MOPIC distinction should be drawn. Only a relative few of the reported cases, however, involve clearly MOPIC or non-MOPIC speech. What is needed, therefore, is a theory for the unavoidably close, difficult, middle-ground cases that are tried and appealed.

The middle-ground cases are, on the theory developed in this chapter, allowed to be decided on what might be thought of as strategic grounds due to the unavoidable closeness and difficulty of the MOPIC or non-MOPIC issues involved. It violates no one's rights, and is sound policy, to decide issues of MOPIC speech vel non, in the middle-ground close cases, with an eye toward promoting the range of values or purposes underlying speech rights.

Specifically, this chapter seeks to increase consistency and predictability in this range of close cases in a way that will promote first amendment values by means of judicially structured incentives for potential speakers in both public employee speech-based dismissal cases and in defamation cases. The basic concept at the heart of this theory as applied to these middle-range cases is to ask whether the speaker, the alleged defamer or the dismissed public employee, could, under all the circumstances, at a practical and low cost, have made the judicial issue of MOPIC vel non easier to resolve.

Costs for the speaker, under our theory, include those factors which involve the distortion of any political message the speaker cares to convey, as well as the financial costs borne by the speaker. In an ideologically neutral way, the potential scope or breadth of the speaker's remarks can be considered, as well as the nature and size of the speaker's potential audience.   If all else is equal, it is more advantageous in terms of free speech values, on which the litigant is in some sense seeking to rely, if the litigant's speech is richer or more general in its implications, rather than more narrow or particular. It is also more advantageous in terms of free speech values, all else equal, if the speech is directed to more than one relevantly potentially concerned person, if for no other reason than that democratic decision making requires broader public discussion.

The all-else-equal qualifications cover a large number of important factors, and the costs faced by a speaker who contemplates broadening his or her speech can take a variety of forms. We have no desire to penalize, for example, a litigant because his or her notes, or the first preliminary draft of a speech was not intended for any audience, or because the litigant chose to pursue an employment-related matter first through authorized channels, rather than immediately firing off a letter to the editor or speaking to a newspaper reporter on the basis of unripe, undocumented suspicions.

A number of possible objections are dealt with below, in the context of particular cases. For the moment, it may suffice to note that it is undesirable that a judge evaluate the importance or the cogency of the speech at issue. The risk of decision on the basis of ideological bias in this area outweighs any possible advantages. In addition, the judge should not ask whether the speech at issue was, as uttered, general or not general in some absolute sense. Under our analysis, the free speech clause should offer protection not only to ambitious, sweeping abstraction and theory, but, in the common middle range of cases, to those speakers who have done their reasonable, cost-effective best under the circumstances to generalize the content and audience of their allegedly protected speech. The term "generalizing" does not mean to identify or encourage making a speech simply more vague, or robbing a speech of particularity, concreteness, and detail. Instead the term "generalizing" means the drawing or suggesting of broader inferences, richer implications, or of more encompassing conclusions by the speaker or audience. It is instead simpler to say whether a speaker, given his or her actual abilities, could easily have further generalized the speech, with the qualifications outlined above. Under the MOPIC distinction, the speaker, rather than the creative audience, is responsible for the generality of the speech.[24] There is, however, a limit to how far we will require the speaker to generalize the speech before it becomes a clear case of speech on a MOPIC.

Certain anomalies are admittedly possible under the MOPIC/non-MOPIC approach. For example, imagine two separate speech instances that are neither easy MOPICs nor easy non-MOPICs. Both are therefore within the middle range cases that result in doubtful, unpredictable decisions such as the cases discussed above. Suppose that speech instance A is closer on the spectrum to being a clear MOPIC speech than speech instance B. But suppose that B, but not A, is speech that cannot be further generalized at low cost under the circumstances. This would mean, in effect, that a judge could say of A, but not of B, that the speaker could easily have further generalized the message, or could have easily expanded the potential audience, but failed to do so. Under this approach, B, and not A, would be ruled speech on a matter of general or public interest and concern.

This result, however, is hardly upsetting. Any upset would depend upon the assumption that the courts can otherwise begin to make principled, accurate, consistent decisions in the common middle-ground cases, a development which shows no signs of arising. The approach outlined here is fair in that it takes speakers as they are, with their limitations, who want to take advantage of the free speech clause, and asks only that they have walked through any open doors toward fuller implication of the values underlying the free speech clause, at least until their speech is clearly on a MOPIC. This incentive-based approach is further justified by the frequent defense raised by speakers to the effect that they should be considered experts on the subject in question, informing the public on matters of potential public significance.[25] It is not amiss to ask experts not to simply disdain opportunities to couch their message more impersonally, or more broadly, in view of the interests they themselves assume to be at stake.

The approach outlined here also has the virtue of avoiding a motive inquiry by courts in difficult cases, where the speaker's motive is often mixed, consisting of a desire to promote both purely personal as well as more impersonal interests.[26] Equally importantly, our incentive-based approach reduces the risk that the uncertainties in our middle-ground cases will tend to chill constructive critical speech,[27] along with reducing the uncertainties themselves. A speaker who wants to be classified as speaking on a matter of public interest, if the case is otherwise close, can formulate a speech in such a way as to bump up against detectable obstacles to further generalization of content and audience. The incentive approach thus lends some measure of non-arbitrary predictability to judicial results, thereby reducing the realistic basis for any chilling effect on protection-worthy speech that this approach encourages. However, speeches of identical content, subject matter, and audience, may or may not be accorded MOPIC status, depending upon the speaker's ability at the time to easily generalize.

THE LIMITED CONTRIBUTION OF CONCEPTUAL ANALYSIS

However the concept of a matter of public or general interest or concern is formulated, the distinctions between the public and the private or personal, and between the various senses of public interest, are

unavoidable.   Such distinctions are notoriously
problematic, but they can help crystalize precisely
what ought to be encouraged in order to promote and
defend the values underlying freedom of speech. ·

It has been rightly recognized that "disputes
over the boundaries between the 'public' and 'private'
realms are among the central issues of public moral
discourse."[28]   Private and public activities may be
thought to be in fact inseparable.[29]   Private and
public may be thought to be simply alternative aspects
of the same interest.[30]   The more general public
versus private distinction has drawn increasing
criticism.[31]

There is much that rings true in Professor Duncan
Kennedy's well-known discussion of the conceptual
disintegration of the public versus private
distinction.[32]   Even if it is true, however, that "one
simply loses one's ability to take the public/private
distinction seriously as a description, as an
explanation, or as a justification of anything,"[33] it
is hardly clear what follows from this line of
reasoning.   The distinction, in the abstract, between
the public and the private may in fact be prone to
unravel.   Adjectives are not employed, however, simply
in the abstract.   The terms public or private, in this
sense, have referents.   There is no inherent dynamic
of staged decline in the concept of, for example, a
public telephone.   An individual can walk into a
drugstore today, inquire after a public phone, and
provoke no greater demand for clarification today, or
tomorrow, than fifty years ago.   If the concept of
public telephone is not pellucid and sharp-edged, it
is at least serviceable and can be widely employed in
consistent fashion.   The question then becomes whether
public and private interests are more like the concept
of public and private phones, or like the concept of
public and private in the abstract.

For the skeptics, the concept of a public
interest, or the public interest, is hardly more
tractable than how Professor Kennedy would view the
broader public-private distinction.   It has been said,
for example, that "there is no public-interest theory
worthy of the name...."[34]   More specifically, the
argument has been made that judges are unable to make
principled distinctions between public interests and
private interests.[35]   The concept of public interest
may indeed be in a "state of confusion,"[36] but it may
equally clearly be indispensable, in light of our
collectively accepted values.[37]   Fortunately, the
concept of the public interest need not be entirely
clear and unequivocal in order to do some practical
work, and it need not be made so in order to make

progress along the lines suggested by this chapter.

One crucial observation, validated by examining the relevant case opinions, is that the concept of public interest may be used in some contexts in a subjective sense, what does the public actually care about, or concern itself with?[38] "Public interest," however, is also used in a more objective sense, in which something may be a matter of public interest even if no one, or only a few people, happen to recognize it as such, or subjectively care about the matter.[39] For example, an obscure scientist may draft an early paper on the depletion of the ozone layer, or an obscure political group may publish its radical manifesto. Both are on matters of public interest, whether or not the public, or any significant segment of the public, cares about either the speech or the subject matter.

The recognizable free speech value may be implicated by at least some speech on matters of public interest in the subjective sense.   It is equally clear, however, that such free speech values may be deeply implicated by some speech that concerns a matter of public interest in only the normative or objective sense. A contrary result would mean that a government that successfully brainwashed or intimidated the public into indifference with regard to political matters could rightly claim that discussion of such matters was then not on any matter of public interest. Dissenting speech would, on such a theory, fail the tests of <u>Connick</u> and <u>Greenmoss</u>, as the speech would not draw significant attention and comment. Any sensible theory of free speech must pose greater problems for a totalitarian regime than that.

The role of the more objective sense of public interest should emphasize the potentially misleading quality of the more subjective formulation of matters of public concern.   It is true that cases such as <u>Connick</u> and <u>Greenmoss</u> refer more commonly to public "concern" rather than to public "interest." The logic of these two cases commits them, however, to attend to more than merely subjective concerns of the public. Both the Supreme Court and lower federal courts have treated public concern as synonymous with public interest.[40] Even where the Court refers to "speech on matters of public concern,"[41] it is evident that the Court desires to protect "speech that matters" or speech concerning "the legitimacy of the political process,"[42] whether or not the speech is popularly accepted, or whether or not the speech rouses the attention of the media, or of any significant element of the public.

The Court should inquire not into whether the

speech itself matters, but, as a minimum improvement, whether the subject of the speech matters. The latter inquiry, though still controversial, is somewhat less subject to ideological abuse. It is easier to say that speech from an unpopular political viewpoint does not matter than it is to say that its subject, the legitimacy of the political process, for example, does not matter. Similarly, any judicial inquiry into whether the speech is important, or even on an important issue or concern, should be avoided. While an "important/unimportant" distinction has some judicial currency,[43] the potential for arbitrary or politicized use of such a classification renders it unworkable.[44]

To the extent that courts may prefer to think in terms of matters of public interest rather than matters of public concern, they should, from the perspective of promoting and defending free speech values, construe public interest in a broad sense. Professor David Braybrooke has pointed out, for example, that some issues, desegregation or slavery versus emancipation, are discussed and debated in terms of human rights, the demands of justice, or freedom, rather than through consideration of the public interest.[45] Narrowly conceived, the public interest may seem too calculative or merely too aggregative to capture what is at stake in such debates. Such matters, whether anyone is actually concerned about them or not, must count as MOPICs on any credible theory.

While the term public interest should be broadly construed in this sense, the aim to promote and defend the values underlying the free speech clause may lead to a decline in application of the term in some cases in which it would seem literally applicable. Media gossip about celebrities, for example, is often a subject in which much of the public happens to take a temporary actual subjective interest or concern. If such gossip is, and is intended to be, merely entertaining, without any implication for any public issue or potential public issue, then there is a case to be made for declining to recognize such speech as speech on a matter of public interest and concern. One should consider anew the classic fusillade of Warren and Brandeis:

> [T]he supply creates the demand....Even gossip apparently harmless when widely and persistently circulated, is potent for evil. It both belittles and perverts. It belittles by inverting the relative importance of things, thus dwarfing the

thoughts and aspirations of a people....Easy of comprehension, appealing to that weak side of human nature which is never wholly cast down....no one can be surprised that it usurps the place of interest in brains capable of other things. Triviality destroys at once robustness of thought and delicacy of feeling.[46]

Warren and Brandeis show few qualms about presuming to distinguish the important from the unimportant. While this is a course not without risk, it can be said in their defense that they are not seeking to distinguish important from unimportant political viewpoints, or issues. They would not claim for themselves, or entrust to others, the power to neutrally and reliably sort out important from trivial political ideas. Some judgments as to relative importance in the realm of public policy are, however, both defensible and inevitable. Generally, a constitutional right is more judicially important than a conflicting nonconstitutional right or claim. The values commonly thought to underlie the free speech clause may reasonably be said to be, for free speech purposes, more important than other, unrelated values.

Even true mere gossip of the sort decried by Warren and Brandeis may be said to not significantly promote, or in fact to inhibit, the realization of the basic purposes underlying the free speech clause, even if multitudes happen to take an interest in the matter. It is difficult to imagine how mere gossip promotes self-development, contributes to the pursuit of public or political truth, furthers democratic decision making, helps balance social stability and change, or restrains governmental tyranny, any more than a wide variety of other activities not protected by the free speech clause.

Rather than dwell upon this perhaps unsympathetic point, we may note instead that there is one other question on which some progress can be made at the conceptual level. This is whether speech that is commercial in content, or that is about some commercial matter, can count as speech on a matter of public interest. Despite the contemporary expansionist inclination to protect, or even strongly protect, speech that goes beyond proposing a commercial transaction, but is still essentially commercial in nature,[47] we should be skeptical in this regard, in view of the minimal or nonexistent relationship between much commercial speech and the recognized free speech values. This question however, cannot be answered sensibly in the abstract. One cannot simply take an instance of speech, see what broad type or category the speech falls into, and grant or deny the speech MOPIC status on that basis. There is a relevant difference between a price proposal by A to B and a Mobil op-ed discussion of energy independence. One should instead, in applying the theory outlined here, look to the breadth or narrowness of the particular speech, as actually formulated by the speaker. In a close case, it should be determined whether the speech could have been further generalized, under the circumstances, by the speaker.

Focusing on the subject matter of the speech, rather than on the speech itself, encourages the judicial error of unduly emphasizing the category of the speech, with the category being taken by the court at its broadest, most expansive level. This error is illustrated by the declaration of the New Jersey Supreme Court in Dairy Stores, Inc. v. Sentinel Publishing Co.,[48] that "matters of public interest include such essentials of life as food and water."[49] The Court reasoned simply that "[a]s an essential of human life, drinking water is a paradigm of legitimate public concern. For this decision, it suffices to conclude that drinking water is such a subject."[50]

It is possible to do better than this, even without any judicial inquiry into the importance or cogency of the particular speech at issue. There is a detectable difference in level of generality of implication between "the town's only drinking well is polluted," and "this particular bottle of mineral water was flat." It need not be determined whether the speech may be easily generalized to establish that these two statements, although they both address a subject essential to human life, need not be considered equally speech on matters of public interest, in any context.

This skepticism as to the usefulness of a broad categorization of a speech as economic or commercial in order to resolve whether the speech is on a matter of public interest does not imply, of course, that economics and commerce are invariably utterly alien to free speech values. Free speech protection rightly extends beyond the realm of the political, narrowly conceived.[51] One reason for this is that for many or all citizens, speech about some economic or commercial matters may contain a considerable breadth of implication concerning matters central to the social order.

The reasoning of the recent Supreme Court decision in Greenmoss[52] should be viewed with suspicion because the decision tends to unduly exclude the economic or broadly commercial from the realm of matters of public interest. Of course, a coal company statement broadly disclaiming responsibility for acid rain, or a gasoline company advertisement discussing fuel conservation would normally be thought to implicate the public interest. However, one portion of the <u>Greenmoss</u> plurality's reasoning was that Dun & Bradstreet's credit report, falsely reporting the bankruptcy of Greenmoss Builders to five subscribers on the stipulation that the report was to be disseminated no further, was classifiable as "hardy" speech.[53] It was thought to be "hardy" speech, in the sense that the speech was less likely to be deterred by the threatened effects of state libel law, since it was "solely motivated by the desire for profit."[54]

The plurality's theory was that profit-motivated speech is less likely to be deterred than speech from other motives.[55] This theory, despite judicial acceptance,[56] does not carry sufficient plausibility to help with the MOPIC distinction. Common sense suggests the possibility that speech motivated by principle, as opposed to profit, may often be hardier. Ideological or religious commitment, unto the extreme of martyrdom, might be crudely defined in terms of the willingness of the speaker to risk substantial state-imposed costs for speaking. Much profit-driven speech, however, may be barely worthwhile to the speaker, even in the absence of additional state regulation. It should be expected that profit-driven speech would tend to be deterred, or in fact to cease, in situations where the anticipated costs exceed the marginal revenues anticipated,[57] where the profit-motivated speech qualifies as a public good,[58] and where it does not. Even if a speaking corporation is able to obtain payment for the social benefits created by its profit-driven speech, the speech may well be on a matter of public interest. An example might be one oligopolist's timely reporting that all of the production of a fellow oligopolist has been poisoned.

The assumption that profit-driven speech tends to be relatively hardy, therefore, is doubtful. There is no need to overreact, however, by being oversolicitous of all commercial speech. It has been argued, for example, that "there is a high degree of public interest in the kind of information obtained"[59] in credit reports. The point is that courts easily can and should look beyond the kind of speech involved, for example, a credit report, to the actual and potential scope of the audience and the message. At least some credit reports, perhaps leaving unsurprisingly unchanged the credit status of a small firm in a big city, where the audience for the credit report is vanishingly small, involve speech that is simply not on a matter of public interest in the relevant constitutional sense.

The limited circulation of a credit report is a legitimate consideration that is entitled to some weight in the decision as to whether the credit report should qualify as speech on a matter of public interest. Limited circulation of an idea, or even its purely private memorialization, of course does not necessarily bar MOPIC status to the speech. If all other factors are equal, however, the larger the percentage of the relevant potential audience that the speaker chooses to address, the more constitutionally significant the speech becomes. Again, if for no other reason, broader dissemination implies a chance for wider participation, by a greater audience, in democratic decision making. Thus it is an overstatement to conclude, as the Tenth Circuit has in Sunward Corp. v. Dun & Bradstreet, Inc.[60], a recent libel case, that "the reports in Greenmoss and 340 reports here have no constitutional significance."[61] The scope of intended audience is of some weight under our theory, though perhaps not of decisive weight in the Tenth Circuit case.

Overall, those who have expressed anxiety over the Court's refusal to find speech on a matter of public concern in Greenmoss can take some comfort from the developing case law. Even in the face of Greenmoss, lower courts recently have found speech that is largely about economic or commercial matters to be speech on a matter of public interest. These recent cases involve such matters as the propriety of a bank's loans to its former president and founder,[62] a magazine's loosely described "investment advice" about a rival investment opportunities magazine,[63] a local timeshare condominium controversy where the libel plaintiff was simultaneously running for town council,[64] and newspaper articles describing the financial dealings of private plaintiffs who were then the subject of numerous regulatory and law enforcement investigations.[65] There evidently has been no judicial rush to conclude that the presence of economic or commercial subject matter elements disqualifies the speech at issue from MOPIC status.

APPLYING THE READY GENERALIZABILITY TEST TO THE PUBLIC EMPLOYEE DISCIPLINE CASES

The number of cases in the federal appellate courts in which a public employee has sought redress for being disciplined allegedly because of what the employee asserts to be speech on a matter of public interest is quite substantial and is growing rapidly. Here, the ready generalizability speech test can only be illustrated rather than fairly tested. There will be some public employee speech dismissal cases which can be easily decided and in which the particular theory used to reach the result, against or in favor of MOPIC status, will be largely immaterial.[66] There is, however, at least one case in which the speech could have been determined as on a MOPIC under any theory, but the court, contrary to all logic, failed to find the speech to be on a MOPIC. The best that can be hoped for is that this case is simply a rare aberration, defensible on no cogent theory.

This incongruous case, Mings v. Department of Justice, may best be explained as a judicial overreaction to unattractive facts. The petitioner in Mings had been removed in 1985 from his job as a border patrol agent in Lubbock, Texas.[67] The petitioner's removal was based in part on the content of a letter he wrote on official stationery to an agency assistant district director for investigations. The Merit Systems Protection Board and the federal circuit found the letter to contain "insulting and abusive language disparaging Catholics, Hispanics and agency employees."[68]

The letter partially focused on a particular agency form, I-293, which was used nationwide by the Immigration and Naturalization Service to notify aliens of the holding of hearings and the dates and locations of those hearings. The letter's references to this form may help account for why the letter was sent to a responsible internal official, rather than to a newspaper, for example, if any such explanation is required. The thrust of the petitioner's letter was much broader than a simple quibble over the drafting of some obscure internal government form.

The transition from a complaint about a form to a sweeping complaint about a broad, plainly controversial, government policy began with the petitioner's assertion that "[a]ll the I-293 accomplishes is to give an illegal alien more time to become further entrenched and hinder the Service efforts in removing him."[69] The focus of the letter then broadened to a level of panoptic generality: the petitioner's study of the history of predominantly Catholic countries had allowed him to conclude that "all of them are corrupt, backward, beggarly countries."[70] The essential thrust of the letter, however, was unmistakable; that the Service is too lax, from the point of view of the broad national interest, in processing and deporting undocumented aliens, due to factors such as endemic, pervasive ignorance, disloyalty, or incompetence.

This brief summary of the letter in question fairly depicts its thrust. At points, the level of generality that is reached is nearly Weberian. It is clear that the writer was concerned preeminently with the merits of broad national policy, and not simply with the technicalities of forms, internal procedures, intra-office bickering, or individual cases and officers. It would also be disingenuous to claim that the subject of the undue laxity, or undue severity or oppressiveness, of treatment of alleged illegal immigrants along the Mexican border was not a matter of public interest in 1984, at least to a significant sector of the public.

Mings represents an obvious case, as it seems readily manageable on any theory of MOPIC speech, and can fall under the ready generalizability theory as well, as it seems impertinent to ask whether the border control agent who wrote the letter could have cheaply broadened the relevant scope of his focus. Unfortunately, the Court of Appeals reached a flatly contrary result. The Court conceded that although the letter was understandably directed to a responsible agency official rather than to the public at large, that fact would not preclude a finding of MOPIC status.[71] The Court concluded, however, that the content of the letter was more in the nature of a personal, internal agency grievance relating to a particular agency form, and that the petitioner's speech was therefore on a matter of only personal interest, rather than on a matter of public concern or debate.[72]

A fair reading of the letter as reported by the Court of Appeals makes the Court's conclusion in this respect strained at best. Clearly the problem is that it is not easy to give the letter a fair reading. Certain statements in the letter are scurrilous. A fair-minded court could read the letter and conclude that the Service did not act unreasonably in removing the petitioner from his position on other grounds. The letter itself suggests the petitioner's inability to perform satisfactorily in certain job-related respects.

What the court of appeals could have done instead, as Connick v. Myers[73] makes quite clear, is to have decided the case against the speaker without the absurd conclusion that the actual content of the letter did not relate to a matter of legitimate public concern. Under Connick, as derived from Pickering v. Board of Education,[74] the Court could have granted the fact that the petitioner's speech addressed a matter of public interest. The Court could then have barred his recovery by finding, as a matter of law, that the employee's free speech interest in this case was outweighed by the Service's interest in the fair and efficient operation of its programs.[75] The Court of Appeals in this case, though well aware of this escape route,[76] chose not to use it, perhaps out of an unconscious distaste for the viewpoint expressed in the letter.

In any event, Mings can be fairly characterized as a rare aberration.[77] Few legal tests on central, frequently litigated matters can effortlessly account for all judicial opinions, without exception. The operation of the ready generalizability approach will be illustrated next by filling in the cells of the matrix of possibilities.

CLOSE CASES ON THE MOPIC ISSUE IN THE CONTEXT OF PUBLIC EMPLOYMENT DISCHARGE

One difficulty in testing the normative appeal of our approach is that the courts are not in a position to retroactively adopt this theory, and therefore their published opinions have often not focused on, or even reported, the actual language used by the speaker, but instead label the general category the speech might be said to fall into. Rather than examining the degree of generality of the actual speech, some courts simply describe the speech at issue and do not reproduce the language employed. Not having the actual language, or excerpts therefrom, reproduced in the opinion, one can only guess as to how the MOPIC issue would be decided under the proposed theory in this chapter. In some cases, though, a call can be hazarded.

As a reminder, the theory is intended only for the quite common, middle-ground, close cases on which reasonable minds differ. The hope is not to show the unreasonableness of contrary judicial results, but to legitimately encourage more valuable speech activity and to reward or sanction the speaker in a given case based on the speaker's reasonable utilization of the speech opportunities available under the circumstances.

With this caveat, we may consider the recent case of Ohse v. Hughes.[78] In this case, the plaintiff was terminated from his job as an Adult Probation Officer. From one perspective, it seems appropriate, based on the reported facts, to view the case as simply a garden variety intra-office squabble based on the speaker's own interests being thwarted in circumstances either caused or exacerbated by friction between the plaintiff speaker and the Chief Probation Officer. The plaintiff's speech, however self-serving or otherwise questionably motivated, and however unrelated to the genuine causes of his dissatisfaction, bears some examination.

The appellate court, while not reproducing the language actually employed, indicated that the plaintiff detailed, primarily to relevant supervisors, serious abuses in a publicly funded probation office that were later admitted to be true by the chief of the office. Ohse revealed the drinking of alcohol by probation employees during business hours, the falsifying of mileage charges to cover meal expenses, the inappropriate taking of sick and vacation days, situations where chief probation officer Hughes misappropriated public funds for unauthorized uses, and that members of the office were sleeping on the job.[79] While these alleged abuses might be considered unsurprising or petty when viewed individually or even collectively, the Seventh Circuit found it clear that these occurrences involved matters of "public concern which would trigger 'debate...vital to an informed decision making by the electorate.'"[80]

The crucial determinant under the ready generalizability theory would require an inquiry into whether, under the circumstances, the employee-speaker could, without distorting his message and without changing his own basic, personal capabilities, have significantly generalized his message, at low cost, so as to more clearly or significantly implicate the basic free speech values. In Ohse, apparently no significant low cost generalization was possible. It was not that the plaintiff's speech focused on isolated incidents or mere particular personalities, where a broader lesson was begging to be drawn. The theme of the plaintiff's speech appeared to describe a continuing, systemic pattern of modest corruption or abuse of the public trust. It is simply not clear where the plaintiff would be expected to go in terms of significant further generalization. Putting the matter in broader historical or sociological perspective would not ordinarily be expected of someone in the plaintiff's position. Any such exertion on the part of the plaintiff would seem gratuitous and contrived. Similarly, the plaintiff could reasonably have been chastised for broadening the audience for his accusations to include the general public at this stage, before the responsible officials had a chance to examine and evaluate his charges.

As has been demonstrated, there need be no fear that deciding close MOPIC issues in this fashion will allow culpable public employees to hide behind a smokescreen of talk on matters of public interest.

The Court may decide as a matter of law[81] that the
interest of the plaintiff in speaking out on matters
of public concern is outweighed by the government's
interest, as employer, in efficiently organized public
offices.[82]   One can only assume, of course, that
courts also take into consideration the public's
interest in the speech, as well as the interests of
the speaker, and that courts appreciate that the
plaintiff's speech might tend to enhance, as well as
impair, the efficient operation of the agency.[83]

As a further test of the ready generalizability
theory, the related close cases may be considered in
which the theory would find a MOPIC, but in which the
Court did not in fact so find. A possible example of
this sort of case is Smith v. Wythe-Grayson Regional
Library Board.[84] In Smith, the plaintiff alleged that
she had been terminated from her position as a public
librarian based at least in part on her
constitutionally protected speech. The Court,
however, held that her speech did not address a matter
of public concern. The Court indicated in this regard
that

> at a Library Board meeting, Mrs. Smith felt
> the amount being offered to the library
> system by the United Way was not adequate
> and hardly worth pursuing. I believe that
> this kind of statement in reality does not
> deal with a matter of public concern in that
> the public would probably have little or no
> interest, other than tangentially, in the
> exact amount of money that came to the
> library system through the United Way.[85]

This appears to be a close case, and under our
theory it is difficult to resolve without a more
precise account of what the plaintiff actually said.
Clearly, the plaintiff was not focusing essentially on
some personal grievance. The Court may in fact be
unfairly degeneralizing the speaker's remarks, as
described above, by characterizing them as focused on
"the exact amount of money" involved.[86] The Court's
own prior description seems to suggest the possibility
that the speaker was, in a broader sense, advocating
that the library system consider dropping out of the
United Way entirely. It may be said that the
speaker's remarks could be generalized even further,
by arguing that the logic of the library system's
dropping out of the United Way should apply to other
United Way participants as well. There is no
indication, however, that the speaker was in a
position to responsibly make such a generalization.

Smith may therefore represent a close case of speech that should be considered as being on a matter of public interest.   Other recent public employee discipline cases may also fall into this category, despite the courts' holding otherwise. Representative examples may include Fiorillo v. United States Department of Justice[87] and Yoggerst v. Hedges.[88] Fiorillo is of special interest because of the Court's conclusion that "[i]t is the nature of the whole communication that must be reviewed to determine whether it is of 'public concern', not sentences taken in isolation."[89]   This rule has the appearance of noncontroversial common sense, but on reflection, it cannot be entirely right.

Imagine a long speech in which the speaker utters exactly one sentence that, in isolation, was clearly and indisputably on a matter of public interest. The Court may, under the Fiorillo approach, decide that the speech as a whole was not on a matter of public interest. If so, the case is over, and the employee loses. What if, however, the employer cared only about the single sentence that in isolation was on a matter of public interest? What if the employer fired the speaker for only that sentence, with no other grounds? The underlying policy logic of the case law and the values underlying the free speech clause would require the kind of interest-balancing inquiry between employer and employee that is only triggered after the initial finding of speech on a matter of public interest.

To balance out the examination of the public employment discipline cases, the categories of close cases in which the ready generalizability theory would yield a finding of no speech on a matter of public interest should be examined. The judicial resolution of the recent reported cases is mixed, with some courts finding speech on a MOPIC where application of the ready generalizability theory would have resulted in a finding of non-MOPIC speech. McKinley v. City of Eloy[90] is representative of these cases. McKinley involved a probationary police officer who was dismissed for allegedly criticizing, in a news interview and at a city council meeting, the City's decision not to give police officers an annual raise. The Ninth Circuit began by correctly refusing to judicially close the class of potential matters of public interest, recognizing instead the constitutional intent "to permit the public to decide for itself which issues and viewpoints merit its concern."[91]   The Ninth Circuit may have erred under our theory, however, by apparently itself generalizing the speech for the speaker.

Because the Ninth Circuit opinion does not indicate the level of generalization of the plaintiff's remarks, it is not entirely clear how broad the plaintiff's actual or fairly implied focus was, and how much breadth was simply supplied by the court on review.[92] To the extent that the plaintiff's speech focused on the strength of desire of the police officers for an annual raise, and their frustration, anger, or disappointment with the City over this issue,[93] his speech seems readily generalizable, hence not MOPIC speech under the theory. The Court's own observation that at least beyond some point, "compensation levels undoubtedly affect the ability of the city to attract and retain qualified police personnel"[94] merely indicates how easily the speaker could have added, through relevant further generalization, to the clarity of the MOPIC issue, assuming his speech did not in fact address such issues.

A case bordering this category, and on which the Supreme Court has recently shed some light, is Rankin v. McPherson.[95] Plaintiff McPherson was terminated from her clerical position at a county constable's office when, upon learning of the attempted assassination of President Reagan, she stated to a co-worker, "If they go for him again, I hope they get him."[96] The trial court found that the language was seriously meant and not merely political hyperbole, that the plaintiff's language was not speech on a matter of public interest, and that the constable's office need not be "required to employ a person who 'rides with the cops and cheers for the robbers.'"[97] The Fifth Circuit reversed, however, finding the plaintiff's speech to be on a matter of public interest, and that her position was too ministerial to be expected to have significant potential for office disruption, or significant effects on office efficiency or morale.

The Supreme Court in affirming the Fifth Circuit focused on the undoubted truth that "the life and death of the President are obviously matters of public concern."[98] The plaintiff's speech, however, was causally remote from the actual assassination event, or any subsequent events. Under the ready generalizability theory, her speech would probably not be considered speech on a matter of public interest, unless several assumptions are made. If her remarks were simply a bare expression of preference, devoid of any even minimal attempt at elaboration, reasoning, justification, or explanation, a court could find that the speech was not on a matter of public interest. After all, the plaintiff's speech in such a case would be almost purely self-referential, autobiographically reporting a certain mere undefended emotive preference of the speaker, however intensely held.   That the plaintiff simply feels strongly about some important hypothetical event need not in itself be a matter of public interest, and her own speech reporting her strong feeling need not be speech on a matter of public interest.

There is of course the possibility that the plaintiff would have elaborated upon, or generalized, her declaration but for her being situationally blocked from doing so, or that she did in fact so elaborate upon her comments.   Our theory does not require generalization where generalization was in fact prevented by immediate interrogation by a speaker's supervisor.   In addition, the possibility of what might be called contextual or antecedent generalization must also be recognized.   In this case, the plaintiff testified without contradiction that her statement about the attempted assassination was made at the end of a discussion about the President's policies with a co-worker.[99]   The preceding discussion by the plaintiff supplies generalization under the ready generalizability theory.   On these assumptions, it seems unlikely that the plaintiff's speech could in fact be easily generalized to a further degree, but that the plaintiff frivolously cast opportunities for further generalization away.   McPherson would under the ready generalizability theory therefore involve non-MOPIC speech only if the plaintiff's speech was a passing, unpursued, unintroduced remark, but should be considered MOPIC speech under the facts presented.[100]

The burden of showing no easy further generalization of the speech should logically rest on the speaker, as the party asserting the constitutional defense to the job discipline.   However, for practical reasons, it seems best to require the employer to bear the burden of showing further generalizability, in some particular respect.   Otherwise, the speaker is placed in the logically demanding position of having to negate an infinite set of possible further ready generalizations.

The final category of the public employment discipline cases, which need not be dwelled upon, consists of close cases in which the proposed approach and that of the actual deciding court converge on a finding of speech not on a matter of public interest. An example of such a case is Rowland v. Mad River Local School District.[101]   In this case, the plaintiff Rowland's contract as a public school guidance counselor was not renewed allegedly at least in part because she informed school personnel of her bisexuality.[102]

While the rights of bisexual teachers may well be a matter of public concern generally, and while this particular case may have become something of a local <u>cause</u> <u>celebre</u>,[103] this case illustrates the application of the ready generalizability theory. The plaintiff apparently reported her sexual preferences in a narrowly autobiographical, contextless way. Apparently the plaintiff declined the opportunity to even begin to tie her own circumstances to any broader concerns.[104] That the plaintiff chose to only disclose a personal fact rather than to elaborate in even a limited way, within the limits of her ability under the circumstances, is significant. Not every civil rights case is also a free speech case.

CLOSE CASES ON THE MOPIC ISSUE IN THE LIBEL LAW CONTEXT

The approach to the MOPIC issue in the defamation cases precisely parallels those cases discussed above in connection with the public employment discipline cases. Many of the recent cases, of which <u>Greenmoss</u> is preeminent, have been referred to above, and the reader is invited to trace out the implications of the ready generalizability approach for any number of cases.

If enough confidence can be developed in the ability of this approach to sort out close MOPIC versus non-MOPIC cases in the defamation area, there may be a significant special payoff. It may then be possible to dispense with any consideration of the often difficult issue of whether the plaintiff in a defamation case is a private figure or a public figure of some sort. If the speech is on a matter of public interest, it may be worth a given level of protection through the free speech clause, regardless of the status of the plaintiff. If the speech is not on a matter of public interest, it should presumably receive a lesser degree of constitutional protection, even if the plaintiff in the libel action is a public figure. This approach would correspond with the underlying concern for the defense and pursuit of the values underlying the free speech clause. It would also dispense with the embarrassing legal fiction that public figures have consented to, or assumed the risk of, not merely harsh public evaluation, but also grossly negligent defamation.[105]

With the possibility of increased clarity and logic in the constitutional law of defamation at stake, consider a brief contrast in outcomes under the ready generalizability theory in two defamation cases,

both of which involve allegations of organized crime
associations.   In <u>Mutafis v. Erie Ins. Exchange</u>,[106]
the speech at issue was an insurance company
employee's placing a memorandum in internal company
claim files stating that Mutafis was "associated with
mafia very heavily."[107]   In <u>Philadelphia Newspapers,
Inc. v. Hepps</u>,[108] the speech was that of a
Philadelphia newspaper that, in a series of articles,
asserted that Hepps had ties to organized crime and
used those ties to influence Pennsylvania state
governmental processes.[109]

Both of these instances of alleged defamatory
speech focus on organized crime.   Organized crime is
undoubtedly a matter of public interest and concern.
Yet under the ready generalizability theory, the
speech in <u>Mutafis II</u> is best categorized as easily
non-MOPIC speech, and the speech in <u>Hepps</u> as easily on
a MOPIC.   Neither is a close case appropriate for the
ready generalizability approach.   <u>Hepps</u> involved wide
dissemination of speech illuminating alleged
corruption in state government.   Any plausible theory
one cares to enlist must find this to be speech on a
matter of public interest.   <u>Mutafis II</u>, however,
involved speech that was not intended for circulation
at any point to more than a handful of insiders, and
the speech had no institutional point or implication
other than to discourage unwarranted financial
exposure by the insurance company in the case of a
single individual.

It is possible to argue that if <u>Mutafis II</u> can
somehow be seen as a close case and therefore
appropriate for our theory, the defendants' speech in
<u>Mutafis II</u> should be classified as on a matter of
public interest based on our theory, as it would be
costly or impractical for the speaker in <u>Mutafis II</u>
either to circulate his thoughts more widely, as to
competitors, or to expand his remarks into an essay on
the insidiousness of organized crime.   All of this
analysis demonstrates that the case is in fact not
close, because the institution of the confidential
insurance files, in nature and purpose, is largely
foreign to the service or exercise of our basic free
speech values.   The speaker may have bumped up against
the speech-value enhancing limitations of the
institution of the insurance company, but the
confidential insurance company files, by their nature
and purpose, have little to do with the aims
underlying the free speech clause.[110]

CONCLUSION

This chapter has offered an illustration of a free

speech values-based, incentive-oriented approach to resolving questions of inclusion and exclusion at the borders of protected free speech. In the particular context we have examined, the ambiguity of the concept of the public interest, and the difficulty of consistent application of this concept in close cases, does provoke a certain natural impatience. The concept is widely used in the law, however, and is in fact indispensible, in that it captures genuinely fundamental concerns. Any conceivable replacement for the concept would involve much the same difficulty of application. Disposing of the concept would not make the legal landscape less ambiguous and more logical, but simply unrecognizable. This chapter has therefore recommended a principled yet pragmatic approach to resolving the increasing number of the most difficult sorts of issues involving this distinction in the important areas of public employee discipline based on speech, in defamation, and less explicitly, but by the same logic, in privacy cases[111] and, by extension, in other free speech areas as well. The aim has been to lend some additional predictability and consistency to the decisions, while strategically promoting the values that lead us to constitutionalize free speech rights in the first place.

Of course, there are other unrelated possible general mechanisms for deciding close free speech cases. Among academics particularly, there may be some sympathy, for example, for a rule that would decide some or all close free speech cases with an eye toward reducing a perceived bias, inequality, skewing, or impoverishment of the societal practice of freedom of speech in favor of well-entrenched, powerful, wealthy interests. The aim of such a rule would be to promote egalitarianism in the exercise of freedom of speech, for the sake of equity, enlightenment, or a "richer" debate on public issues.[112]

We cannot address here the broad question of the extent to which the logic of freedom of speech, itself or in combination with other sound ethical principles, requires that practical speech opportunities be equalized. We can suggest, however, the impracticality of resolving close cases of freedom of speech with the aim of equalizing speech opportunities, or reducing the illegitimate suppression of institutionally disfavored speech.

It is one thing, in our theory, for a judge to ask whether a speaker could easily have been less narrowly personally focused in her remarks. It is another thing for a judge to ask whether a particular ruling will reduce unjust inequality, or "skew," or bias, in the distribution of practical speech opportunities. Obviously, the judge cannot merely consult or recur to the determination of the market, or of the ballot box, or of some apparent societal consensus, as the legitimacy of these institutional influences is precisely what is being called into question. But if no such reference is intended, it becomes unclear how the judge is to recognize "skew," or unfairness, or "repressive tolerance" except on dismayingly controversial assumptions.

At a practical level, how would the judge be expected to recognize "skew," or tainting? Should the judge focus on processes of repression, or on suspicious end-states? Why not insist on whatever pattern of speech that would emerge from equalization of incomes, or of wealth? How much equalization? Should the judicial system as a whole be aiming at an ideal of less procapitalist and more prosocialist speech? Would half-capitalist and half-socialist speech be the best distribution? How should the judge allocate speech subsidies within an obviously fragmented generally socialist or progressive camp? Should we give a full subsidy to a particular Trotskyite group, and then another full subsidy to a variant Trotskyite group claiming that the first group does not speak for them? Is there a case for enhancing diversity or richness by judicially encouraging or promoting the speech of arguably underrepresented but plainly nonprogressive forces or groups? How do we recognize progressivity, or whatever it is we are to be enhancing? We will of course need some sort of theory explaining why promotion of the speech of the marginalized political left is more justifiable than promotion of the speech of the marginalized political right.

Such an approach to strategically deciding close free speech cases, it would seem, simply presumes an exceptionally controversial general theory of politics. The approach outlined in this chapter, in contrast, while not wholly ideologically neutral, at least offers the virtue of theoretical unambitiousness, if not modesty.

NOTES

1. Gallie, Essentially Contested Concepts, 56 Proc. of the Aristotelian Society 167 (1956).

2. See, e.g., Rosenbloom v. Metromedia, Inc., 403 U.S. 29, 32 (1971) (plurality opinion) ("the report of an event of 'public or general interest'") (citing Warren & Brandeis, The Right to Privacy, 4 Harv. L. Rev. 193, 214 (1890)).

3. See Warren & Brandeis, supra note 2.

4. 472 U.S. 749 (1985) (plurality opinion).

5. 461 U.S. 138 (1983).

6. See Mount Healthy City School Dist. Bd. of Educ. v. Doyle, 429 U.S. 274 (1977).

7. 472 U.S. at 759. See also Meiklejohn, Public Speech and Libel Litigation: Are They Compatible?, 14 Hofstra L. Rev. 547, 551-52 (1986).

8. 472 U.S. at 759.

9. Id. at 763.

10. 472 U.S. at 761 (quoting Connick, 461 U.S. at 147-48). This is an inquiry of law, rather than fact. See Connick, 461 U.S. at 148 n.7, 150 n.10.

11. 472 U.S. at 786 (Brennan, J., dissenting).

12. Id. See also Langvardt, Public Concern Revisited: A New Role for an Old Doctrine in the Constitutional Law of Defamation, 21 Val. U.L. Rev. 241, 258 (1987) (standards for whether a particular speech addresses a matter of public concern as being the "chief question left unanswered by Greenmoss").

13. See, e.g., Sisler v. Gannett Co., 104 N.J. 256, 268, 516 A.2d 1083, 1089 (1986) (quoting Dairy Stores, Inc. v. Sentinel Publishing Co., 104 N.J. 125, 144, 516 A.2d 220, 229 (1986)).

14. Diversified Management, Inc. v. Denver Post, Inc., 653 P.2d 1103, 1111 (Colo. 1982) (en banc) (Erickson, J., dissenting). See also Meiklejohn, supra note 7, at 551.

15. Allen v. Scribner, 812 F.2d 426, 430 (9th Cir.), modified, 828 F.2d 1445 (9th Cir. 1987).

16. McKinley v. City of Eloy, 705 F.2d 1110, 1113 (9th Cir. 1983).

17. See Note, The Public Employee's Right of Free Speech: A Proposal for a Fresh Start, 55 U. Cin. L. Rev. 449, 449 (1986) [hereinafter Note, The Public Employee's Right of Free Speech] ("The lower federal courts have had difficulty applying the Supreme Court's balancing test. Therefore, the decisions in

this area are often times irreconcilable."); Note, Connick v. Myers: _New Restrictions on the Free Speech Rights of Government Employees_, 60 _Ind_. _L.J_. 339, 358-59 & n.143 (1984-1985) [hereinafter Note, _New Restrictions on the Free Speech Rights_] (characterizing the distinction as unworkable; collecting assertedly mutually inconsistent federal court cases).

18.   _See_ _Greenmoss_, 472 U.S. at 759-60.

19.   _Id_. at 760; _Connick_, 461 U.S. at 146-47.

20.   _See_ NAACP v. Claiborne Hardware Co., 458 U.S. 886, 913 (1982); Carey v. Brown, 447 U.S. 455, 467 (1980).

21.   Garrison v. Louisiana, 379 U.S. 64, 74-75 (1964), _quoted_ _in_ both _Greenmoss_, 472 U.S. at 759 _and_ _Connick_, 461 U.S. at 145.

22.   _Greenmoss_, 472 U.S. at 759; _Connick_, 461 U.S. at 146-47.

23.   _See_ Nixon v. Fitzgerald, 457 U.S. 731, 734 (1982); Renfroe v. Kirkpatrick, 722 F.2d 714 (11th Cir.) (per curiam) (teacher's unwillingness to share a job with another teacher), _cert_. _denied_, 469 U.S. 823 (1984).

24.   It may be that a person's demanding something for himself commits him to the more general implication that everyone relevantly similarly situated is similarly so entitled. _See_ the development of similar conceptions of moral reasoning in M. _Singer_, _Generalization in Ethics_ 17, 19-20, 24 (1961) _and_, over time, in R. _Hare_, _The Language of Morals_ (rev. ed. 1961); R. _Hare_, _Freedom and Reason_ (1963); R. _Hare_, _Moral Thinking: Its Levels, Method and Point_ (1981).

25.   _See_ Pickering v. Board of Educ., 391 U.S. 563, 572 (1968); Note, _The Public Employee's Right of Free Speech_, _supra_ note 17, at 454.

26.   _Cf_. _Connick_, 461 U.S. at 148 (undertaking a rather subtle inquiry into the discharged speaker's subjective motivations).

27.   _See_ Note, _New Restrictions on the Free Speech Rights_, _supra_ note 17, at 340.

28.   Brest, _Constitutional Citizenship_, 34 _Clev_. _St_. _L_. _Rev_. 175, 177 (1986) (emphasis in original).

29.   See Kreimer, Allocational Sanctions: The Problem
of Negative Rights in a Positive State, 132 U. Pa. L.
Rev. 1293, 1294-96 (1984); Seidman, Public Principle
and Private Choice: The Uneasy Case for a Boundary
Maintenance Theory of Constitutional Law, 96 Yale L.J.
1006 (1987).

30.   See Aleinikoff, Constitutional Law in the Age of
Balancing, 96 Yale L.J. 1006 (1987).

31.   See Seidman, supra note 29, at 1007.

32.   See generally Kennedy, The Stages of the Decline
of the Public/Private Distinction, 130 U. Pa. L. Rev.
1349 (1982).

33.   Id. at 1357.

34.   G. Schubert, The Public Interest 223 (1960).

35.   Farber & Frickey, The Jurisprudence of Public
Choice, 65 Tex. L. Rev. 873, 925 (1987).

36.   V. Held, The Public Interest and Individual
Interests 18 (1970).

37.   See id. R. Flathman, The Public Interest 13 (1966).

38.   See R. Flathman, supra note 37, at 16-17. It is
in this sense that the alleged restaurant behavior of
a celebrity such as Carol Burnett may be a matter of
public interest. See Burnett v. National Enquirer,
Inc., 144 Cal. App. 3d 991, 193 Cal. Rptr. 206 (1983),
appeal dismissed, 465 U.S. 1014 (1984). But see
Meiklejohn, supra note 7, at 557 (discussing arguable
public interest implications of defendant's speech for
Burnett's anti-alcoholism activities).

39.   See R. Flathman, supra note 37, at 17. Sorauf,
The Conceptual Muddle, in V Nomos: The Public
Interest 183, 186 (C. Friedrich ed. 1962).

40.   See, e.g., Pickering v. Board of Educ., 391 U.S.
563, 568 (1968); Altman v. Hurst, 734 F.2d 1240, 1244
(7th Cir.), cert. denied, 469 U.S. 982 (1984).

41.   Philadelphia Newspapers, Inc. v. Hepps, 475 U.S.
767, 774 (1986).

42.   Id.

43. See Greenberg v. Kmetko, 811 F.2d 1057, 1061 (7th
Cir.), reh'g granted, vacated en banc, 820 F.2d 897
(7th Cir. 1987); vacated, remanded in part and aff'd
in part, 840 F.2d 467 (7th Cir. 1988) (en banc); Note,
The Evolution of a Public Issue: New York Times
Through Greenmoss, 57 U. Colo. L. Rev. 773, 775 (1986).

44. See Schauer, "Private" Speech and the "Private"
Forum: Givhan v. Western Line School District, 1979
Sup. Ct. Rev. 217, 231 (P. Kurland & G. Casper eds. 1980).

45. See Braybrooke, The Public Interest: The Present
and Future of the Concept, in V Nomos: The Public
Interest 129, 131 (C. Friedrich ed. 1962).

46. See Warren & Brandeis, supra note 2, at 196.

47. See Board of Trustees of State Univ. v. Fox, 109
S. Ct. 3028, 3036 (1989).

48. Dairy Stores, Inc. v. Sentinel Publishing Co.,
104 N.J. 125, 134, 516 A.2d 220, 230 (1986).

49. Id.

50. Id.

51. See Rosenbloom v. Metromedia, Inc., 403 U.S. 29,
41 (1971) (plurality opinion); Meiklejohn, supra note
7, at 54-55.

52. See Greenmoss, 472 U.S. at 762-63.

53. Id. at 762.

54. Id.

55. Id. (citing Virginia State Bd. of Pharmacy v.
Virginia Citizens Consumer Council, Inc., 425 U.S.
748, 771-72 (1976)). See also Langvardt, supra note
12, at 250; Note, The Evolution of a Public Issue,
supra note 43 at 789.

56. See, e.g., Sunward Corp., 811 F.2d at 534
(commercial credit reports are hardy speech, unlikely
to be deterred by state regulation).

57. See R. Posner, Economic Analysis of Law ch.1 (3d
ed. 1986).

58. See Posner, Free Speech in an Economic
Perspective, 20 Suffolk U.L. Rev. 1, 20-23 (1986).

59. Langvardt, _supra_ note 12, at 256.

60. _Sunward Corp._, 811 F.2d at 533.

61. _Id._

62. Sisler v. Gannett Co., 104 N.J. 256, 516 A.2d 1083, 1089 (1986).

63. J. F. Straw v. Chase Revel, Inc., 813 F.2d 356, 362 (11th Cir. 1987).

64. McCabe v. Rattiner, 814 F.2d 839, 843 (1st Cir. 1987).

65. Diversified Management, Inc. v. Denver Post, Inc., 653 P.2d 1103, 1104, 1106 (Colo. 1982) (en banc) (pre-_Greenmoss_).

66. _See, e.g._, Nixon v. Fitzgerald, 457 U.S. 731 (1982).

67. 813 F.2d 384 (Fed. Cir. 1987).

68. _Id._ at 386, 388.

69. _Id._ at 386.

70. _Id._

71. _See id._ at 388 (citing Givhan v. Western Line Consol. School Dist., 439 U.S. 410, 413 (1979)).

72. _See id._

73. 461 U.S. 138 (1983).

74. 391 U.S. 563 (1968).

75. _See_ 461 U.S. at 142; Mount Healthy City School Dist. Bd. of Educ. v. Doyle, 429 U.S. 274 (1977).

76. _See Mings_, 813 F.2d at 837, 838-39.

77. _Cf._ Jungels v. Pierce, 638 F. Supp. 317 (N.D. Ill. 1986) _aff'd in part, rev'd in part_, 825 F.2d 1127 (7th Cir. 1987).

78. 816 F.2d 1144 (7th Cir. 1987), _vacated and remanded_, 108 S. Ct. 1070 (1988), _on remand_, 836 F.2d 22 (7th Cir. 1988) (per curiam).

79. _Id._ at 1151.

80.   Id. (quoting Pickering, 391 U.S. at 572).

81.   See, e.g., Connick, 461 U.S. at 148 n.7, 150 n.10 (deciding as a matter of law, and in light of the entire record, that a government employee's office questionnaire concerning office policy involved, in part, an issue of public concern); Allen v. Scribner, 812 F.2d 426, 430 n.8 (9th Cir.), modified, 828 F.2d 1445 (9th Cir. 1987) (deciding as a matter of law that an entomologist's public criticism of an insect eradication project was of public concern).

82.   See Ohse, 816 F.2d at 1151.

83.   As additional possible examples of close cases that may involve speech on MOPICs, under the proposed theory and as found by the court, consider Allen v. Scribner, 812 F.2d 426 (9th Cir.) (protecting public criticism by state entomologist focusing on alleged understatement of extent of California medfly infestation), modified, 828 F.2d 1445 (9th Cir. 1987); Wren v. Spurlock, 798 F.2d 1313 (10th Cir. 1986) (protecting request by teacher and nine others for official investigation of public school principal on thirty-five grounds), cert. denied, 107 S. Ct. 1287 (1987).

84.   657 F. Supp. 1216 (W.D. Va. 1987).

85.   Id. at 1220.

86.   Id.

87.   795 F.2d 1544 (Fed. Cir. 1986) (petitioner's claim that prison was still saturated with corruption found by the court to be stale news).

88.   739 F.2d 293 (7th Cir. 1984) (petitioner's expression of happiness to co-worker concerning her superior's discharge not protected; petitioner was penalized by Seventh Circuit for failing to articulate assumptions that were presumably clear to the listener from previous conversations with the speaker).

89.   Fiorillo, 795 F.2d at 1550. See also Greenberg v. Kmetko, 811 F.2d 1057, 1062 (7th Cir.) (comments made by speaker are to be considered as a whole), reh'g granted, vacated en banc, 820 F.2d 897 (7th Cir. 1987), vacated, remanded in part and aff'd in part, 840 F.2d 467 (7th Cir. 1988) (en banc).

90.   705 F.2d 1110 (9th Cir. 1983).

91.   Id. at 1114.

92.   Id.

93.   Note that alleged employee frustration and morale concerns did not reach the level of matters of public interest in Connick v. Myers, 461 U.S. 138 (1983).

94.   McKinley, 705 F.2d at 1114.

95.   107 S. Ct. 2891 (1987) (5-4 decision).

96.   Id. at 2895.

97.   Id. at 2902.

98.   Id. at 2897.

99.   Id. at 2895.

100. For other examples of possible non-MOPIC speech under this theory, where the court found otherwise, consider Koch v. City of Hutchinson, 814 F.2d 1489 (10th Cir. 1987) (plaintiff's official investigatory conclusion that a particular fire involved arson), cert. denied, 109 S. Ct. 262 (1988); Johnson v. Town of Elizabethtown, 800 F.2d 404 (4th Cir. 1986) (challenge before Town Board by clerk as to use of facsimile stamp, notarization procedure, etc.).

101. 730 F.2d 444 (6th Cir. 1984), cert. denied, 470 U.S. 1009 (1985).

102. Id. at 448.

103. See id. at 452, 453 (Edwards, J., dissenting).

104. See id. at 449.

105. See Curtis Publishing Co. v. Butts, 388 U.S. 130 (1967) (plurality opinion).

106. 775 F.2d 593 (4th Cir. 1985) (per curiam). See also 728 F.2d 672 (4th Cir. 1984) [hereinafter Mutafis I]

107. Mutafis I, 728 F.2d at 673.

108. 475 U.S. 767 (1986) (plurality opinion).

109. Id. at 769.

110.   For cases compatible with this result, in the context of credit reports rather than insurance company confidential files, see Dun & Bradstreet, Inc. v. Greenmoss Builders, Inc., 472 U.S. 749 (1985); Sunward Corp. v. Dun & Bradstreet, Inc., 811 F.2d 511 (10th Cir. 1987).

111.   See Warren & Brandeis, supra note 2, at 214; Sidis v. F-R Publishing Corp., 113 F.2d 806 (2d Cir.), cert. denied, 311 U.S. 711 (1940).

112.   On the desirability of such a state of affairs, see, e.g., Fiss, Free Speech and Social Structure, 71 Iowa L. Rev. 1405 (1986). For some underlying social theory, see, e.g., Ingber, The Marketplace of Ideas: A Legitimizing Myth, 1984 Duke L.J. 1.

8

The Pathological Complexity of Free Speech Regulation

INTRODUCTION

Free speech case law permits the government to impose a wide range of restrictions on a similarly wide variety of forms of speech. The judicial tests employed to control or legitimize such restrictions have become increasingly complex. Even if we were all to agree on the precise purposes of the free speech clause, as well as on what constitutes speech in the first place, many cases involving government restriction of speech would still be unavoidably difficult. This is because no plausible approach to defining the limits on governmental power to restrict speech can avoid controversial valuations or controversial predictions of the future consequences of deciding a case in a particular way. But the unavoidable difficulty of some free speech cases does not, by itself, explain why the legal tests or doctrines applied should be as complex and multifaceted as the courts have made them. There is no reason in principle why admittedly difficult problems are necessarily better adjudicated by relatively complex tests.[1]

Free speech doctrine tends toward excessive, unjustified complexity for several reasons. The first is the fallacy that difficult problems are necessarily best resolved judicially through complex formulas. Second, our legal culture often places such a high value on freedom of speech that a judicial standard requiring a government seeking to restrict speech to meet a series of conjunctive requirements may be adopted so as to drive additional nails into the coffin of improper government regulation of private speech. As well, the decision making dynamics of multimember courts, in which voting coalitions must be patched together in a potentially unstable fashion, may encourage a process in which the particular concerns of various individual justices are more or less mechanically aggregated, rather than critically distilled, into a compound formula commanding the agreement of a majority. Thus, a judge will join a coalition if her own concerns are incorporated, however awkwardly, into the ultimate formulation of the legal test, rather than leave the coalition on the ground that the new formulation is now unnecessarily complex, poorly focused, or unwieldy. This will result in unnecessarily complex tests with overlapping elements and no single unifying theme or rationale. Finally, there is the inescapable sense that part of the unnecessary complexity flows from judicial inattention to the reasons for constitutionally valuing speech in the first place. To the extent that clarity as to the purposes of free speech has received insufficient attention by the courts, we might anticipate diminished clarity in the case law itself.

This chapter documents the unnecessary complexity of the judicial formulations most frequently used in resolving the most common kinds of free speech regulation cases. The free speech regulation cases are often dubiously decided partly because of the sheer distraction of considerations that are really tangential to justifying restrictions on speech. Therefore, this chapter recommends a more concentrated judicial focus on free speech cases. The better analysis measures the gains and losses in the fulfillment of the purposes underlying the free speech clause, both from the subjective standpoint of the speaker and from the standpoint of other affected parties. These gains or losses due to governmental regulation of speech should be the central judicial concern. They should be measured in light of the purposes underlying the free speech clause, focusing particularly on the value of the options or choices available to speakers and their audiences before and after implementation of the governmental regulation in question.

One important implication of this approach is that if a regulation does not impair a speaker's ability to pursue his or her own free speech values, because it leaves open some sufficient channel other than the one being regulated, then the speaker cannot cogently claim a violation of free speech rights. This is so even if the government acted with a malicious or repressive intent, failed to substantially further any legitimate state interest, or failed to tailor its regulations so that there would be the least amount of impingement on the number, variety, or range of speech channels available to the speaker. Similarly, even if the speaker strongly prefers, for extraneous reasons, to use his or her original means of speaking without the government regulation, the presence of a fully adequate alternative channel renders the speaker's free speech claim baseless.

Adjudicating free speech cases will often remain difficult, even after all distracting considerations are set aside. This chapter will consider the unavoidable difficulties of determining when speech and speech-related activity partially disserve free speech values by taking on a broadly coercive character or by abandoning the goal of persuasion altogether. This chapter will also briefly address some difficult issues of burden of proof and standard of appellate review in free speech cases. To illustrate and clarify the approach recommended above, some attention will be given to the troubling issues involved in restrictions on picketing in residential neighborhoods. The simplified approach suggested in this chapter generates reasonably sensitive results in a parsimonious way, while minimizing distractions and minimizing any need for recourse to futile judicial attempts to balance the right of free speech against a right to privacy.

THE COMPLEXITY OF CURRENT FREE SPEECH TEST FORMULATIONS

The Scope of the Problem

Over the past forty years or so, free speech jurisprudence has spawned concepts and categories of varying scope and dimension. Thus, it has become common for the courts to distinguish between time, place, and manner restrictions on speech and absolute bans;[2] between content-based and content-neutral restrictions;[3] between viewpoint-based and viewpoint-neutral restrictions;[4] and between direct and incidental burdens on speech.[5] The courts have also developed tests for governmental restrictions on commercial speech,[6] for symbolic conduct or mixed speech and conduct cases,[7] as well as for regulating speech in various kinds of government forums.[8] Central to many of the judicial tests for the legitimacy of speech regulations are concerns for the furtherance of some governmental interest of some degree of weight and legitimacy as well as for whether the governmental interest is being pursued by only narrowly tailored means or by the available means least restrictive of freedom of speech.[9] Often, but hardly invariably, the test formulation incorporates a concern for the alternative speech channels, or the remaining means of communicating, left to the speaker burdened by the regulation. This concern, however, is considered to be at most only one of several relevant inquiries.[10]

This chapter develops the thesis that an inquiry into the available channels or media of speech left open to the speaker, suitably developed and refined, should do most of the work in the jurisprudence of free speech regulation. The other distinctions, tests, and factors typically do not even pull their own weight. Beyond their unavoidable doctrinal imprecision and confusion, many of these considerations lead to an improper analytical focus, introduce unnecessary arbitrariness and unpredictability, and invariably raise more subsidiary questions than they answer.

Time, Place and Manner Restrictions

To begin to illustrate these effects, we may consider one of the most frequently encountered and logically inclusive categories, that of governmental restrictions on the time, place, or manner of speech. A governmental restriction on speech is a time, place, or manner restriction if it does not absolutely ban the restricted speech activity in question.[11] Of course, time, place, and manner restrictions will sometimes verge upon, if not be practically tantamount to, an absolute ban.[12] At some point along the continuum, the time, place, and manner regulations undeniably become severe enough to be equivalent in effect to a well-enforced prohibition on the speech activity in question.[13] Therefore, it is hardly clear why much should turn on the distinction between time, place, and manner restrictions and absolute prohibitions, or why different legal tests should be applied to these two categories. From a practical standpoint, the more crucial distinction would be between relatively modest time, place, and manner restrictions on the one hand, and relatively severe or burdensome time, place, and manner restrictions as well as absolute bans on the other.

Of course, we may care about factors other than the degree of severity of the restriction. Under the rubric of freedom of speech, we may also be concerned with the distribution of the burden, or the differential impact, of a speech restriction. Time, place, and manner restrictions as well as absolute bans both may be based on or motivated by a desire to

suppress or disadvantage one side in an ongoing
debate. Put somewhat differently, the distinction
between content-neutral and content-based restrictions
cuts across the distinction between time, place, and
manner restrictions and absolute bans.[14] Our initial
feeling may be that absolute bans are generally more
suspicious than time, place, and manner restrictions.
Still, it is far from clear why even an absolute ban
on a particular form of expression that is plainly
motivated or justified by considerations irrelevant to
the content or viewpoint of the speech should be given
more exacting judicial scrutiny than a time, place,
and manner restriction that is evidently intended
solely to muzzle opposition to a government policy.

The Time, Place, and Manner Analysis. The
purpose of maintaining the time, place, and manner
distinction has never been clarified, partly because
of the continuing lack of clear guidance from the
Supreme Court as to the precise standards for
adjudicating these restrictions.[15] Typically,
however, the courts work through a time, place, and
manner restriction in the following manner. The court
first determines whether the time, place, and manner
restriction is content-based or content-neutral.[16] If
the restriction is deemed content-neutral, the court
considers whether the restriction serves,[17] or is
designed to serve,[18] a significant[19] or substantial[20]
governmental interest.
    Whether a regulation actually serves, or even is
designed to serve, a given interest will often be a
largely speculative inquiry inviting courts to uphold
or strike down the regulation by unconsciously
manipulating the level of rigor, magnitude, and
concreteness with which the service of the interest
must be shown. Even if a regulation serves a
sufficiently weighty governmental interest, there then
remains the issue of whether the regulation is
sufficiently "narrowly tailored" in serving that
interest, and whether the sufficiency of the tailoring
is judged by relatively demanding[21] or lax[22]
standards.
    In Ward v. Rock Against Racism,[23] a concert sound
control case, the Court majority sought to establish
with greater clarity the appropriate test for "narrow
tailoring." The Court rejected the view that some or
all content-neutral time, place, and manner
restrictions must be the least restrictive or least
intrusive means available of promoting the
government's interest. The Court also determined,
however, that the restriction must not "burden
substantially more speech than is necessary to further

the government's legitimate interests."[24]

For the moment, the test would seem to be more accurately characterized as one of "fairly narrow tailoring." What this amounts to in particular cases is of course difficult to specify in advance. A revealing case would involve a content-neutral regulation that promotes a substantial and legitimate governmental interest with generally great efficiency, but which burdens some speakers in exchange for only a trivial promotion of the legitimate governmental interest at stake. The question might be phrased as one of whether the government's legitimate interest can be "substantial" in a particular case if it is only minimally furthered by the application of the regulation to a particular definable class of speakers where the regulation at issue is more meaningfully furthered by its application to other speakers.

In the case of content-based restrictions, the Court has settled on a "least restrictive means" approach to the narrow tailoring requirement,[25] but even this least restrictive means test may inevitably involve some sort of evaluative balancing of the marginal furtherance of the generally compelling interest against the disvalue of the restriction on speech.[26] Finally, if the regulation has passed muster on the preceding requirements, the Court often, but not invariably,[27] goes on to impose the further requirement either that the speaker be left with one or more alternative channels[28] with which to disseminate his or her message, or that the remaining alternative means of speaking not be unreasonably limited.[29] The courts are unfortunately divided on the verbal formulation of the inquiry into alternative speech channels. They are also substantively divided on the question of how one measures the constitutional adequacy of an alternative speech channel and on the degree to which the alternative channel must be available, either formally or realistically, to the speaker. Working through some of these problems, and establishing why it is important to do so, is central to this chapter.

The time, place and manner inquiry, which is of doubtful utility itself, engenders a series of derivative inquiries which are themselves of limited value. As we have seen, after it is determined that the speech restriction goes to time, place, and manner, the Court then determines whether the restriction is content-based or content-neutral,[30] a distinction that surprisingly often sparks controversy in particular cases, and tells us very little. As this distinction has evolved, the courts must consider the predominant purpose of the ordinance.[31]

Determining the governmental body's predominant purpose, particularly in the absence of legislative history, is of course an inquiry fraught with difficulty.[32]

Restrictions on Primary Versus Secondary Effects of Speech.

Once the predominant purpose of the regulation is somehow judicially ascertained, the Court then asks whether such purpose is aimed at the content of the speech in question, or instead at the "secondary effects" of the speech[33] in such a way that the regulation is justified without reference to the content of the speech.[34] Thus, a restriction that is intended to prevent persons from considering or adopting what the legislature considers fallacious or dangerous ideas is a content-based restriction whereas a restriction that is intended to allow, for example, residential homeowners to sleep undisturbed, or to be spared the expense of picking up mountains of leaflets discarded in the streets, is aimed at the "secondary effects" of the speech.[35] This means that we cannot know, without further investigation, whether a statute that by its express terms restricts only speech promoting, for example, conservative Republicanism, is content-neutral or not, since we do not yet know the legislature's predominant intent, or what secondary effect, if any, of conservative Republican speech the legislature had in mind.

However the courts conceive of content-neutrality, the concept will often be difficult to apply, even if the courts satisfactorily determine the predominant legislative intent.[36] Distinguishing a primary from a secondary effect of a restriction is probably more difficult than is commonly recognized. In Linmark Associates, Inc. v. Township of Willingboro,[37] for example, the Court confronted the constitutionality of a ban on residential "For Sale" signs. The Court held that under the circumstances, including the community's desire to prevent "panic" home sales and maintain a racial balance in the community, the ban was content-based.[38] This may seem correct, on the Court's theory that the community "proscribed particular kinds of signs...because it fear[ed] their 'primary' effect, [i.e., seeing them] will cause those receiving the information to act upon it."[39] But on reflection, it is far from obvious why the ordinance could not be equally well described as aimed predominantly at secondary effects. The community is not attempting to keep apart willing buyers and sellers who would otherwise be brought together by the signs. There is no allegedly dangerous or controversial idea that the community seeks to suppress. The community may simply be attempting to prevent the kind of panic selling that may be irrational from the general standpoint of buyers, sellers, and all segments of the community. It may be that rapidly changing community demographics, attributable to panic selling, is regarded as undesirable by all concerned persons. If so, the community ordinance seems more aptly characterized as aimed at a secondary effect.

The Court in Sable Communications v. FCC[40] similarly assumed that the restrictions on access of juveniles to "dial-a-porn" were content-based. But with a bit of imagination and some pointed congressional testimony, presumably the same restrictions struck down in Sable could be reenacted on content-neutral grounds justifying the regulations by reference to predicted juvenile criminal behavior caused or facilitated by dial-a-porn, and not stemming from congressional disapproval of any juvenile's agreement with any dial-a-porn message or viewpoint.

To take another example, forbidding the construction of temporary structures such as anti-apartheid shanties on college campuses, based upon the presumed secondary effect of preventing aesthetic injuries, constitutes another sort of apparently easy case.[41] But one might argue that if a student group constructs an anti-apartheid shanty, it may be difficult to show that the aesthetic justification for removing the shanty is wholly independent of everyone's reactions to the merits of the view being expressed. If the community were deeply, emotionally convinced of the merits of the anti-apartheid message, would it so readily view the shanty as an aesthetic affront that befouls the landscape? Suppose a family lived in a building designed after the fashion of Thomas Jefferson's Rotunda, and a child had built a tree house in the yard. Would a neutral passerby be likely to find the tree house an aesthetic affront?

One might argue, however, that anti-apartheid protesters waive such an issue because they invariably stipulate that the shanty is meant to be ugly, that it is intended to evoke an arresting contrast between the squalor of those persons disenfranchised under apartheid and the privilege and splendor surrounding the shanty. This response, even if it establishes convincingly that the regulation is content-neutral as applied, merely further illustrates the point that a content-neutral regulation may well have a disproportionate, if not devastating, effect on one side of a political debate, while leaving an opposing side essentially untouched.[42] In this context, poorer groups must resort to noisier, messier, more disruptive means of communicating than wealthier groups.   Thus, it is hardly coincidental that the group barred from sleeping in public parks favored greater, rather than lesser, attention toward resource expenditure on the problem of homelessness.[43] Content-neutrality may thus be neutral in form, but in practical effect it is predictably biased in its consequences against particular groups and their associated viewpoints.

From the standpoint of this chapter, however, the overriding criticism of the content-neutrality category is not that it fails the test of general ideological neutrality, but that the concept suffers from an equal and opposite flaw of essential indeterminateness.   Knowing that a particular regulation of speech is content-neutral tells us very little about the laxity or rigor by which the regulation will be judged, and gives us little ground for predicting whether the regulation will be upheld or struck down.[44]   Instead, the fundamental flaw of the content-neutrality inquiry is its almost complete insensitivity to what should genuinely matter in free speech adjudication.   Dean Stone has provided a comprehensive taxonomy of four distinct formulations of the legal standards applicable to content-neutral restrictions on speech.   Each formulation can be supported by recent Supreme Court authority.   The four formulations emphasize the considerations of reasonableness, broad interest balancing, the weight of the government's interest, and the breadth or narrowness of the regulation's incursion into otherwise protected speech, in light of the regulation's purpose.[45]   Of these four formulations, only one considers the availability of alternative means of communicating for the speaker affected by the regulation.[46]   On the approach taken in this chapter and discussed at greater length below, this single consideration, suitably defined and elaborated, is really of predominant importance.[47]

Content-Based Restrictions.   The courts are generally suspicious of content-based restrictions,[48] and are inclined to include in that category restrictions based on the subject matter under discussion,[49] while often singling out restrictions based on the viewpoint of the speaker as being of central concern.[50]   Even if it is assumed, however, that content-based restrictions tend to be more dangerous to free speech than content-neutral restrictions, judicial suspicion of content-based restrictions is only imperfectly focused.   Put simply, there does not seem to be any particularly severe danger to free speech if an admittedly content-based restriction, whether or not it is narrowly tailored to effect its purpose, leaves fully available to the speaker the best practical means, from the speaker's standpoint, of promoting the speaker's message, without impairing the purposes or values underlying the free speech clause from the standpoint of other affected parties.

If the courts determine that a given regulation leaves the speaker's primary free speech channels essentially unimpaired, the regulation has in that respect no significant practical effect on what we have referred to as free speech values. Thus, the courts should be extremely reluctant to strike the regulation down as unconstitutional, let alone apply a heightened, content-based test in doing so. The inclination of the courts to ignore this logic largely stems from the preoccupation, in content-based speech restriction cases, with distracting inquiries into the importance of the state interest and into the tailoring of the restriction to the state interest.[51]

Focusing on the content-based nature of the speech restriction, as opposed to the free speech value of alternative speech channels, led to an odd analysis in Regan v. Time, Inc.[52] Regan involved a challenge to federal statutes making it a crime to photograph United States currency except where certain conditions were met and where the photograph was intended for publication "'for philatelic, numismatic, educational, historical, or newsworthy purposes in articles, books, journals, newspapers, or albums...'"[53] The Court found this "purpose" restriction unconstitutional merely because it determined that the restriction permitted the government to discriminate on the basis of content; that is, photographic reproduction of currency in connection with "newsworthy" articles would be permitted, whereas photographs not falling under this or any other exception would be prohibited.[54]

The Court thus struck down the purpose exception peremptorily as content-based. Even if this result itself is defensible, the analysis seems misfocused. Even the most controversial distinction under the statute, between newsworthiness and nonnewsworthiness, is hardly foreign to constitutional adjudication.[55] Furthermore, the Court did not pretend to detect any substantial progovernment bias in the distinction itself, nor did it find that the distinction significantly correlated with particular viewpoints. In light of the purposes underlying the free speech clause, it would have been natural and appropriate for the Court to have considered whether the statutory restrictions on photographs of United States currency left the speakers with alternative modes of conveying undistortedly their intended message, provided those modes were not significantly disadvantageous in promoting the recognizable free speech values of the affected persons. To oversimplify, could <u>Time</u> make whatever point it intended to make essentially as well without violating the statute? If so, as seems intuitively likely, it is far from clear why the purpose restriction should be said to violate the free speech clause.

   <u>Narrow Tailoring</u>. To this point, the analysis has in fact understated the complexity, manipulability, uncertainty, and even arbitrary irrelevance of much contemporary free speech law. Time, place, and manner restrictions must not only serve some significant or substantial governmental interest, but they must do so with some degree of effectiveness in a way that is more or less narrowly tailored to serve that interest. To suggest that the Court has provided less than consistent guidance in this area is not a matter of descending to linguistic quibbling.   There is a substantial practical difference between a narrow-tailoring rule, requiring merely that the restriction strike directly at the precise evil in question, and a rule requiring that the government employ the means of striking at the evil that is least restrictive of freedom of speech.
   The Court's equivocal direction in this respect is undeniable,[56] and it has resulted in inconsistent decisions at the circuit court level.[57]   Thus, while the Court "has required 'narrow tailoring' even within the area of content-neutral regulations, it is not clear what level of exactitude is appropriate."[58]   At times or for particular kinds of speech, the Court has seemed to adopt a stringent requirement that the restriction be the least speech-restrictive means of practicably[59] achieving the government purpose.[60]   At other times, or for other, presumably less valuable or more vulnerable sorts of speech, the narrow-tailoring requirement is deemed met if the restriction aims at and directly promotes the governmental interest[61] or promotes that interest more, by some unspecified greater or lesser degree, than would be possible in the absence of the regulation[62] or "if it targets and eliminates no more than the exact source of the 'evil' it seeks to remedy."[63]
   The more exacting "least restrictive means" formulation of the narrow-tailoring requirement is sometimes criticized as being virtually impossible to

meet.[64]   While this fear is overstated,[65] the test
does seem susceptible to judicial manipulation,
consciously or unconsciously, in that a court in a
nondeferential mood may adopt its own view of whether
one regulation is really more or less restrictive than
another, or simply pronounce itself unconvinced by the
evidence that all less restrictive means have been
ruled out.   A court can always point out that the
government failed to adopt a marginally less
restrictive conceivable regulation, or has failed to
take some further issue or objection into
consideration, thereby second-guessing a complex
policy decision undertaken by an elected body familiar
with relevant local circumstances.

The less stringent formulations of the
narrow-tailoring requirements are also questionable,
however.   Requiring only that the regulation promote
the governmental interest more effectively than would
be the case in the absence of the regulation[66] could,
by itself, lead to harsh results.   Such a test, for
example, could justify the government's enacting some
hideously severe regulation on the ground that a
draconian regulation would promote the governmental
interest better than no regulation at all.   Of course,
an unduly severe regulation might be struck down on
some other element of the free speech test as
applied.[67]   The point, however, is that an unduly
oppressive and needless restriction on speech, even if
it qualifies under the less stringent formulation, is
the very antithesis of "narrowly tailored" in any
literal sense.

Requiring instead that the regulation target and
eliminate no more than the precise evil in question,
or its source,[68] is also problematic.   This
formulation fails to recognize that if one has a
choice between using either a sledge hammer or a fly
swatter in dispatching a group of insects, there is a
sense in which the sledge hammer is not narrowly
tailored for the job, even if the hitting surface area
of the hammer and the fly swatter are equal and no
greater than necessary.   If, for example, a government
were to narrowly target the problem of campaign
literature littering by imposing strict liability in
the form of a mandatory ten-year prison sentence on
the campaign organizers, such a criminal statute,
while perhaps being aimed at the precise problem,
could well be unduly burdensome on free speech rights
because of its excessive repercussions on the conduct
and activities of campaign organizers.   The view that
"an ordinance is sufficiently well tailored if it
effectively promotes the government's stated
interest"[69] endorses the unnecessary use of sledge

hammers.

Although it should be possible to settle on a single most popular version of the narrow tailoring requirement or to specify which version is to be applied in precisely which circumstances, this leaves the central problem untouched. No matter how it is formulated, the concept of narrow tailoring is inconsequential from the standpoint of promoting the purposes underlying the free speech clause. The breadth or narrowness of a regulation and its impact on speech activities is one thing, while the extent to which the speaker can effectively express his or her message, or pursue free speech values despite the regulation, is quite another.[70] It is perhaps debatable whether these two inquiries are closely related, but it clearly goes too far to suggest that they are nearly equivalent.

One way of illustrating the distinction between a narrow-tailoring requirement and an analysis focusing on available alternative speech channels is to note that a government restriction on speech might not even approach being narrowly tailored on any formulation, and yet might leave open a wide range of valuable, effective alternative channels, that are superior to the channels that are regulated. A government regulation might, for example, severely burden or prohibit free speech avenues A and B, where the regulation is either ineffective, or could accomplish its purposes just as well by regulating only avenue A. The same regulation could leave free speech channels C and D entirely unimpaired, with channels C and D being in all respects the best options available to the speaker and to all affected parties.

A regulation, therefore, might not be narrowly tailored, but might well leave open the best free speech channels. Accordingly, if those superior channels are left unimpaired, that should normally be the end of the inquiry. Despite the lack of narrow tailoring, there would be no cognizable harm from the standpoint of free speech values. Free speech tests that concern themselves centrally with any form of narrow tailoring are thus misfocused. Free speech tests that require some form of narrow tailoring, but ignore entirely any question of available alternative speech channels left open to the speaker,[71] are even more seriously flawed for the reasons discussed above.

It should be appreciated that speakers are often motivated to speak in particular ways for reasons other than to most effectively, or most cost-effectively, promote the free speech values of the speaker or others. As this chapter will discuss below, it may well be the case that a speaker objects vehemently to a regulation that deprives one of only those means of speaking known to be relatively undesirable or cost-ineffective from a free speech value standpoint.   One might, for example, prefer a particular kind of picketing not for any advantage in promoting free speech values from one's own perspective, but because that kind of picketing combines speaking out with a great ability to coerce unwilling, unconvinced targets to act in accordance with one's will.   The test for restrictions on commercial speech, mixed speech and conduct, and symbolic conduct tend to require narrow tailoring while ignoring the presence of alternative speech channels.

Burden of Proof Analysis.   There are certain unresolved problems that attend not only approaches emphasizing narrow tailoring, but also those, as is argued for in this chapter, that rely almost exclusively on alternative speech channel analysis. For example, to the extent that either of these approaches is less than crisply objective, the legal standard of review on appeal becomes important. Currently, the standard of review to be applied to trial court findings of fact in free speech cases in which the trial court struck down the restrictions as unconstitutional, is particularly controversial.[72] Similarly, there are difficult burden-of-proof issues associated with both the narrow tailoring and alternative speech channels inquiries.   The courts have been seriously split on whether the government or the challenging speaker should bear the burden of proof on the issue of narrow tailoring.[73]   Allocating the burden of proof on the issue of narrow tailoring is inherently difficult because, while the government will generally be in a better position to offer evidence on this point, courts may well be reluctant to saddle governments with the often practically impossible task of showing by a preponderance of the evidence why some slightly narrower, less speech-burdensome regulation would not have been equally effective in promoting the statutory goal.   In a range of cases, such a burden on the government would seem nearly impossible to meet.[74]

Allocating the burden of proof on the issue of the sufficiency of the remaining alternative speech channels is admittedly also a matter of controversy. The Court has appeared to place the practical burden of showing the constitutional adequacy of the alternative speech channels on the government.[75]   Dean Stone has noted that an opposite approach, requiring speakers to show the insufficiency of the remaining alternatives, tends to result in decisions against the speaker, at least in close cases.[76]

We, as a society, may so fear deciding free speech cases incorrectly against the speaker that this fear alone dictates the placement of the burden of proof on this issue. Avoiding governmental inroads on free speech is important, but the similarly important goal of preventing racial discrimination by the government has not led the courts generally to require the government to prove its own nondiscriminatory intent.[77] On the issue of the adequacy of alternative channels, logic suggests that the burden of proof belongs at the most crucial point on the speaker. This should not be disturbing, because the reason for allocating the burden to the speaker on this issue actually reflects our sensitivity to the speaker's own free speech interests. While neither the government nor the speaker is generally in a superior position to bring forth evidence on the free speech case as a whole, the speaker will generally be in a much better position to cast light on the issue of the adequacy of the alternative speech channels. This is because the Court is centrally concerned with the adequacy of the speaker's alternatives, and with their practical availability to the particular speaker. The Court must focus on the relevant free speech values from the subjective perspective of the parties involved.

It may be, for example, that an alternative of distributing leaflets is, for the particular speaker, infeasible, inherently distortive of the message, or not suited to the target audience. All of this is more likely to be peculiarly within the knowledge of the speaker and a matter of conjecture for the government. While the speaker should of course not be required to address in turn the inadequacy of the infinite number of distinct alternative ways in which he or she might conceivably communicate the message, the speaker should be required to show the inadequacy, from his or her own standpoint, of any plausible alternative channels actually affirmatively suggested by the government, with the government also being responsible for such matters as showing that the speaker's own preferred channel involves impairing the free speech values of third parties.

FOCUSING ON THE ADEQUACY OF ALTERNATIVE CHANNELS

In the contexts discussed above, as well as in others,[78] the courts improperly de-emphasize or even ignore the availability or lack of availability of alternative channels that are as advantageous to the speaker's own free speech values as the channel being

restricted.   Unnecessary complexity and misfocused
analysis results. Disencumbering free speech analysis
of the distractions discussed above and focusing on
alternative speech channels restores proper focus and
reduces analytical complexity.

Free speech law, however, even then retains some
unavoidable analytical complexity.   The government
cannot and should not be permitted to successfully
defend its regulation merely on the ground that some
sort of alternative speech channel, of whatever
quality or practicality, exists.   While the case law
is clear that the government may not simply point to
some technically available alternative speech channels
in support of its regulation,[79] it is not clear how
much this means beyond a rejection of some obviously
unsatisfactory universal rule that an ability to
exercise one's speech rights in "some other place"
invariably suffices.[80]   On such a broad theory,
unpopular speakers could be vexatiously chased across
the country from jurisdiction to jurisdiction,
impairing their ability to speak effectively.

On the other hand, it is unclear why a regulation
denying the use of a particular undistinctive square
foot of sidewalk, or requiring protesters to move an
inconsequential six inches to the left, could not be
so trivial in its effects on the speaker's free speech
values that the regulation could not be upheld without
consideration of any other extraneous factors.   Just
as the Court has held that a particular book may be
constitutionally protected in one urban bookstore but
not in another,[81] so the Court has in fact sensibly
considered whether a speaker can speak in "another"
place in passing on the constitutionality of a
regulation preventing her from speaking in some
designated place.   In Heffron v. International Society
for Krishna Consciousness, Inc.,[82] for example, the
Court considered, among other factors, whether
alternative forums were available to the speaker.[83]
The Court explicitly observed that the challenged
restrictions on solicitations at the state fairgrounds
did not prevent the respondents from engaging in their
communicative activity "anywhere outside the
fairgrounds."[84]   The government is thus plainly not
invariably barred from the plea that the regulated
party may speak in "some other place."

Constitutionally adequate alternative speech
channels, however, will not always be realistically
available.[85]   It is even possible for a government
regulation to be narrowly tailored, or to be the least
restrictive means for attaining the legislative goal,
without ensuring that a speaker is left with any
adequate alternative speech channels.   The least

restrictive means test, therefore, cannot be generally described as a "more stringent"[86] test than the alternative speech channels test.

Evaluating the Adequacy of Alternative Speech Channels

Evaluating the constitutional adequacy of an alternative speech channel would take the following form. Just as each speaker may have "a variety of speech interests"[87] that may require consideration, so reasonable speakers may wish to consider more than one dimension of the adequacy or inadequacy of potential alternative speech channels, insofar as each dimension bears on each speech interest. These dimensions might include the size of the actual or potential audience,[88] the prestige of an alternative channel,[89] the "quality" or likely appreciativeness of the audience reachable through an alternative channel,[90] financial cost,[91] flexibility of the alternative channels,[92] immediacy or personalization of impact,[93] and certainly the degree to which the alternative permits greater articulation or detail of presentation. Thus, the courts should consider qualitative as well as quantitative aspects of the available alternatives[94] against the backdrop, or baseline standard, of the free speech values otherwise available in the absence of the government regulation.

The basic free speech values that will be involved, such as the pursuit of truth, participation in the process of democratic self-government, and self-realization, should be examined from the subjective standpoint of the actors involved. It may go too far, however, to give independent weight to the speaker's own choice of means of speaking, merely because it is his or her own choice. Although there will doubtless be some tendency for speakers to choose effective rather than ineffective means of speaking, courts should also consider the possibility that the speaker may prefer one means of speaking rather than another for reasons unrelated to, or which actually disserve, free speech values. A speaker may seek a greater potential for sheer annoyance or coercion of a captive, disfavored audience, or some other target of the speech.

Similarly, the courts should not give independent weight to the speaker's choice of means merely on the ground that as the speaker's own choice, that channel embodies and reflects the speaker's interest in his or her own self-fulfillment or self-realization. The courts should, where necessary, consider which of two media better promotes self-realization in and through its use, from the standpoint of the affected parties.

They should not assume, however, that free speech values are enhanced simply by allowing persons to choose their own means of expression or to act as they please.   This would amount to a dubious claim that respect for free speech implies a broad conduct libertarianism.   Free speech does not necessarily imply a general realm of laissez faire.   On such a libertarian view, respecting someone's decision to drive to work rather than take a bus would become a free speech matter because failing to respect that autonomous choice would impair the value of self-realization or self-fulfillment.   This line of argument is not to deny, of course, that certain means of speaking may, under the circumstances, be more conducive to self-realization than others in the course of use.   Presumably, prayer and fasting at a tyrant's doorstep, for example, may tend to promote self-realization more than sticking an obscene bumper sticker on one's vehicle.

Once the relevant considerations are clarified, alternative speech channel analysis becomes a matter of proper application.   At this stage, a number of problems appear.   One problem involves the proper analysis of alternatives that are allegedly not financially or commercially viable.   Although the financial cost or practical affordability of an alternative will normally be considered in assessing its adequacy, the mere fact that, for example, the alternative sites must be bid for by the speaker, or are already occupied by tenants, does not render the sites necessarily inadequate.[95]   Speakers must presumably be prepared to compete in the economic marketplace on fair terms or on the same terms as anyone else.

It goes too far, however, to suggest that the "economic impact" of the restriction on the speaker is never a relevant issue.[96]   There will inevitably be difficult cases falling between the two extremes. While it will obviously be inadequate to inform a welfare-rights group that its sole alternative option is buying network television time, it is not necessarily a speech restriction attributable to the government if a particular group's message is so distasteful that it cannot profitably sell its literature from any commercially zoned property. Obviously, even nontotalitarian governments may intentionally or unintentionally shape the political preferences of the citizenry.   However, governments do not necessarily unconstitutionally impair free speech rights by failing to guarantee responsive markets. The cases between these two extremes are unavoidably fact-sensitive and value-sensitive.   The touchstone must be an overall sense of whether, taking concerns for free speech of all the affected parties into account (including the audience of willing and unwilling listeners, as well as any ways in which the government regulation may actually enhance the free speech value of some affected person), there has been a significant[97] net diminution[98] in free speech values on the whole.   Of course, one person's freedom of speech may not be unfairly diminished for the sake of enhancing someone else's, but this is really an issue in the law of equal protection.   In close cases, this will of course be a complex, difficult call.   But it is useful to remember that this sort of judgment will amount to only a fraction of the complexity and difficulty encountered with the currently entrenched free speech tests.

Adequate Alternatives and the Problem of Residential Picketing

To illustrate this inquiry, it may be useful to discuss the role of free speech value analysis and the analysis of available alternative speech channels in the particular context of the conscientious picketing of home residences by the use of public sidewalks or public streets.   In attempting to resolve such cases, the courts apply the sort of unnecessarily multifaceted tests discussed above, but now are additionally encumbered by the complication of public forum analysis.[99]   The public forum doctrine, which is controversial in this context,[100] begins by at least implicitly assuming that all public streets in all settings are presumptively alike for free speech purposes, and that they are quintessential public forums in the same category as public parks and public sidewalks.[101]

Perhaps some of the reluctance to categorize sidewalks in front of only downtown public buildings as public forums, but not to categorize bucolic residential neighborhood lanes without sidewalks as such, stems from the fear that such a distinction "would represent a radical departure from the general direction of first amendment jurisprudence.   Such a holding would effectively place vast areas of this country out of the reach of the protection of the first amendment."[102]   Of course, holding residential streets to be public forums does not guarantee protection for all peaceable speech activity.[103]   It would not matter, however, from the standpoint of free speech values, whether a certain percentage of turf fell into a less protected category if all speakers had equally good or perfectly adequate alternative speech forums readily available to them.   The genuine issue then, is whether restricting someone's speech on a street or sidewalk leaves that speaker with adequate alternative means, from the speaker's own perspective, to convey a message.

In cases of residential picketing, however, the legal issue is ordinarily stated as a matter of balancing the constitutional right of speech or communication against a more amorphous, but undoubtedly important, right of privacy.[104] The approach advocated herein, while treating some of the same considerations, focuses a bit more manageably on the furtherance or nonfurtherance of recognized free speech values, and on the conflicts between these values. The analytical overlap of these approaches stems in part from recognizing that while the private home may be considered to be the locus of privacy or a safe haven,[105] it may also, relatedly, provide a crucial environment for reflection,[106] which is in itself a vehicle for the exercise of free speech values.

An approach to the problems inherent in residential neighborhood picketing requires both a sensitivity to the particular free speech values involved, especially from the distinctive standpoint of the protester, and a recognition that perhaps not every aspect of the protester's activity, or even of the protester's speech, can be said to unequivocally promote free speech values. A sensitivity to the free speech values embodied in the protester may lead us to recognize that the alternatives of picketing at a downtown business location,[107] communicating through "direct mail, radio, television, newspapers or telephone,"[108] or even picketing in a less focused and concentrated manner in front of the target's own residence[109] could conceivably represent a significant impairment in free speech values of the protester. For example, a prolife picketer may, as a matter of conscience or tactics, prefer not to reach large numbers of people with a message,[110] but instead to confront personally a physician who performs abortions. Not all prolife picketing, of course, will be carried on this way, but doing so, rather than, for example, communicating through radio advertisements, is potentially fully legitimate and may well be preferable from the point of view of the protester's own free speech values.

On the other hand, certain aspects of a residential picketer's tactics, even though they are preferred by the picketer, either may not detectably advance free speech values, or may be positively inconsistent with free speech values, at least from the standpoint of a target or victim. This concern would include not just the familiar "captive audience" problem,[111] but all attempts to merely embarrass, inflict suffering, coerce, intimidate, or bully an unconsenting[112] target, directly or through adult or child third parties, in ways that essentially "bypass" or ignore the process of reasoned or even impassioned persuasion that appeals to the judgment of the target on the merits of the issue.

The Limited Utility of the Concept of Coercion

It may be tempting to suppose that the Court's concern for free speech values requires that the residential picketer's "speech" or other activity be classified as itself impairing free speech values if and only if the picketer's speech or other activity can be characterized as "coercive." The concept of coercion, however, turns out to be both too amorphous and too controversial to serve this role. While coercion as a concept is helpful in free speech analysis because it can be generally distinguished from the process of more or less reasoned persuasion[113] that is central to free speech, the question of whether coercion is itself morally neutral has been left unclear by the literature.[114] This is a matter of some importance. If residential picketers contend that their picketing is aimed at preventing moral evil or the violation of moral rights of others by their target, then on a moralized conception of what coercion means, the picketers cannot be said to be engaging in coercion, regardless of how extreme their tactics are.

Without presuming to resolve this issue of the status of coercion, it seems clear that coercion in the context of residential picketing will often involve the subversion and impairment of the free speech values of the direct or indirect target of the coercion, whether the attempted coercion is successful or not.[115] Even unsuccessful attempts at coercion could impair free speech values from the standpoint of the target if, for example, the target is so tormented and distracted by the incessant din of the picketing that he or she is unable to reflect on or reason about the merits of the underlying issue raised by the picketers. The opportunity to reflect on and consider the merits of public or moral issues is plainly central to various free speech values.

The recognition that coercive speech can substantially impair the free speech values of a target, or that speech can be "persuasion bypassing," casts serious doubt on the Supreme Court's repeated claim that speech that is coercive does not lose its constitutionally protected character.[116] Of course, some coercive speech may be justifiable on independent grounds, as perhaps when necessary to save lives or avoid injuries.   It is also perfectly possible to protect coercive speech in a given case on the ground that the degree to which it impairs free speech values is minimal compared with the degree to which it is expressive of other free speech values, particularly those of the speaker.   But this would, if pushed too far, run contrary to our proper skepticism about permitting a speaker unilaterally to redistribute free speech values in his or her own favor.   While public debate should doubtless be "uninhibited, robust, and wide-open,"[117] and while persuasive, emotional, and even offensive speech, as well as purely descriptive speech, are important to public debate, these and similar considerations certainly do not support a broad immunization of coercive speech.[118]

The crucial problem with focusing on the concept of coercion in this context, however, is its insufficiently inclusive character.   A residential picketer might, for example, impair free speech values by means other than coercion in any narrow sense of the term.[119] One might manipulate, or condition, or even socially pressure a target into compliance, in a way that does not involve persuasion and in fact impairs free speech values, without exercising coercion as that term is normally understood.[120] If a residential picketer, by means other than coercion, can intentionally or unintentionally undermine free speech values or the purposes underlying the legal institution of freedom of speech, then an analytical focus on coercion by speakers is necessarily too narrow.

CONCLUSION

This chapter has suggested that current free speech law is unnecessarily complex, in ways that risk unnecessary arbitrariness, unpredictability, and sheer manipulability of result.   More deeply, there is some risk that unnecessarily complex judicially created free speech doctrine will eventually make it more difficult for ordinary citizens to comprehend or profoundly subscribe to freedom of speech as an overridingly important constitutional value.[121] Whatever the magnitude of these risks, they need not be taken.   Focusing instead, as this chapter has suggested, on the availability or lack of availability of adequate alternative speech channels, from the standpoint of the speaker and other affected parties, is itself an adequate alternative to current free speech regulation doctrine.

No free speech test formulation can be guaranteed to be immune from judicial abuse for repressive ends, but the simpler the test, the fewer the possibilities for disguising repressive ends.   By its nature, the practically-available-alternative-speech channel analysis above is both inescapably central to what we should be preeminently concerned about in most free speech cases, and inescapably formulated so as to discourage, rather than promote, repression of disfavored ideas.   To pass the alternative speech channel test as outlined above, there must in effect be no relevant constitutionally cognizable harm in the regulation.   In the absence of the government restriction on speech, the speaker will be able to present a particular message in a particular way to a particular audience, thereby promoting, from his or her own standpoint, if that of no other person, such free speech values as the search for truth, political participation, and self-realization.   If the government restriction is to pass the alternative speech channel test discussed above, the restriction must leave practically open to the speaker, or as open as the now restricted alternative would have been, at least one alternative that, from all relevant persons' standpoints, is not significantly less promotive, overall, of the relevant free speech values.   There may, of course, be times when the government is justified in impairing freedom of speech, as when this is required to avoid some moral catastrophe, but the problem of specifying the circumstances under which a given degree or kind of restriction on free speech can be justified is inescapable on any theory.

Of course, our approach is not simple in any absolute sense.   Close, difficult cases involving obscure value trade-offs may arise.   The proffered alternative speech channel may offer the possibility, for example, of greater articulateness, but to a less u s e f u l   a u d i e n c e ,   c r e a t i n g   p r o b l e m s   o f commensurability.   But in the broad run of cases, it will be reasonably clear whether some overall roughly equivalent alternative speech channel exists from the speaker's standpoint.   If theoretical problems remain, they are problems that cannot be avoided on any more complex, multifaceted theory than that argued for in this chapter.

NOTES

1. For a sense of the fallacy of assuming that difficult legal problems are invariably met optimally by highly nuanced, multifactor judicial tests, see Epstein, The Risks of Risk/Utility, 48 Ohio St. L.J.

469 (1987).

2. See, e.g., City of Renton v. Playtime Theatres, Inc., 475 U.S. 41, 46 (1986).

3. See, e.g., Stone, Content-Neutral Restrictions, 54 U. Chi. L. Rev. 46, 115-17 (1987).

4. See, e.g., Stone, Content Regulation and the First Amendment, 25 Wm. & Mary L. Rev. 189, 197-200 (1983).

5. See, e.g., Linmark Assoc's, Inc. v. Township of Willingboro, 431 U.S. 85, 94 (1977).

6. See, e.g., Central Hudson Gas & Elec. Corp. v. Public Serv. Comm'n, 447 U.S. 557, 563-66 (1980).

7. See, e.g., United States v. O'Brien, 391 U.S. 367, 376-77 (1968).

8. See, e.g., Perry Educ. Ass'n v. Perry Local Educators' Ass'n, 460 U.S. 37, 45-46 (1983).

9. See, e.g., Clark v. Community for Creative Non-Violence, 468 U.S. 288, 293-94 (1984).

10. See, e.g., Frisby v. Schultz, 108 S. Ct. 2495, 2501-02 (1988).

11. See City of Renton, 475 U.S. at 46; Tollis, Inc. v. San Bernardino County, 827 F.2d 1329, 1332 (9th Cir. 1987).

12. The various time, place, and manner restrictions, in their cumulative effect, might have approached an absolute ban in the Nazi protest march case of Collin v. Smith, 578 F.2d 1197, 1199-1202 (7th Cir.), cert. denied, 439 U.S. 916 (1978).

13. See Collin, 578 F.2d at 1201-2.

14. See, e.g., City of Renton, 475 U.S. at 46-47 (classifying the ordinance in question as a time, place, and manner restriction, but going on to consider its character as content-neutral or content-based).

15. See City of Watseka v. Illinois Pub. Action Council, 796 F.2d 1547, 1551 (7th Cir. 1986), aff'd mem., 107 S. Ct. 919 (1987).

16. See, e.g., Stone, supra note 3, at 115-17.

17. _See_ _Clark_, 468 U.S. at 293 (referring to a test of serving the public interest or purpose, rather than merely being intended to serve it).

18. _City of Renton_, 475 U.S. at 47 (referring to design or intention behind the restriction).

19. _Clark_, 468 U.S. at 293 (characterizing the required governmental interest as "significant").

20. _City of Renton_, 475 U.S. at 47 (adopting a formulation of "substantial" governmental interest).

21. _See_ City of Watseka v. Illinois Pub. Action Council, 796 F.2d 1547, 1553 (7th Cir. 1986),_aff'd mem_. 107 S. Ct. 919 (1987) (imposing a stringent "least restrictive" governmental means test). _See also_ ACORN v. City of Frontenac, 714 F.2d 813, 818-19 (8th Cir. 1983); New York City Unemployed and Welfare Council v. Brezenoff, 677 F.2d 232, 237 (2d Cir. 1982).

22. _See_ _City of Watseka_, 107 S. Ct. at 920 (White, J., dissenting) (rejecting a least restrictive means test for narrow tailoring (citing _Clark_, 468 U.S. at 293-94)).

23. 109 S. Ct. 2746 (1989).

24. _See_ _id_. at 2758.

25. _See_ Sable Communic. v. FCC, 109 S. Ct. 2829, 2836 (1989).

26. _See_ _id_. at 2839 (Scalia, J., concurring).

27. _See_ _Brezenoff_, 677 F.2d at 236-40 (not requiring the availability of adequate alternative speech channels).

28. _See_ _Clark_, 468 U.S. at 293; Heffron v. International Soc'y for Krishna Consciousness, Inc., 452 U.S. 640, 648 (1981) (requiring as one element the availability of alternative speech channels).

29. _See_ _City of Renton_, 475 U.S. at 47.

30. _See_, _e.g._, _id_. at 46-47.

31. _See_, _e.g._ Tollis, Inc. v. San Bernardino County, 827 F.2d 1329, 1332 (9th Cir. 1987).

32. _See_, _e.g._, Easterbrook, _Statutes' Domains_, 50 _U. Chi_. _L_. _Rev_. 533 (1983).

33. See City of Renton, 475 U.S. at 47. A "secondary effect" of speech might be, for example, an alleged increase in crime attributed to the presence of the "speech" of one or more porno shops in a downtown area. Id. at 48.   Another illustration is the increase in auto accidents associated with distracting highway billboards.   Wheeler v. Commissioner of Highways, 822 F.2d 586, 594-95 (6th Cir. 1987), cert. denied, 108 S. Ct. 702 (1988).

34. See City of Renton, 475 U.S. at 47-48.   This approach to content neutrality is criticized as too speech-restrictive in Stone, supra note 3, at 115-17 n.5.   For an argument that the Renton approach to content neutrality should be confined to restrictions on the basis of subject matter, but not applied to restrictions on the basis of viewpoint, see Note, The Content Distinction in Free Speech Analysis After Renton, 102 Harv. L. Rev. 1904 (1989).

35. See Clark, 468 U.S. at 293.

36. See, e.g., Redish, The Content Distinction in First Amendment Analysis, 34 Stan. L. Rev. 113, 139-42 (1981) (discussing the application of the content distinction to Cohen v. California, 403 U.S. 15 (1971)).   For the arguments raised by the opposing parties, see Wheeler v. Commissioner of Highways, 822 F.2d 586, 589 (6th Cir. 1987), cert. denied, 108 S. Ct. 702 (1988).

37. 431 U.S. 85 (1977).

38. Id. at 94.

39. Id.

40. 109 S. Ct. 2829 (1989).

41. See, e.g., Students Against Apartheid Coalition v. O'Neil, 838 F.2d 735 (4th Cir. 1988).

42. For a balanced discussion of this criticism, see Stone, supra note 4, at 199.

43. See Clark v. Community for Creative Non-Violence, 468 U.S. 288 (1984).

44. See, Stone, supra note 3, at 48-50.

45. See id.

46. See id. at 49 ("[s]ome content-neutral restrictions are constitutional if 'they are designed to serve a substantial governmental interest and do not unreasonably limit alternative avenues of communication'"). Note that this test could conceivably be met by a merely "substantial" governmental interest where the speaker is, under the circumstances, left with no practically usable means of conveying his or her message.

47. But see, e.g., United States v. Albertini, 472 U.S. 675, 687-88 (1985).

48. See, e.g., City of Renton, 475 U.S. at 47.

49. See, e.g., Carey v. Brown, 447 U.S. 455, 462 n.6 (1980).

50. See City of Renton, 475 U.S. at 48-49.   The distinction between restrictions on the basis of subject matter and restrictions on the basis of the speaker's viewpoint is pressed in Note, The Content Distinction in Free Speech Analysis After Renton, 102 Harv. L. Rev. 1904 (1989).

51. See, e.g., Boos v. Barry, 108 S. Ct. 1157, 1164 (1988) (content-based restriction on political speech in a public forum).

52. 468 U.S. 641 (1984). The photograph at issue in this case appeared on the front cover of Sports Illustrated and depicted $100 bills falling through a basketball hoop.

53. 468 U.S. at 644 (quoting 18 U.S.C. § 504(1) (1982)).

54. Id. at 648-49.

55. See, e.g., Dun & Bradstreet, Inc. v. Greenmoss Builders, Inc., 472 U.S. 749 (1985) (relying on a distinction between matters of public concern and those not of public concern in the libel law context); Connick v. Myers, 461 U.S. 138 (1983) (relying on the same distinction, but in a public employee dismissal case).

56. See SDJ, Inc. v. City of Houston, 837 F.2d 1268, 1275-76 (5th Cir. 1988) (discussing the Court's apparent variations in this area).

57. See id. at 1275.

58. _Id_. at 1275-76.   For the Court's most recent pronouncement in this area, see Ward v. Rock Against Racism, 109 S. Ct. 2746 (1989).

59. The restriction on speech is not typically held defective because a conceivably less restrictive alternative exists.   _See_ Albertini, 472 U.S. at 688.

60. _See_, _e.g._, Village of Schaumburg v. Citizens For a Better Env't, 444 U.S. 620, 637 (1980) (imposing requirement that the restrictions serve the state interests "without unnecessarily interfering with First Amendment freedoms" and noting the availability of "less intrusive" measures).

61. See _SDJ, Inc._, 837 F.2d at 1276.

62. See _Albertini_, 472 U.S. at 689.

63. Frisby v. Schultz, 108 S. Ct. 2495, 2502 (1988) (citing City Council v. Taxpayers for Vincent, 466 U.S. 789, 808-10 (1984)).

64. _See City of Watseka_, 796 F.2d at 1564 (Coffey, J., dissenting).

65. _See_, _e.g._, New York City Unemployed and Welfare Council v. Brezenoff, 677 F.2d 232, 238 (2d Cir. 1982) ("least restrictive efficient method" test successfully met by the government restriction).

66. _See_, _e.g._, _Albertini_, 472 U.S. at 689.

67. An unduly severe regulation might, for example, be suspected of being an attempt to suppress the idea or point of view being advocated, thus engendering extremely strict judicial scrutiny.   _See_, _e.g._, _City of Renton_, 475 U.S. at 48.

68. _See e.g._, Frisby v. Schultz, 108 S. Ct. 2495, 2502 (1988).

69. _SDJ, Inc._, 837 F.2d 1268 at 1276.

70. For the distinction between these two inquiries, _see e.g._, Project 80's, Inc. v. City of Pocatello, 876 F.2d 711, 716 n.7 (9th Cir. 1989); City of Watseka v. Illinois Pub. Action Council, 796 F.2d 1547, 1577 n.4 (7th Cir. 1986) (Coffey, J., dissenting). _But cf_. _Clark_, 468 U.S. at 298, 308 n.6 (finding little difference between the time, place, and manner restrictions as opposed to the four-factor standard

used in the draftcard burning case of O'Brien v. United States, 391 U.S. 367 (1968), which notably does not incorporate any consideration of any alternative means of communicating left open to the speaker).

71. See, e.g., the test formulation in Central Hudson Gas & Elec. Corp. v. Public Serv. Comm'n, 447 U.S. 557, 563-66 (1980); see also Don's Porta Signs, Inc. v. City of Clearwater, 829 F.2d 1051, 1052 (11th Cir. 1987), cert. denied, 108 S. Ct. 1280 (1988) (making no reference to alternative speech channels in a commercial speech test); United States v. O'Brien, 391 U.S. 367, 376-77 (1968); Clark, 468 U.S. at 294.

72. See Don's Porta Signs, Inc. v. City of Clearwater, 108 S. Ct. 1280, 1280-81 (1988) (White, J., dissenting from denial of certiorari). See also Lindsay v. City of San Antonio, 821 F.2d 1103, 1107-8 (5th Cir. 1987), cert. denied, 108 S. Ct. 707 (1988); Schultz v. Frisby, 807 F.2d 1339, 1341 n.14 (7th Cir. 1986), rev'd, 108 S. Ct. 2495 (1988). But cf. Garcia v. Gray, 507 F.2d 539, 543 (10th Cir. 1974), cert. denied, 421 U.S. 971 (1975) ("[t]rial court findings, including those involving constitutional rights, may not be set aside on appeal unless they are clearly erroneous"); Bering v. SHARE, 106 Wash. 2d 212, 220-21, 721 P.2d 918, 924 (1986) (en banc), cert. denied, 107 S. Ct. 940 (1987) (substantial evidence standard applied on appellate review of fact under state law even though trial court had imposed restrictions on freedom of speech).

73. Compare, e.g., Tollis, Inc. v. San Bernardino County, 827 F.2d 1329, 1333 (9th Cir. 1987) (burden on government) and ACORN v. City of Frontenac, 714 F.2d 813, 818, 818 n.6 (8th Cir. 1983) (citing Schad v. Borough of Mount Ephraim, 452 U.S. 61, 74 (1981)) (same) and Brezenoff, 677 F.2d at 240-41 (same) with Don's Porta Signs, 829 F.2d at 1054 (citing Harnish v. Manatee County, 783 F.2d 1535, 1540 (11th Cir. 1986)) (placing the burden on the speaker) and M.J.M. Exhibitors, Inc. v. Stern (In re G. & A. Books, Inc.), 770 F.2d 288, 298 (2d Cir. 1985) (same).

74. See, e.g., Wheeler v. Commissioner of Highways, 822 F.2d 586, 590 (6th Cir. 1987) (regulation permitting off-premises urban area signs if they are "more than 660 feet from the interstate highway").

75. See Taxpayers for Vincent, 466 U.S. at 819-20. See also Pennsylvania Alliance For Jobs and Energy v. Council of Munhall, 743 F.2d 182, 193 (3d Cir. 1984)

(Becker, J., dissenting) (citing Perry Educ. Ass'n v. Perry Local Educators' Ass'n, 460 U.S. 37 (1983)).

76. See Stone, supra note 3, at 80.

77. See, e.g., Washington v. Davis, 426 U.S. 229 (1976).

78. See, e.g., Perry Educ. Ass'n v. Perry Local Educators' Ass'n, 460 U.S. 37, 45-46 (1983) (not referring to the availability of alternative channels in connection with "designated" public fora, as opposed to traditional public fora).

79. See Meyer v. Grant, 108 S. Ct. 1886, 1893 (1988); Consolidated Edison Co. v. Public Serv. Comm'n, 447 U.S. 530, 541 n.10 (1980).

80. See, e.g., United States v. Grace, 461 U.S. 171, 185 (1983) (Marshall, J., concurring part and dissenting in part) (statute requiring protester to move across the street from the Supreme Court if she wished to display a sign); Schad v. Borough of Mount Ephraim, 452 U.S. 61, 76-78 (1981) (Blackmun, J., concurring) ("Were I a resident of Mount Ephraim, I would not expect my right to attend the theater or purchase a novel to be contingent upon the availability of such opportunities in 'nearby' Philadelphia, a community in whose decisions I would have no political voice."); Virginia State Bd. of Pharmacy v. Virginia Citizens Consumer Council, Inc., 425 U.S. 748, 757 n.15 (1976) ("We are aware of no general principle that freedom of speech may be abridged when the speaker's listeners could come by his message by some other means such as seeking him out and asking him what it is"); Southeastern Promotions, Ltd. v. Conrad, 420 U.S. 546, 556 (1975) (apparently no equally good theater available for musical); Spence v. Washington, 418 U.S. 405, 411 n.4 (1974) (quoting the widely cited language from Schneider v. State, 308 U.S. 147, 163 (1939) that "one is not to have the exercise of his liberty of expression in appropriate places abridged on the plea that it may be exercised in some other place").

81. See, e.g., Smith v. United States, 431 U.S. 291, 301 (1977) (patent offensiveness of an allegedly obscene work must be measured by contemporary community standards).

82. 452 U.S. 640 (1981).

83. Id. at 654-55.

84.   Id. at 655.

85.   The Court has rightly focused on the realistic, as opposed to the merely formal, availability of alternative channels. See, e.g., Meyer v. Grant, 108 S. Ct. 1886, 1893 (1988); Township of Willingboro, 431 U.S. at 93.

86.   Pennsylvania Alliance For Jobs and Energy v. Council of Munhall, 743 F.2d 182, 185 (3d Cir. 1984).

87.   Village of Schaumburg v. Citizens For A Better Env't, 444 U.S. 620, 631 (1980).

88.   See Meyer, 108 S. Ct. at 1892.

89.   Tacynec, 687 F.2d at 798.

90.   See id.   But see Township of Willingboro, 431 U.S. at 93 (perceived advantage in using "For Sale" signs to reach persons not actively seeking sales information).

91.   See, e.g., Township of Willingboro, 431 U.S. at 93.

92.   See Lindsay, 821 F.2d at 1111.

93.   This factor should often be relevant in cases involving conscience-based residential picketing, as in Frisby v. Schultz, 108 S. Ct. 2495 (1988). But cf. City Council v. Taxpayers for Vincent, 466 U.S. 789, 820 (1984) (Brennan, J., dissenting) (some advantages of signs over more articulate handbills from a free speech value standpoint).

94.   See e.g., Taxpayers for Vincent, 466 U.S. at 803 n.23 (quantitative analysis); City of Watseka, 796 F.2d at 1553 (qualitative analysis). One occasionally relevant "second-order" consideration would be the alternative's relative vulnerability to particularly subtle, practically undetectable government censorship. See City of Lakewood v. Plain Dealer Pub. Co., 108 S. Ct. 2138, 2145-46 (1988) (newsracks versus pamphleteers).

95.   See City of Renton, 475 U.S. at 53-54.

96.   But see id. at 54.

97.   Presumably, insubstantial restrictions on freedom of speech, however burdensome or objectionable they may be in other respects, are generally not

actionable. <u>See</u> Kev, Inc. v. Kitsap County, 793 F.2d 1053, 1061 (9th Cir. 1986) (slight diminution in 250 effectiveness of erotic message, due to ten-foot separation requirement between dancers and patrons, does not constitute significant impairment).

98. Of course, the diminution in free speech or in free speech values need not be to zero in order to be actionable. <u>See</u>, <u>e.g.</u>, Christy v. City of Ann Arbor, 824 F.2d 489, 492 (6th Cir. 1987) (city may not set proportional limits on the percentage of non-obscene erotic materials sold at bookstore).

99. Criticism of the utility and focus of public forum analysis is found in Farber & Nowak, <u>The Misleading Nature of Public Forum Analysis: Content and Context in First Amendment Adjudication</u>, 70 <u>Va. L. Rev.</u> 1219, 1223-24 (1984) (public forum doctrine often irrelevant, confusing, or crude). Occasionally, public forum analysis can be simply bypassed. <u>See</u>, <u>e.g.</u>, Board of Airport Comm'rs v. Jews for Jesus, 107 S. Ct. 2568, 2571 (1987).

100. <u>See</u>, <u>e.g.</u>, the obvious ambivalence of the court in Pursley v. City of Fayetteville, 820 F.2d 951, 955 n.5 (8th Cir. 1987). It is possible to read such criticism as suggesting that public forum analysis is either not useful or that the street in question was either a limited purpose public forum or a nonpublic forum. <u>See</u> Perry Educ. Ass'n v. Perry Local Educators' Ass'n, 460 U.S. 37, 45-47 (1983).

101. <u>See</u>, <u>e.g.</u>, Frisby v. Schultz, 108 S. Ct. 2495, 2500 (1988).

102. Schultz v. Frisby, 807 F.2d at 1347, <u>rev'd</u>, 108 S. Ct. 2495 (1988).

103. <u>See</u>, <u>e.g.</u>, <u>Frisby</u>, 108 S. Ct. at 2504.

104. <u>See</u>, <u>e.g.</u>, Haiman, <u>Speech v. Privacy: Is There a Right Not To Be Spoken To?</u>, 67 <u>Nw. U.L. Rev.</u> 153, 154 (1972).

105. <u>See</u>, <u>e.g.</u>, Carey v. Brown, 447 U.S. 455, 471 (1980).

106. <u>See</u> <u>id</u>. at 489 (Rehnquist, J., dissenting).

107. <u>See</u>, <u>e.g.</u>, <u>Pursely</u>, 820 F.2d at 953.

108. See Schultz v. Frisby, 807 F.2d 1339, 1356 (7th Cir. 1986) (Coffey, J., dissenting),rev'd, 108 S. Ct. 2495 (1988).

109. See Frisby v. Schultz, 108 S. Ct. 2495, 2501 (1988).

110. But cf. Schultz v. Frisby, 807 F.2d at 1371 (Coffey, J., dissenting) (focusing in this context on size of audience), rev'd, 108 S. Ct. 2495 (1988).

111. See, e.g., Lehman v. City of Shaker Heights, 418 U.S. 298 (1974).

112. While the target of picketers may generally be presumed to prefer that the picketers leave, the issue of consent may perhaps be somewhat more problematic in the case of residential picketing of high public officials. For a discussion of similar facts, see Garcia v. Gray, 507 F.2d 539 (10th Cir. 1974), cert. denied, 421 U.S. 971 (1975) and Gregory v. City of Chicago, 394 U.S. 111 (1969).

113. See, e.g., Gert, Coercion and Freedon, in XIV Nomos: Coercion 30, 44-45 (J. Pennock & J. Chapman eds. 1972).

114. For what seems to be a well-grounded, familiar approach, see Wolff, Is Coercion Ethically Neutral?, in XIV Nomos: Coercion 144, 146 (J. Pennock & J. Chapman eds. 1972) ("[C]oercion is degrading.   To coerce a man rather than persuade him is to treat him as a thing governed by causes rather than a person guided by reasons.").   However, the philosophical literature is sharply divided on the extent to which the concept of coercion has built into it a negative moral evaluation or a sense of prima facie unjustifiability. Compare, e.g., Ryan, The Normative Concept of Coercion, 89 Mind 481, 483-84 (1980) (no coercion if no violation of one's obligations or the rights of those acted upon) and Carr, Coercion and Freedom, 25 Am. Phil. Q. 59, 63 (1988) (a justifying moral convention can render what would otherwise be coercive into noncoercive activity) with A. Wertheimer, Coercion 188 (1987) (rejecting Ryan's approach in this regard) and Lyons, Welcome Threats and Coercive Offers, 50 Phil. 425, 427 (1975) (arguing that a person might be coerced into acting fairly). Robert Nozick leaves open the degree to which the concept of coercion necessarily refers to some moral baseline in Nozick, Coercion, in Philosophy, Science, and Method 447 (S. Morgenbesser, P. Suppes, & M. White eds. 1969).

115. It is often argued that there can be no unsuccessful coercion; that if the target does not comply with the would-be coercer's threat or demand, he or she has not been coerced, or even made subject to coercion. See, e.g., Bayles, A Concept of Coercion, in XIV Nomos: Coercion 16, 17 (J. Pennock & J. Chapman eds. 1972); Gunderson, Threats and Coercion, 9 Can. J. Phil. 247, 256 (1979) and other authorities cited in Westen, "Freedom" and "Coercion", Virtue Words and Vice Words, 1985 Duke L.J. 541, 562 & n.79. Professor Westen himself thinks this approach is inaccurate. See id. at 562. Attempted, but unsuccessful, coercion is in any event often blameworthy. See Bayles, supra, at 19.

116. See, e.g., NAACP v. Claiborne Hardware Co., 458 U.S. 886, 909-11 (1982); Organization For a Better Austin v. Keefe, 402 U.S. 415, 419 (1971).

117. New York Times v. Sullivan, 376 U.S. 254, 270 (1964).

118. See Bering, 106 Wash. 2d at 258, 721 P.2d at 944 (Anderson, J., dissenting in part) (persuasive speech as losing constitutional protection when it becomes coercive). But cf. Kamin, Residential Picketing and the First Amendment, 61 Nw. U.L. Rev. 177, 212 (1966) (raising the possibility that simple distribution of leaflets could be coercive if the leaflets were accepted because of the imposing bulk of the person distributing them).

119. See, e.g., Carr, supra note 114, at 59 ("not all interferences with one's freedom involve coercion"). Cf. Bering, 106 Wash. 2d at 219, 721 P.2d at 923 (picketing that causes physicians and patients emotional distress and a substantial risk of physical and mental harm is coercive).

120. See, e.g., McCloskey, Coercion: Its Nature and Significance, 18 S.J. Phil. 335 (1980). But cf. Day, Threats, Offers, Law, Opinion and Liberty, 14 Am. Phil. Q. 257, 165 (1977) (including threats and intimidation as coercive modes of influence, but excluding punishment or deterrence from the category of coercion). The question of whether there are circumstances in which making someone an "offer" could impair free speech values is as intriguing as, but probably no more easily resolved than, the related question of whether an "offer" could ever be coercive. See, e.g., Benditt, Threats and Offers, 58 Personalist 382, 383-84 (1977) (yes); Day, supra at 259 (offers not curtailing liberty). For commentary on Benditt,

see Richards, _Acting Under Duress_, 37 _Phil_. _Q_. 21, 35-36 (1987).

121.   _See_ Blasi, _The Pathological Perspective and the First Amendment_, 85 _Colum_. _L_. _Rev_. 449, 470-73 (1985).

Conclusion:
The Future of Freedom of Speech

The picture of free speech law sketched thus far has been a bit more dour than most. In our view, the free speech expansionist project has put dangerous stresses on the edifice of free speech law. Of course, any or all of the judicial decisions decried above might in principle be overruled or otherwise rendered harmless, but the picture would, for the long term, still be gloomy. The crucial problem instead lies at the very foundations of the theory of freedom of speech.

We have assumed throughout this book that freedom of speech is not simply some totemic object of adoration. Freedom of speech is protected for a reason, or for some more or less complex calculus of reasons. Promoting what we have referred to as free speech values is, in at least some essential measure, the point of constitutionalizing freedom of speech, whether or not we might also promote those same values in various other ways, and whether or not judges do or should think about those values when deciding free speech cases.

More for the sake of argument than on any definitive basis, we have assumed that the free speech values include the ascertainment of truth, promotion of political democracy, and self-realization or development, or some related considerations, or some subset thereof. It is to be expected that as a society changes its understanding of these values, or of the reasons for the rule of free speech, the law of free speech will itself, over time, tend to reflect those changes.

Now, a society, and more particularly, the judges who decide free speech cases on behalf of society, will tend to change their understanding of notions such as truth, democracy, and self-realization in response to any number of different sorts of influences. But it is plausible to imagine that judges are not immune in particular from the influences, at least with some time lag, and at least indirectly, of the society's past and present "academic scribblers,"[1] and in our context, ultimately of those philosophers and other writers who focus their attention on ideas such as truth, democracy, and self-realization.

If so, we should expect our most profound understandings of freedom of speech to face some jeopardy, at least over the long term. It is relatively uncontroversial that modern philosophy (and twentieth-century philosophy to an unprecedented degree) has presented us, from its mainstream, with an increasingly attenuated understanding of what it means for something to be true, or why democracy is desirable, or why self-realization is a worthy or meaningful aim. Increasing numbers of the most highly respected, lucid, insightful, mainstream scholars closest to the center of intellectual gravity have begun to offer us only what, to the ordinary person, would inevitably seem an unsatisfactorily impoverished view of such matters.

But this is not itself the most ominous development from the standpoint of the long-term vitality of the institution of freedom of speech. What is most striking about the contemporary philosophical understanding of the values underlying freedom of speech, and of freedom of speech itself, is the obvious and undeniable practical instability, the sheer fragility, of any institution of free speech nourished only by such sources. The contemporary mainstream philosophical answer to the question of why we should revere, or even adhere at any significant cost, to the familiar institutions of freedom of speech, is so thin, so desiccated, so ultimately uninspiring that freedom of speech is ultimately rendered insecure.

At least until recently, the ordinary person has tended to believe that notions such as truth, democracy, and self-realization were more or less objectively recognizable, that they were good, and that this judgment of goodness was itself not merely ultimately arbitrary, or simply conventional, or true only relative to a given culture. Democracy, for example, could in such a view be said to be "really" good; the goodness of democracy was somehow and somewhere ultimately grounded in some sort of objectively true foundational belief, or at least somehow rationally justified. Usually, this ultimate grounding or other rational justification of moral belief was explicitly theistic.[2]

It is probably fair to say that the weight of the most influential contemporary philosophy no longer supports such an approach, or any other approach that would place freedom of speech at less than serious risk.[3] Now, the claim that the trend in contemporary philosophy is toward views which generate only a fragile, unstable practical context for an institution of freedom of speech may not seem unusual or troubling. Every transiently preeminent trend in moral philosophy has been fragile and unstable itself, in that it has given way historically to some successor view, and the idea of freedom of speech has thus far nonetheless persisted.

The problem, however, is that the succession of unstable world views implicit or explicit in Milton, Locke, Kant, Hegel, and John Stuart Mill tends to conceal the fact that, at each stage, the successor view has retained sufficient metaphysical or motivational depth and power to authoritatively guide human-kind. It is not obvious why this must continue to be so. If contemporary philosophy itself has not already reached that critical stage, it may well be that its successor generation will prove to have fallen beneath some critical minimum level of metaphysical depth and motivational power such that society can no longer sustain a recognizable institution of freedom of speech. In the past, modern philosophical instability has generally effected only a manageable shift in our reasons for preserving freedom of speech. At our stage, however, the remaining reasons may ultimately prove too weak.

It may be, therefore, that for the future, the most grievous threat to freedom of speech will be neither the crude and perhaps increasingly aberrant depredations of Stalinist censorship and rewriting of history, nor the mind control of some insidious technological dystopia, but the predictable unraveling and inadequate replacement of a benignly intended, but philosophically truncated and motivationally ineffectual, descendent of modern liberalism itself.

What might graphically be referred to as the "shriveling" of moral philosophy is of course not a new phenomenon. The process has been underway at least since the Enlightenment, and the shriveling has had ample time to manifest itself in highly developed form in the discipline of the law. Justice Holmes is probably the most conspicuous exemplar of this process, in his report to Harold Laski:

> I often think of the way our side shrieked
> during the late war at various things done
> by the Germans such as the use of gas. We
> said gentlemen don't do such things, to
> which the Germans: "Who the hell are you?
> We do them." There was no superior tribunal
> to decide, so logically the Germans stood as
> we did.[4]

We have seen similar thoughts expressed by various
members of today's Supreme Court at numerous points
above. Even Chief Justice Rehnquist has gone so far
as to write that "[t]here is no conceivable way in
which I can logically demonstrate to you that the
judgments of my conscience are superior to the
judgments of your conscience, and vice versa."[5]
     The generally diminishing ambitiousness of modern
moral philosophy, and the inevitable eventual
reflection of this trend in our constitutional
jurisprudence, seem clear. What remains to be shown
is the distinctively pernicious potential in the
continuation of this process. To show this, we might
consider in some detail the relevant writings of the
entirely representative, unimpeachably mainstream,
benevolently liberal, exceptionally astute and
sophisticated contemporary theorist Richard Rorty. In
focusing in particular on Rorty, our point is of
course not to seek to in any sense refute his
particular view. Rather, the point is that if freedom
of speech faces eventual tough sledding even in
Rorty's ideal world, the theory of which eschews the
extremism of logical empiricism, emotivism, and
outright moral skepticism, then freedom of speech
probably faces tough sledding in any real future world
that is likely to eventuate.
     The overall theme of our examination of Rorty's
theory and Rorty's utopia will be that any widespread
commitment by ordinary persons in Rorty's utopia to
familiar principles of freedom of speech is likely to
be transitory, and to be felt ultimately to be
gratuitous and unnecessarily costly. It seems evident
that while Rorty's utopia may begin with a societal
consensus favoring freedom of speech, that consensus
can be no stronger than a mere psychological vestige,
a product of cultural inertia, a set of beliefs
parasitically dependent upon discarded prior beliefs
in the form of some sort of moral objectivity or
realism explicitly cast aside and disavowed by Rorty's
theory and Rorty's utopia. Rorty's utopia involves

abandoning the search for any universal or bindingly, objectively authoritative grounds for moral principles, but the cultural or psychological inheritance carried by those who have only now foresworn such a search or such commitments is not immediately dissipated. A change in belief does not immediately effectuate a change in motivation congruent with those beliefs, and a change in a person's most general beliefs does not immediately radiate out to bring all of a person's other, subsidiary beliefs into line with the changed general belief.[6] Rorty's utopia can thus give the appearance of liberalism and stability, but only for a time.

Rorty's prolific writings have left the outline of his approach reasonably clear.[7] A most concise summary has been offered by Professor Milton Fisk, who writes that on Rorty's "uncompromising pragmatism, all efforts to find the true, the good, and the beautiful outside the strictly nonphilosophical practices of scientists, politicians, and artists are vain efforts to transcend the communities in which those practices go on."[8] In Rorty's own words, "I do not think there are any plain moral facts out there in the world, nor any truths independent of language, nor any neutral ground on which to stand and argue that either torture or kindness are preferable to the other."[9] As for what has often been referred to as human nature, Rorty suggests we "avoid the self-deception of thinking that we possess a deep, hidden, metaphysically significant nature which makes us 'irreducibly' different from inkwells or atoms."[10] More generally, Rorty joins in the project of "preventing man from deluding himself with the notion that he knows himself, or anything else, except under optional descriptions,"[11] while crediting the Enlightenment with appreciating that "anything could be made to look good or bad, important or unimportant, useful or useless, by being redescribed."[12]

What Rorty leaves us with is admittedly not relativism, at least not in the sense in which an ambitious claim is made that one idea is "really" as good as any other.[13] Nor does Rorty embrace nihilism or moral skepticism.[14] What Rorty offers, as he cannot, on his own terms, "argue" for or against anything,[15] is a world of more and less attractive conversations employing vocabularies of greater and lesser utility or appeal. These conversations, or the one with which a vaguely defined "we" may care to identify ourselves, may well seem familiar, in that husks of traditional ethical and metaphysical terminology may be employed. Thus we may continue to talk of moral rightness and wrongness, or of good and

evil, but these usages will be merely
"sociologized,"[16] or intra-conversational references
or strategies, with the traditional metaphysical
content having been drained off. The morally wrong
reduces, as in Holmes's reference quoted above,[17] to
the sort of thing our group simply does not do.[18]

Rorty does explicitly link truth to freedom of
speech, but he does so in an ultimately uninspiring
way. Rorty recommends, if that term is not
excessively freighted with metaphysical baggage, that

> openmindedness should not be fostered
> because, as Scripture teaches, Truth is
> great and will prevail, nor because, as
> Milton suggests, Truth will always win in a
> free and open encounter. It should be
> fostered for its own sake. A liberal
> society is one which is content to call
> "true" whatever the upshot of such
> encounters turns out to be. That is why a
> liberal society is badly served by an
> attempt to supply it with "philosophical
> foundations."[19]

Of course, part of the price to be paid for adopting a
purely definitional linkage between freedom of speech
and the attainment of truth is that it becomes absurd
to defend, or justify, or even somehow merely to
prefer, freedom of speech for the alleged instrumental
reason that it will tend to lead, better than
alternative regimes, to the discovery or creation of
truth.

Thus it becomes impossible to coherently value
freedom of speech, in Rorty's utopia, on truth-seeking
grounds. Nor can freedom of speech be meaningfully
valued as contributing to the value of individual
self-realization, at least in any familiar sense. As
we have seen, there is no objective discernible higher
self for us to express, develop, or realize.[20] Free
speech might be useful for the operation of a
democratic society, but by this point, the status and
moral point of democracy as well have become
alarmingly attenuated.

Hilary Putnam has sought to retain the linkage
between democracy and freedom of thought by observing,
on assumptions at least loosely similar to Rorty's,
that universal freedom of thought aptly reflects our
recognition that we are all "in the same
predicament,"[21] and that we all have a need for, and a
capacity for, free moral thought.[22] One obvious
problem, however, is that while we are all equal in
certain respects, we are unequal in others. And in

Rorty's utopia, we have abandoned the appeal to some transcendent schema allowing us to objectively conclude that some way, or ways, in which we are alike really outweigh those in which we differ. Why should those who fancy themselves superior in some relevant respect accord equal free speech rights to their inferiors, even if we assume that the latter want to speak and have at least some capacity to do so? What if the presumed superiors find it genuinely painful or tiresome to listen? Perhaps things could be arranged technologically so that the presumed inferiors are left under the gratifying perpetual illusion of having spoken freely and equally. Such a state of affairs would hardly amount to undominated, undistorted communication, but, metaphysically, so what?

Our historical experience suggests that Rorty's utopia, which is assumed to closely parallel familiar non-Rortyian, metaphysical liberalism in being characterized by equality, freedom, tolerance, diversity, empathy, expanded sensitivity, and aversion to cruelty and humiliation, would, once the patterns of thinking, inhibitions, taboos, and prejudices developed in a lifetime of metaphysical, grounded moral thinking wore off, reflect the mere preferences of some or all of the society. In a world of Rortyian pragmatism, we may be confident that at least some sorts of brute pleasures and pains would remain as motivators.

Whether freedom of speech would survive in any recognizable form, let alone be enhanced or perfected, seems doubtful. Rorty does not offer us any guarantees in exchange for trading in a metaphysical for a pragmatic culture. At one point, he grants that "[w]e do not know how it would feel. We do not even know whether, given such a change in tone, the conversation of Europe might not falter and die away. We just do not know.[23] Surely Rorty cannot assume the stability of any recourse to a Platonic "noble lie" in which society's intellectual elite recognizes that Rorty is right, but the plodding masses are nonetheless taught traditional values on traditional grounds.

Rorty does make, however, an intriguing argument, or what looks like an argument, for the view that the society he envisions is not disastrously unstable. Rorty submits that the weakening of religious faith has historically had the effect of strengthening, rather than weakening, the bonds of liberal society, and that the demise of objective, universal, or transcendent morality would have no more deleterious effect.[24] This is, to put it mildly, an issue on which much might be said. But even if Rorty's premise

is assumed to be true, we have reason for doubting his
conclusion.   Abandoning religious faith may, on
Rorty's premise, be analogized to having used up half
a tank of the sort of fuel required to drive a
society.   Abandoning both religious faith and all
objective morality, and one suspects that the
abandonment of the former eventually requires the
abandonment of the latter, would be the equivalent of
driving on empty.   Going without untoward incident
from full to half full does not allow us to infer that
we can always afford to burn half a tank full,
regardless of how much we start with.
     The   crucial   disanalogy   seems   to   be   this.
Theistic explanations for why one occasionally ought
to do something distasteful, such as tolerate
unpleasant speech, can, on their own terms, strike one
as complete, sensible, and motivating.   At least for a
time, it may seem that a variety of secularly-based
objective moralities can provide some sort of
complete, sensible, motivating substitute explanation.
But as a matter of human psychology, the line is
crossed when the   only reason offered for refraining
from censorship of painful speech rises no higher than
that which Rorty can offer.   Certainly, one might
accept a Rortyian reason because it happened to strike
one as somehow aesthetically appealing to do so.   Why
such compliance should be common, though, is hardly
clear.   Some things, such as the prospect of a large
financial   profit,   tend,   in   modern   societies,   to
motivate.   Other things, such as the prospect of a
Hero of Socialist Labor medal, or a handshake from
Fidel, simply tend to have less motivating power.
Rorty's utopia does not offer much reason for
self-sacrifice.
     Some commentators have not found Rorty's utopia
particularly attractive.[25]   On the positive side, it
may be said that the Rortyian utopia is barren ground
indeed for the moral fanaticism of a Hitler or a
Stalin.   It is difficult to envision a Hitler or
Stalin who makes no appeal to concepts of objective
morality.   One suspects that for a time, the Rortyian
utopia would have an open, progressive quality.
Certainly, the first generation of utopians would not
simply fail to see any point in it all and plug in, en
mass, to the perpetual sensory gratification machines
we may expect some entrepreneur, perhaps the last
entrepreneur, to provide.   But it is hardly obvious
why the second or third generation would not.   More
gratification seems more appealing than less.   There
is certainly no deep reason associated with, for
example, human dignity, not to do so.   The elder
generation may protest against the   choice, but that

preference is merely their own current preponderant cultural practice, without any pretension to any deeper warrant. Ultimately, the characteristic sound of Rorty's utopia is likely not that of free and equal debate, but the uniform electronic hum of the gratification machines.

Again, the point of all this is not to show that Rortyianism in particular would jeopardize the future of any recognizable institution of freedom of speech. We have merely singled out Rorty as one of the most sophisticated, sympathetic, and influential mainstream contemporary philosophers. The point is rather that Rorty fairly illustrates the general drift of much of modern moral philosophy, and that the future of free speech is unsafe in the hands of those generations who will be influenced by such philosophers.

NOTES

1. See J.M. Keynes, The General Theory of Employment, Interest and Money, ch. 24, at 383 (1964).

2. See Boyd, How to Be a Moral Realist, in Essays on Moral Realism 208 (G. Sayre-McCord ed. 1988). Professor Boyd finds this theistic grounding to be a profound mistake. See id. For a contrary view, see Wright, Legal Obligation and the Natural Law, 23 Ga. L. Rev. 997 (1989). See also Neuhaus, The Moral Delegitimation of Law, 4 Notre Dame J.L., Ethics & Pub. Policy 51 (1989).

3. For a sense of the at best limited metaphysical ambitions of many of today's mainstream ethical philosophers, see, e.g., B. Ackerman, Social Justice in the Liberal State 11 (1980) ("[n]o reason is a good reason if it requires the powerholder to assert... that his conception of the good is better than that asserted by any of his fellow citizens..."); D. Gauthier, Morals By Agreement (1988) (developing a subjectivist-relativist theory); Harman, Moral Relativism Defended, 84 Phil. Rev. 3 (1975); A. MacIntyre, After Virtue 6 (2d ed. 1984) ("[t]here seems to be no rational way of securing moral agreement in our culture"); J.L. Mackie, Ethics: Inventing Right and Wrong 15 (1977) ("[t]here are no objective values"); Rawls, Justice as Fairness: Political Not Metaphysical, 14 Phil. & Pub. Aff. 223 (1985) (disclaiming any ambitious "grounding" of his theory of justice); B. Williams, Ethics and the Limits of Philosophy 22-26 (1985) (discussing the difficulty of persuasively undermining the views of the ethical skeptic who wishes simply to consistently opt out of

the use of all moral language).

4.   2 Holmes-Laski Letters: The Correspondence of Mr.
Justice Holmes and Harold J. Laski 1238 (M. DeWolfe
Howe ed. 1953) (letter to Laski of April 18, 1930)
(emphasis in the original).

5.   Rehnquist, The Notion of a Living Constitution, 54
Tex. L. Rev. 693, 704 (1976).

6.   See G. Harman, Change in View (1986).

7.   The gist of what is relevant for our purposes can
be drawn from R. Rorty, Contingency, Irony, and
Solidarity (1989);   R.   Rorty,   Consequences   of
Pragmatism (1982); R. Rorty, Philosophy and the Mirror
of Nature (1979).   Among Rorty's most relevant journal
articles   are   Rorty,   Postmodernist   Bourgeoise
Liberalism, 80 J. Phil. 583 (1983); Rorty, Thugs and
Theorists: A Reply to Bernstein, 15 Pol. Theory 564
(1987) (replying to Richard Bernstein's One Step
Forward, Two Steps Backward: Richard Rorty on Liberal
Democracy and Philosophy, in id. at 38); Rorty, Unger,
Castoriadis, and the Romance of a National Future, 82
Nw. U.L. Rev. 335 (1988).   See also Rorty, The
Priority of Democracy to Philosophy, in The Virginia
Statute for Religious Freedom 257 (M. Peterson & R.
Vaughn eds. 1988).

8.   Fisk, The Instability of Pragmatism, 17 New Lit.
History 23, 23 (1987).

9.   R. Rorty, Contingency, Irony, and Solidarity 173
(1989).   See also H. Putnam, The Many Faces of Realism
77-78 (1987) ("our moral beliefs, in my view, are not
approximations to The Universe's Own Moral Truths...").

10.   R. Rorty, Philosophy and the Mirror of Nature 373
(1979).

11.   Id. at 379.

12.   R. Rorty, supra note 9, at 7.

13.   See R. Rorty, Consequences of Pragmatism 166 (1982).

14.   See generally Stick, Can Nihilism Be Pragmatic,
100 Harv. L. Rev. 332 (1986) (emphasizing the
discontinuities between nihilist or irrationalist
legal scholarship and Rorty's views).

15.   See R. Rorty, supra note 9, at 44.

16.   See id. at 83 n.4.

17.   See supra text accompanying note 4.

18.   See R. Rorty, supra note 9, at 59.

19.   Id. at 52 (emphasis in the original).   See also H. Putnam, supra note 9, at 51 (rejecting ethical foundationalism).

20.   See supra text accompanying notes 8-12.

21.   H. Putnam, supra note 9, at 50.

22.   Id. at 51.

23.   R. Rorty, supra note 13, at 174 (emphasis in the original).

24.   R. Rorty, supra note 9, at 85.

25.   See, e.g., Moore, The Interpretive Turn in Modern Theory: A Turn for the Worse?, 41 Stan. L. Rev. 871, 904 (1989).

Selected Bibliography

The literature on freedom of speech is, fittingly, massive. A few of the most timely and intriguing books discussing free speech law are listed below. For other relevant books, and for a sampling of the immense law review literature on the subject, the interested reader is invited to examine the references listed in the endnotes following each of the chapters above.

Baker, C. Edwin, <u>Human Liberty and Freedom of Speech</u>
     (1989)
Barendt, Eric, <u>Freedom of Speech</u> (1985)
Bollinger, Lee, <u>The Tolerant Society: Freedom of
     Speech and Extremist Speech in America</u> (1986)
Chevigny, Paul, <u>More Speech</u> (1988)
Emerson, Thomas, <u>The System of Freedom of Expression</u>
     (1970)
Kalven, Jr., Harry, <u>A Worthy Tradition: Freedom of
     Speech in America</u> (J. Kalven ed. 1988)
Meiklejohn, Alexander, <u>Political Freedom</u> (1965)
Redish, Martin, <u>Freedom of Expression: A Critical
     Analysis</u> (1984)
Richards, David, <u>Toleration and the Constitution</u>
     (1986)
Schauer, Frederick, <u>Free Speech: A Philosophical
     Enquiry</u> (1982)

Index

About the Author

R. GEORGE WRIGHT is Associate Professor of Law at Samford University's Cumberland School of Law, and former Bigelow Teaching Fellow and Lecturer in Law at the University of Chicago Law School. He is the author of numerous articles on free speech law and other legal topics.